W9-APR-075

With Our Own Eyes

Note: The names of the Central American refugees mentioned in this book have been changed to protect families and friends still threatened by violence in their home countries.

With Our Own Eyes

Don Mosley
with Joyce Hollyday

HERALD PRESS
Scottdale, Pennsylvania
Waterloo, Ontario

Library of Congress Cataloging-in-Publication Data
Mosley, Don, 1939-
  With our own eyes / Don Mosley with Joyce Hollyday.
    p. cm.
  ISBN 0-8361-9050-5 (alk. paper)
  1. Church work with refugees—United States. 2. Jubilee
Partners—History. 3. Sanctuary movement—Georgia—Comer.
4. Refugees, Political. 5. Mosley, Don, 1939- . I. Hollyday, Joyce.
II. Title.
BV4466.M67 1996
261.8'32—dc20   96-24455
                                                                            CIP

The paper used in this publication is recycled and meets the minimum
requirements of American National Standard for Information Sciences
—Permanence of Paper for Printed Library Materials, ANSI Z39.48-
1984.

All Bible quotations are used by permission, all rights reserved, and are
from CPV, *The Cotton Patch Version of the Bible,* translated by Clarence
Jordan, © New Wind Publishers, 1963; NEB, *The New English Bible,* © The
Delegates of the Oxford University Press and the Syndics of the
Cambridge University Press 1961, 1970; © NRSV, *The New Revised Standard Version of the Bible*, copyright © 1989 by the Division of Christian
Education of the National Council of the Churches of Christ in the
U.S.A.; KJV, from *The Holy Bible, King James Version.*

WITH OUR OWN EYES
Copyright © 1996 by Herald Press, Scottdale, Pa. 15683
    Published simultaneously in Canada by Herald Press,
    Waterloo, Ont. N2L 6H7. All rights reserved
Library of Congress Catalog Number: 96-24455
International Standard Book Number: 0-8361-9050-5
Printed in the United States of America
Book and cover design by Jim Butti

05 04 03 02 01 00 99 98 97 96 10 9 8 7 6 5 4 3 2 1

To Carolyn, my wife and best friend

Contents

Author's Preface and Acknowledgments

What you are about to read is much more than one person's story. Though it is told from my perspective, it is a story in which literally thousands had a part. No two would have told it exactly the same way.

The events on which this story is based have centered on the people who make up Jubilee Partners, an international Christian service community in northeast Georgia. Visitors, volunteer workers, and refugees from all over the world enrich our daily life together. But the continuity comes from a small core of "resident partners" who share the central vision and the risks of the work of Jubilee.

We are like nothing else so much as a large family. These are my sisters and brothers. As you will sense at times while you read this book, I love them and appreciate the privilege of sharing my life with them. This is their story as much as mine.

Beyond the boundaries of the Jubilee community there are good friends and co-workers too numerous to mention. Only a random few appear in the following pages. I hope the rest will not be too disappointed.

A few must be mentioned here, however. Among

them are Dale and Connie Nash. Their special encouragement and hospitality allowed this book to begin taking form in the little writing shack in the woods behind their house in the Blue Ridge Mountains.

Without the help of Joyce Hollyday, I doubt the book would have been completed. For more than three years I worked to get the book on paper in whatever brief snatches of time I could find. Sometimes I worked literally on the run—I would compose a section mentally while jogging, then write it down when I returned home. Much of the book was written in quiet hours before sunrise and the day's distractions. Joyce came along at just the right time to help bring order to what I had accumulated. Wherever you run across a touch of special eloquence in the following pages, you are probably looking at one of Joyce's contributions. She has been less than a ghost writer but more than an editor.

Finally, I must express my deepest gratitude to my own family. Carolyn has been a patient, prayerful, vigorous, and graceful part of all that has happened at Jubilee since the time when it existed only as an idea shared by the two of us. With our son Tony and daughter Robyn, we had a tiny backpacking tent as our only home for a time. Then we celebrated together as we progressed over the next two years to a pop-up camper, a single room in Jubilee's main building, and finally a small house just for our own family! Even then, as this book documents, some of the hardest times still lay ahead.

Carolyn, Tony, Robyn—I love you and thank you. If they knew the whole story, so would thousands of refugees and others who have benefited from your endurance.

—*Don Mosley*
Comer, Georgia

Introduction:
Love Is "Comeing"

by Joyce Hollyday

Dark was descending as I crossed into Madison County, Georgia. Out beyond the shadows, the red clay earth stretched on for miles.

On this Easter Eve, the local Christian radio station was playing Handel's "Messiah" from beginning to end. As the jubilant strains of the "Hallelujah Chorus" began filling my car, I glanced off to my left and saw the rising moon—a huge, orange ball crawling up over the eastern horizon.

I turned up the radio a notch and quickened my pace, flying over northeast Georgia's dusty roads, catching glimpses of the moon between the trees. I stopped at Comer's only traffic light, then in a blink passed through the small town—deserted on a Saturday night. As I turned into the road by the "Jubilee Partners" sign, the voices on the radio launched into "I Know That My Redeemer Liveth."

The triumphant hymn ushered me down the long gravel drive, past two lakes, through a shallow stream, and around a bend. When I got out of the car, the full moon was flooding the Jubilee meadow with white light. I had always felt a thrill at arriving here, but never had I experienced the lighting and background music to match.

Ten hours later, the moon was pink and setting in a predawn sky. The large bell at Jubilee Partners was ringing, beckoning members of the community and assorted guests to the porch off the dining hall.

Blake Byler Ortman read the resurrection account from the Gospel of Luke. Then, like the women bearing spices that first Easter morning, we went in search of the tomb. Expectation burned strong and authentic as we walked across the fields. Only the presence of two beavers swimming in the lake—one slapping its tail on the water and executing an Easter flip—reminded us we were in northeast Georgia, not Palestine.

We came upon a "tomb" created from rocks and tarps in the woods. An "angel," sitting on a rock and playing melodies on a flute, stopped and questioned us. "Why do you look for the living among the dead?" He directed us up a hill.

At the top of the hill, we gathered on homemade pews. Behind a large wooden cross, the sun was peeking over the horizon. As the sky gradually lightened, we sang hymns of praise. We recounted Jesus' life, death, and resurrection in the joyful anthem "He Is Coming."

Suddenly, all eyes went to a corner of the field. Don Mosley appeared in a bright Nicaraguan shirt, carrying a dozen orange balloons. The Jubilee bell beyond the woods rang loud and long as Don approached. He handed out the balloons to the delighted children, while Carolyn Mosley passed out crepe paper streamers and markers. We were all invited to write an "Easter joy" on a streamer.

Behind me, several Muslims—who had recently arrived from Bosnia and were still learning English—asked among themselves, "How do you spell *Jubilee*?" Each of their streamers bore the name of this community that had welcomed them. In front of me, six-year-old Hannah Byler Ortman popped off her pew, turned, and knelt. Using the pew's plank for a writing surface, she carefully penned on a streamer "Love Is Comeing."

We taped the streamers to the balloons. The children lined up next to one another, oldest to youngest. Thirteen-year-old Chris Borgman let go of his balloon and shouted, "Christ is risen!" As it soared into the air, we all exclaimed, "He is risen indeed!"

Down the line, one by one, the balloons were released. When four-year-old Misha Winterfeld shouted, "Christ is risen!" and let go, his balloon lifted a few feet and stopped. His cautious mother had tied his balloon to his little finger to make sure he didn't lose it prematurely. Soon all the balloons soared up and away, over a large oak tree and toward the sun.

When they were out of sight, we walked back to the dining hall. As we entered, a lavish aroma of fresh-baked sweets and the joyful swells of the music of "Pachelbel's Canon," wafted through the air and bathed our senses. The Bosnians had made a honey-and-nut pastry resembling baklava. The Vietnamese refugees had baked cakes, decorated profusely with yellow and orange flowers and the words "Jesus Is Alive." Hot cross buns, sweet rolls, and other pastries filled three tables. Eating and laughter were hearty.

After breakfast I set out alone for a walk. The sun was already hot and high in the sky. The beavers had gone into hiding in the light of day. No trace was left of the balloons. But up on a bench, in the shadow of the cross, Hannah's words remained. Her marker had seeped through the thin crepe paper and left this promise: "Love Is Comeing."

I walked down the hill, past a field recently planted with blueberry bushes, by the chicken coop, where the roosters were still noisily greeting the morning, and then across a small bridge bearing a sign, "Beware! of Trolls." Engraved in the bridge's planks are the names of the community's children—Ben, Misha, Hannah, Eli, Chris, Rachel, Marah.

Beyond the bridge is a retreat shack tucked in the woods, where members of the community come from time to time to pray, rest, or write. And beyond the shack is a grove of tall pines that contains a small cemetery. It is holy ground, a place of honor for men largely despised by this world—refugees, homeless men, death-row prisoners executed by the state. Here they are embraced by the trees and warmed by a blazing sun.

Outside a large shed nearby are scattered several bicycles in all sizes. Inside hangs a homemade hot-air balloon, constructed by Don out of bamboo and sheets of black plastic. His first such creation took off into the sky; even a high-speed chase by car didn't retrieve it. The launchings of the balloons are grand events at Jubilee, usually done in the early mornings before the wind picks up, with a barrel fire and a window fan.

Peeking out from behind the suspended balloon is a huge, hand-painted sign: "Thank You, Comer, for Hospitality—In the Name of One Who Was Also a Refugee." Below these words is written in a long list: "39 Cubans, 30 Laotians, 100 Cambodians, 21 Nicaraguans, 783 Salvadorans, 400 Guatemalans, 80 Hondurans, 14 Afghans, 6 Armenians, 144 Vietnamese, 60 Bosnians."

The sign was attached to the back of the Jubilee Partners float in the 1993 Comer Christmas parade. It is already outdated; many more refugees have come through the community in the months since. The sign is a revelation of the calling of Jubilee Partners. It is a proclamation that at the heart of that calling is Jesus: Jesus, who preached good news to the poor and invited his followers to show compassion to those who suffer; Jesus, who while still an infant was taken by his parents into exile in Egypt to flee the wrath of Herod; Jesus, the refugee.

At the bottom of the sign, an arrow points left and is marked "Bethlehem." An arrow labeled "Egypt" points in the opposite direction. The arrows make clear that Jesus' parents had a choice to make after his birth. The authorities were rattling swords and slaughtering children in an effort to do away with this newborn threat to their power. Mary and Joseph fled to Egypt to save their Son's life.

As I pondered the sign, the quiet was broken by the whistle of a train moving down the tracks not far from Jubilee Partners. Comer is along a major east-west freight route, and trains rumble through several times a day— even on Easter Sunday. The interruption of the whistle was a fitting one, a reminder that the people of Jubilee also have had to make risky choices.

Like those in many southern towns, the train tracks divide Comer's white and black communities. In a different era the town, which lies on the northern edge of the "cotton belt," was home to plantations and slavery. While taking on concerns from the far corners of the world, the folks at Jubilee have also dug in to confront racism right at home in Madison County. On one occasion they even tangled with the Ku Klux Klan. As a result of getting involved in a variety of local projects and at various times attending all four of Comer's churches, Jubilee Partners has been a bridge builder among people who, in most places, remain separate and divided.

The train tracks are a symbol of another concern. For years a special white train carrying nuclear warheads from a weapons plant in Amarillo, Texas, to the naval weapons depot in Charleston, South Carolina, rolled unnoticed through small towns in the South. When Jubilee Partners became aware of it, the community became the tracking center for the eastern half of the country and helped to organize protest vigils all along the route.

Jubilee Partners stood for justice and peace at every turn, often placing the community on a collision course with the powers that be. Whether racing along train tracks at midnight in pursuit of an eerie white train, refusing to pay federal taxes that support war, conducting Central American refugees past Border Patrol barriers, confronting Klan violence—the community offers a courageous witness that the call of Jesus is stronger than the powers of this world. Few other places on earth have experienced the mixture of languages and cultures that has visited this plot of 260 acres in rural Georgia.

As victims of war and torture and all manner of violence have made their way to Jubilee, the community has looked evil in the face. With compassion and sacrificial generosity, its members have steadfastly held to their faith in Jesus Christ. They have welcomed refugees from every corner of the world and sent community members off to Thailand and Nicaragua, to South Africa and Bosnia and Iraq, to bring a peaceful presence to the world's most troubled places.

The Jubilee story is an extraordinary one and inspires down to the bones. It is a testimony to what ordinary people can do when they are willing to live by faith, whatever the cost. That faith is based on resurrection hope, on the belief that Jesus has indeed triumphed over evil and death—even though the evidence often seems to show otherwise.

Later that Easter morning, the Jubilee van dropped off the Vietnamese refugees and several Jubilee volunteers at the Comer United Methodist church. Others of us went on to the First Baptist Church, then to Springfield Baptist, which was still lively with praise when we arrived an hour into the service.

On our return, as we waited outside the United Methodist church for the others, Don nodded toward a statue in a small family cemetery. He said, "See the 'black power angel'?"

Sure enough, there was a marble angel, turned dark by the wear of time, her hand raised in the air in a fist, reminiscent of the militant black power salute of the 1960s. Don laughed and explained that a rock-throwing child had likely knocked off the finger that had pointed heavenward.

He drew our attention to a small headstone that rested just outside the fence of the family plot. "He was a homeless man who died on the streets of Comer many years ago," Don explained about the man beneath the stone. The owners of the cemetery decided to bury him, but didn't feel it was quite right to include him in with the family.

That's the kind of distinction that's likely to upset an angel. It's right that she stands there, looking defiant, fist in the air. That's the kind of division the folks at Jubilee Partners have committed their lives to breaking down. Like that angel, they are gentle in spirit but unwavering about the things that matter.

Above all, they show the world that we are all part of the same family. Vietnamese. Bosnians. Salvadorans. Black. White. Rich. Poor. It doesn't matter. We are all children of God.

Their message is especially timely for our harsh era, when politicians and citizens are rushing to scapegoat all manner of humanity—welfare mothers and "illegal aliens," racial minorities and "criminals"—for a variety of national ills. In a time when so many people believe that the answer to our problems is to build more prisons and raise more fences, we need the witness of those whose lives are rooted in compassion.

Throughout their history, the people at Jubilee Partners have found biblical passages on which to build their life. Perhaps one more for them is found in Hebrews 13:1–2. "Let mutual love continue. Do not neglect to show hospitality to strangers, for thereby some have entertained angels unawares" (NRSV except "unawares" KJV).

The Jubilee folks would be the first to say that angels have passed through their doors. These angels brought with them their stories of sacrifice and courage. Their generosity and hope have been a balm for many a weary Jubilee soul. Like many other Christians before them, the people of Jubilee Partners have learned the truth that, when they set out to minister, they are most often ministered to. They have discovered the power of mutual love.

The world will continue to draw lines and close ranks. And the victims will be legion. The globe's suffering overwhelms, threatening to render us paralyzed and powerless. Where will the next crisis be? What land will next be torn apart by war or ravaged by hunger?

For a group of people in northeast Georgia, the questions come close to home. They refuse to stand by helplessly in the face of the world's anguish. Instead, they have embraced that suffering and been profoundly inspired by its survivors. And with the testimony that follows on these pages, they invite us also to be inspired—and moved to make a difference.

From where will the next stream of refugees make their way to Jubilee Partners? No one can know for sure. Only one thing is certain: "Love is comeing."

With Our Own Eyes

1

Cows, Construction, and Consequences

At first it was only a faint rumbling far away. I snuggled deeper into my warm sleeping bag and clung to my pleasant dream. The sound became a thundering roar; the ground shook. Suddenly the tent jerked violently; I bolted up.

One of the children screamed, "Daddy! What's *happening?*"

Seconds later I was standing in cold, wet grass in front of the tent, waving my arms and shouting as a hundred cows and their calves bolted past. As they charged down the hill toward the ponds, one mother hung back to wait for her small offspring, which had tripped over our tent rope. He got his legs back in order and went bawling after her.

"Looks like we survived another stampede, doesn't it?" Ryan Karis was standing outside his new yellow tent in his underwear. A few feet away Ed Weir was untangling himself from the clothesline he had strung outside his tent the night before. Wet swimsuits and towels were scattered in the mud.

"Yeah, but I don't think I've got enough adrenaline left

for another one," Ed answered. "I can't take such excitement so early in the morning. The electric fence goes at the top of my work list today. Those cows have to go."

I ducked back into my family's tent and started pulling on my shirt and jeans. "I'm going for a little walk," I said in answer to my wife Carolyn's glance. "The sun is just about to come up, and there are lots of pretty places on this land that I haven't explored yet. I'll come back in a few minutes for breakfast."

Tony and Robyn, at ten and six, were still small enough that the four of us could just barely fit into our little backpacking tent—three long sleeping bags pressed in side by side, with Robyn across at our feet. The kids had stayed up with us by the campfire until nearly midnight the night before, too excited to go to bed. Now they were happy to settle back into their sleeping bags for a few extra minutes of sleep.

The first rays of the sun filtered through the trees as I emerged from the tent again. It was early summer, and the northeast Georgia air had been cool and damp during the night. Dewdrops glistened on spiderwebs in the tall grass as the sunlight reached them. A trace of smoke still rose from the embers of our campfire.

A brown thrasher sang a cheerful song from a nearby tree, a welcome change from the persistent calling of the whip-poor-wills all night. As I started down the slope, a flock of crows announced noisily to half the county that a human was invading their meadow.

I felt a surge of joy as I walked along the edge of the woods. We were finally here! It was hard to believe, after all the years of planning and dreaming, countless meetings and trips to hunt for land. After a long search, we had found this beautiful piece of land at the edge of a small town named Comer. Forests and meadows, streams and ponds made up its 260 acres. At first we could reach our campsite only by crossing a neighbor's property and driving across an open field.

Three families set out in the spring of 1979 with the encouragement of our friends back at Koinonia Partners. We were the lucky ones—six adults and six children embarking on a pioneering adventure few people ever have a chance to experience. The truth was that far more adventure awaited than we imagined. But at that moment we had enough to think about just laying out the sites for new buildings and getting the construction work started.

"Jubilee Partners!" We had finally settled on the name for our new community shortly before arriving on the land. As our vision of the community began to take shape, the biblical theme of Jubilee kept coming up in our discussions. We turned often to Jesus' launching of his ministry in the synagogue at Nazareth. Reading from the prophet Isaiah, Jesus announced,

> "The Spirit of the Lord is upon me,
> because he has anointed me
> to bring good news to the poor.
> He has sent me to proclaim release to the captives
> and recovery of sight to the blind,
> to let the oppressed go free,
> to proclaim the year of the Lord's favor."
> —Luke 4:18-19 (NRSV)

The "year of the Lord's favor" referred to the Jubilee year. Every fifty years throughout the history of the Israelites, prisoners were freed, debts forgiven, and the poor given a share of the resources (Lev. 25). Jubilee was a year marked by justice and mercy—themes that throbbed at the center of God's good news from the Old Testament prophets to Jesus. We didn't know yet exactly how we were going to put justice and mercy into action, but we recognized that the ancient vision was a good one to keep before us.

A brook ran the length of the Jubilee property, about a mile from north to south. Near our campsite it broadened into three ponds lying end to end. I sat on a log near where the stream rippled down from the middle pond to the lower one and began to think about the events that had brought us here.

Koinonia Partners near Americus, Georgia, was the ideal place from which to launch Jubilee Partners. It was a bustling Christian community and farm founded almost forty years earlier by Clarence Jordan and others. Koinonia provided dramatic evidence that a handful of Christians can overcome great odds when they hold firmly to their beliefs.

For the first few years, these Christians had been tolerated by their south Georgia neighbors, even admired by some. Clarence Jordan was as southern as grits—he came from a prominent family nearby. He was an ordained Southern Baptist minister with a degree in agriculture and a Ph.D. in New Testament Greek. He was also a gifted storyteller and Bible teacher with a quick sense of humor. For a while he had more invitations to preach in local churches than he could handle.

But Jordan just couldn't help being indiscreet when he preached. At a time when the nation was fiercely proud of its victory over the Germans and the Japanese, Jordan insisted that Christians should love their enemies, not drop nuclear bombs on them. While most folks in the United States were trying to cash in on the economic boom that followed World War II, he was calling for people to live more simply—maybe even (shades of communism!) collectively, like the first Christian *koinonias*, or communities.

Most scandalous of all, Clarence Jordan preached at

every opportunity that churches, black *and* white, ought to be in the forefront of the struggle against racism. Preaching that message in southern white churches in the '40s and '50s soon left Jordan with a lot more time free for his work on the farm.

If Jordan and the others at Koinonia had been satisfied merely to talk about such issues, they might have been ignored and left to work their fields in relative peace. But the primary purpose of Koinonia from the first had been to serve, in Jordan's words, as a "demonstration plot for the kingdom of God." It was common knowledge around Sumter County that at Koinonia black people and white people were breaking longstanding southern rules by worshiping and even eating together.

That was more than the Ku Klux Klan or the White Citizens Council could tolerate. By the late '50s Koinonia had become a favorite target of night riders and dynamiters. Local businesses imposed a boycott; for several years merchants did business with Koinonia only furtively and at considerable peril. One store that dared to sell a load of seed to Koinonia was destroyed the next night by a blast that broke windows all over downtown Americus.

The courage of the community under attack for its faith inspired people around the world, and led to renewed demand for Jordan's message. "So long as the word remains a theory to us and is not incarnated by our actions and translated by our deeds into a living experience," he preached, "*it is not faith*. It may be theology, but it is not faith. Faith is a combination of both conviction and action. It cannot be either by itself."

Jordan had little patience with Christians paralyzed by their fear of what might happen if they really acted on faith. "Faith," Jordan insisted, "is a life in *scorn* of the consequences."

Carolyn and I arrived at Koinonia Partners in the summer of 1970. The overt violence against Koinonia had all but ended. Clarence Jordan had died just months earlier, but under the energetic leadership of a lean, young lawyer named Millard Fuller the community was growing rapidly.

Hundreds of people were streaming through the Koinonia community. Some of them were pulled there by fantasies born of the '60s; others were driven by their hatred of the war that was raging in Vietnam and all they associated with it. Most soon tired of the heat, the gnats, and the hard work, and moved on.

But gradually a stable core of partners coalesced. The community's emphasis shifted toward developing practical solutions to the deeply rooted problems of poverty. Slavery had long since been replaced by sharecropping and similar arrangements throughout the South, but the transition had done little to improve the quality of housing for many rural black families. All around Koinonia dilapidated shacks lined the back roads, many of them in worse condition than the barns that sheltered pigs and chickens on the farms of white neighbors.

In 1968 Clarence Jordan and Millard Fuller had launched the Fund for Humanity, soliciting contributions which then became part of a revolving fund used primarily to finance the construction of modest new houses. Low-income families were charged only the basic cost of the houses, with no profit or interest added. Their monthly payments were put back into the revolving fund and used to build still more homes. It was a radical idea; critics listed plenty of reasons why it wouldn't work.

Jordan had enthusiastically laid off lots for forty houses on the north end of Koinonia's property, but he died of a heart attack six weeks before the first house was completed. With Millard Fuller as director, the housing project continued at full speed. Even at a distance, Koinonia's supporters sensed that something significant was happening, and contributions poured in.

Soon after Carolyn and I arrived at Koinonia, I was put in charge of the housing project. Later Millard and his wife, Linda, decided to go to Africa for three years. We spent most of their last evening at Koinonia brainstorming excitedly about the possibility of starting a housing project there. At one point, Millard sat forward on the sofa and exclaimed, "This could be a historic moment!" Not in our wildest dreams could we foresee then that these ideas would blossom into hundreds of housing projects in cities all over the world within the next few years.

One year later I flew to Zaire to spend a month in Mbandaka with the Fullers, designing and surveying what eventually became the first Habitat for Humanity project. The next year, Ryan and Karen Karis spent two months in a nearby village helping to launch the second such project. Now the Karises were camped up the hill from where I sat, part of another new adventure with a future as unpredictable as Habitat for Humanity's future had been earlier.

Suddenly I realized that it was time to get back to camp and start on the day's work. As I stood up, a deer broke out of the trees and crossed the meadow with long, graceful leaps. She paused and looked back from the woods on the other side, while two spotted fawns jumped from the bushes and ran to catch up with her. A great blue heron lifted from the edge of the pond ahead of me and flew past them and the waiting doe. I felt as though I was getting a glimpse of sunrise in the Garden of Eden.

As I approached the campsite, my idyllic mood was shattered by the news blaring from our transistor radio: "Officials deny charges that Three Mile Island still poses a risk to nearby residents. . . . Khomeini warns the U.S. not to welcome the deposed Shah of Iran. . . . Nicaraguan President Anastasio Somoza shrugs off charges of human rights violations and says his forces are rapidly destroying the Sandinista guerrillas. . . . In El Salvador today, Archbishop Oscar Romero pleaded with. . . ."

Ed turned off the radio as Mary Ruth Weir announced that breakfast was ready. "Now that we've survived one stampede and one news broadcast, why don't we have some pancakes?" she said irritably. All of us shared her frustration. We resented the fact that the world's problems imposed themselves on us even in this pristine setting. But in a little while, we had put the troubles of the rest of the world out of our minds as we went about our work.

As one long day followed another, we established a grueling routine, working from early morning until nearly dark. At first we focused most of our energy on the construction of a two-story house to be shared by the Weirs and the Karises. The older children helped Karen in the new garden or took turns caring for the younger ones. The Georgia sun beat down on all of us as we worked—digging, hammering, painting, and sweating. Sometimes when we felt we just couldn't keep working in the heat, we would break for a while and go for a cool swim in one of the ponds.

Just before dark we would take turns by families and go down to a secluded section of the creek for baths. It took careful coordination for everyone to finish before the mosquitoes came out and made bathing impossible.

As the weeks passed, the novelty of being pioneers wore thin. Some of us checked the calendar from time to time, wondering whether we might lose the race to get everyone housed before winter arrived.

We laugh now about our "pioneering days." Carolyn admits, "If I had known that we were going to be like *Little House on the Prairie* for a year, I might not have been so enthusiastic about it." But there were valuable lessons learned.

"It was a situation in which we didn't know from one day to the next what new adventure we might find," Carolyn says. "When we first arrived, we didn't have any running water or electricity. So every time we got something like that, it was like a miracle. It was good to experience that—to be grateful for the little things, for the things we just took for granted before."

Carolyn and Robyn laugh now about Dawn Weir's sixteenth birthday party. My brother David was visiting for a while to help us with construction. He heated as many gallons of water as he could fit on the woodstove and gave Dawn a bathtub full of hot water as a gift. She was thrilled. For the next hour, she soaked up the luxury of a long hot bath while we called through the door for periodic reports.

By midsummer we were aware that we had one half-finished house, less than $30,000 in our bank account, no paying jobs, and no time even to go look for other work. Crawling into our tents began to change from being fun to serving as a nightly reminder of our precarious situation. We were still confident that it would all work out somehow, but we began to experience in a small way the difference between talking bravely back at Koinonia about "taking a leap of faith" and actually doing it. Somewhere along the way, we began to grasp that "living in scorn of the consequences" might indeed bring consequences.

2

Always More Room

Ironically, it was our growing sense of vulnerability and uprootedness that set the stage for a still larger leap of faith, beyond what rational and prudent people would have recommended.

We had never been able completely to ignore events in the larger world. We began to feel particular kinship with one group of persons, the "boat people" of Southeast Asia. Almost every newscast we heard included a story about yet another tragedy in the South China Sea as refugees tried desperately to reach safety in overcrowded boats. We found it especially painful to consider that our own nation's violence in the Vietnam War had been a primary cause of their dislocation and suffering. Although we were far more secure than those refugees, we were adrift just enough to begin to sense what they must be feeling.

The cover story of the July 2, 1979, issue of *Newsweek* was titled "Agony of the Boat People." Before I even opened the magazine, I was struck by the cover photograph. It showed an open boat crowded with refugees, most of them children. In the middle of the crowd sat a woman with a look of fatigue and hopelessness. A crying child sat in her lap, pulling at her.

The article reported that more than 700,000 people

had streamed out of Indochina in the previous four years, including up to a quarter-million who had crossed by land from Cambodia and Laos and as many who had put out to sea in crowded, leaky boats. Of those trying to escape by boat, an estimated twenty to fifty percent died at sea. Even though the United States was already taking in 7,000 refugees from Indochina each month—more than all other countries combined—President Jimmy Carter was about to raise the monthly quota to 10,000. U.S. refugee agencies were bracing for the increase.

By the time I had read the story through the second time, I was sure we had found our work—or that we had been found by it. The biblical theme of Jubilee—"the poor . . . captives . . . oppressed"—seemed suddenly to take on new meaning. I typed a one-page proposal that we make Jubilee a welcome center for such refugees. While the other five adults passed it around, I went off alone to pray.

When I returned to the construction site a little while later, Karen ran out to meet me. I could tell from her expression that she agreed with the proposal. In minutes Carolyn, Ed, Mary Ruth, and Ryan had joined us and were talking excitedly about the idea.

Two things were immediately obvious to us. The first was that we knew nothing about how to undertake such a project. The second was that our ignorance didn't matter; we *knew* we were on the right track.

The next few weeks were a time of investigation and planning. I began by calling church officials to learn how their refugee resettlement programs worked. Often I had to shout for silence as the hammering and sawing in the next room drowned out our telephone conversations.

Some of the "experts" were unresponsive to our proposal to establish a refugee welcome center. A few told us bluntly that our services weren't needed; it would be better to leave the work to established agencies. On the whole, however, we were encouraged by the national refugee resettlement officers of the major church denominations.

Using their input we began to consider what kinds of facilities we would need before we could take in the first refugees. We decided we needed at least six buildings, a new road more than a mile long, and a water system half that length. The work seemed endless. When we totaled up what we thought the projects would cost by the end of the following May—with ourselves and volunteers doing all the work free of charge—it came to $131,000. Moreover, we estimated it would take between twenty and thirty thousand person-hours of labor to complete.

Shaken somewhat by the growing realization of what we were proposing to take on, I placed a call to Dr. Harry Haines, chairman of Church World Service and head of the United Methodist Committee on Relief (UMCOR). Haines and I had already met several times, and I had great respect for his imagination and his vision of the church's role in helping people around the world. I had seldom heard him speak softly, so I was not surprised when I had to hold the telephone away from my ear slightly.

"Don, I think that's a marvelous idea," he boomed after I described our tentative plans. "Don't listen to anyone who might try to discourage you! There are at least twelve to fifteen million refugees around the world already, and the number is increasing much faster than we can respond. I assure you there will always be more demands on your center than you can meet."

"You know," I continued, "we're getting new insights about what it really means to live by faith. . . ."

"Wonderful!" he cut in. "I recommend that all of you at Jubilee spend some time studying the eleventh chapter of Hebrews."

"As a matter of fact, Harry, we decided just this morning that we should open our first newsletter with Hebrews 11:1."

"That's *splendid*, Don. My advice to you now is simply to go out and *act* on it!"

After a pep talk like that from a man of Haines' experience and stature, we felt ready to take on Goliath. Never mind that after a hard summer of work our accomplishments consisted of little more than a still-unfinished house, a new well, and an outhouse. What did it matter that we had not yet sent out our first newsletter—and lacked even a mailing list?

Our friends at Koinonia Partners and Habitat for Humanity came to our rescue—they allowed us to borrow their mailing lists for our first mailing. After that we used only the addresses of people who responded directly to us.

Early in September we sent out the first "Jubilee Partners Report." Across the top in bold print was this message from Clarence Jordan's *Cotton Patch* (CPV) translation of the Bible.

> NOW FAITH IS THE TURNING
> OF DREAMS INTO DEEDS;
> IT IS BETTING YOUR LIFE
> ON THE UNSEEN REALITIES.
> HEBREWS 11:1

We described our dream of making Jubilee's 260 acres of forests and meadows into a place of hospitality for the homeless, starting with refugees from Southeast Asia. We told of our plans to offer lessons in basic English, orientation classes to help with cultural transition, and contacts with churches that might later host the refugees. We asked for contributions, non-interest loans, and volunteer labor.

After mailing the letters out from Koinonia, we returned to Jubilee and our work. As we went about our tasks, we were preoccupied with one question: Would people respond? If not, we had no idea what we would do next. We tried to be calm and leave the matter in God's hands, but. . . .

A few days later the first letter arrived. It was the most beautiful, welcome letter I had ever received. It was from Willie Mae Champion, a longtime employee and neighbor of Koinonia. She had worked closely with Clarence Jordan to develop the fruitcakes and other mail-order products that helped Koinonia survive the long boycott. Later she and I worked together on one Koinonia project after another.

Now she was writing to tell us how much she loved us and that she would be praying for the success of our work with the refugees. Having grown up in a poor sharecropper's shack made her understand what the refugees were up against. She had no money to contribute, but the letter could not have meant more to me if she had sent a thousand dollars with it.

The next day there were half a dozen responses. The day after that the dam broke! We were astonished as the letters began to pour in faster than we could open and respond to them. In the evenings we sat around the dining-room table and took turns reading them aloud, sometimes laughing, often with tears in our eyes. It was clear that many people had been sympathetic to the refugees but unclear about how they could respond. We began to realize that we were going to have hundreds of true partners in this work.

We were thrilled to find checks in most of the envelopes, but some of our most treasured responses were from people who had no money to offer. One man wrote that he had no money to give because his wife had just died after a long and costly illness; he offered to send us her clothing for the refugee women.

One car after another began to arrive with helpers, offering anywhere from a few hours to a month of free labor. Our little cluster of tents grew and was joined by all kinds of camper trailers and RVs.

The following months were a blur of activity. We divided into several work crews and poured new foundations. In a race against time, we began to frame-in a large community building to protect the growing volunteer crew from winter weather. We kept a small bulldozer busy most of the time, preparing construction sites, burying septic tanks, and clearing brush. A survey crew laid out the site for the refugee cabins, a school building, and a playground. In our rare moments of relaxation, Carolyn and I went to the site of the future Welcome Center to stroll among the survey markers, smiling as we imagined the refugee children who would be playing there in a few months.

To our amazement, people seemed always to show up with the right skills just as we needed them. Each one brought new energy when our own threatened to give out. Three friends came from a Hutterian community in North Dakota and left us breathless as we watched them build half a mile of road through the forest to the Welcome Center—and bury two water lines its full length—all in less than seventy-two hours!

Meanwhile we did our best to build good personal friendships with our neighbors. We had come to the little town of Comer with some apprehension, born of the strained relationships we had experienced so often with white neighbors around Koinonia. We attended services in local churches and participated vigorously in school activities. We requested special meetings with the leaders of each church, the City Council, and the County Commissioners. At each opportunity we explained as fully as we could what we hoped to do and urged people to come for a visit.

Predictably, there was some nervousness about a group of "outsiders" coming into a small Georgia community and establishing an orientation center for refugees from all over the world. Comer was a town of fewer than a thousand people, many of them members of families that had been in the area for generations. What we were bringing into their neighborhood was different from anything Comer had ever experienced.

The mass-suicide "Jonestown massacre" in Guyana was still fresh on everyone's mind. The very mention of "communes" made people uneasy. A reporter from the major newspaper of the region was assigned to write an exposé about Jubilee. She told us later that she had gone back after her visit and told the editor that there was nothing to expose, but the editor was determined to get his story.

We caught our breath when the paper came out with a banner headline across the top of the front page: "CHRISTIAN COMMUNE BEING DEVELOPED." The article itself was bland, with nothing to justify its prominent place on the front page or a provocative headline. There was a brief flurry of worried calls to the Comer City Hall, with a few people asking that the place be shut down by the police. To our great relief, most of our neighbors shrugged it off and continued their competition to get us to join their churches. Our appreciation for the warmth and the genuine hospitality of the people of Comer deepened.

In the spring we had to approach the county health department for approval of our Welcome Center plans. We were nervous, aware that this was the place where the local officials were most likely to impede our work, if so inclined.

We made clear to the health official that we expected people from all corners of the globe to come through Jubilee's facilities. He thought for a few moments, then asked that we give him time to research the matter. The realization of the danger of "exotic diseases" from such a population, he explained, would oblige him to consult with his supervisor in Atlanta.

Several days later he came to Jubilee with a drawing of the septic system we were required to build before the county would allow our Welcome Center to open. I could already see from his manner that he was not bringing good news. When he laid the drawing in front of us, our hearts sank. We were required to build the biggest septic system of its type in the county. We were required to dig field lines three feet wide, three deep, and close to a mile long!

We had been pushing ourselves to the limit for close to a year. Fatigue was becoming a factor in whether we were going to be ready for the refugees as soon as we had hoped. We had already moved our target date back three months, to the end of the summer. Meanwhile we were getting calls from the national offices of the United Methodists and the Lutherans, urgently inquiring how long it would be before we could take our first refugees.

We were not in a position to argue with the health department, so we smiled grimly and said that, of course, we'd get right on it. No problem.

For the next several weeks we worked harder than ever. We kept a bulldozer and rented tractor with a backhoe busy from dawn to dark every day. While two people took their turns on the machines, others hauled barrels of fuel, pushed wheelbarrows, and directed the big dump trucks as they delivered hundreds of tons of crushed stone for the ditches.

In mid-May we were finally ready to call the county inspector to approve the open ditches. We stood at the edge of the big field late one evening and looked out across our work. Before us lay 4,000 feet of parallel ditches, each partly filled with crushed stone surrounding a perforated sewage line. Connector lines tied it all together in a giant zigzag pattern. Everything had been leveled with a transit so liquid would flow through the system as it should. Michelangelo could hardly have felt greater pride in the ceiling of the Sistine Chapel.

That night it began to rain. By the next morning the thunderstorm had become so violent we gave up all hope of returning to the work site. As we watched helplessly, lightning flashed and water poured out of the sky for three days. When it finally slackened enough, we trudged down the muddy road, dreading what we knew we were about to see.

An awful sight awaited us. Not only were all the ditches full of water, many were nearly full of mud. The flexible sewer pipe we had placed so carefully a few days earlier lay tangled at the lower edge of the field; a few sections were still in ditches, buried under tons of mud.

As we looked out over the mess, it seemed for a moment that our dream had just reached a sudden dead end. "That does it," said one tired worker. "We'll never be able to repair all of that." No one was in a mood to argue with him. We turned and slogged the half-mile back through the drizzle to tell the others the bad news.

For awhile discouragement and defeat prevailed. But gradually we started to shift our thoughts from our own bad luck to the suffering of the refugees. We remembered that even as we talked, there were Vietnamese crowded into refugee camps waiting for our help, people who had survived storms at sea in flimsy boats. We remembered that thousands of Laotians and Cambodians were waiting in Thailand. Many of these people had been forced by the brutal Khmer Rouge regime to work in Cambodia's "killing fields" under conditions far worse than we faced—children as well as women and men.

We rented a pump and began emptying water out of the ditches. Since the field was too soggy to support heavy machines, we shoveled mud from the ditches by hand. Taking it one section at a time, we rebuilt the whole system. By the middle of June, we were ready again for the inspector. He rushed out and checked our work. Only after we had safely covered the last ditch did we relax. We had done it!

A short time later I was invited to describe our program at the monthly meeting of our County Commissioners. When I finished, the chairman said, "The health inspector told us about how hard you folks work over there. He says you do things right. I just want to tell you on behalf of the county officials that we appreciate what you are doing. Let us know if you need anything."

I left that meeting walking six inches above the floor. Our years of struggling with local officials at Koinonia made me realize more than ever the significance of what had just happened. We still had two months of hard work ahead of us before we could take in the first refugees, but there was no longer any doubt. We were on our way!

Encouragement continued to come from many sources. One of the strongest words came while I was at the national conference of the Fellowship of Reconciliation in Berea, Kentucky, a few weeks later. FOR Executive Secretary Richard Deats knew we were expecting refugees any day at Jubilee. He preached from Isaiah 54:2-3:

Enlarge the limits of your home,
spread wide the curtains of your tent;
let out its ropes to the full
and drive the pegs home. . . . (NEB).

We were about to learn that in our home, as well as in our hearts, there would always be more room.

3

Cuba Comes to Comer

I hung up the telephone as calmly as I could and went downstairs from my new office in our community building, which we had named the Koinonia House. It was early fall of 1980. Several Jubilee people were taking a break in the large kitchen. At the first lull in the conversation, I said as casually as I could, "Oh, by the way, I just got a call from New York. The Methodist refugee office says that our first fourteen refugees will arrive at the Atlanta airport tomorrow morning."

"Tomorrow morning! But we're still painting their cabin. Their bunks aren't finished. . . ."

For a moment or two, everyone was talking at once, excited that the long wait was over but nervous now that our moment of truth had arrived.

"They are boat people," I said, "but from Cuba. The ones from Southeast Asia will come later."

The change came as no surprise to us. Back in the spring, the first trickle of Cuban refugees had successfully crossed the eighty miles of open sea to Florida. President Carter had welcomed the "freedom flotilla" publicly as a natural part of his emphasis on international human rights, and the U.S. public supported him. But the trickle quickly grew to a torrent, and Cuban leader Fidel Castro saw an opportunity to cut his government's expenses. He opened his prisons and released the inmates to come to the United States along with the others.

By midsummer more than 100,000 newly arrived Cubans were in Florida. The Church World Service (CWS) officials with whom we had been preparing to sponsor Asian refugees now pleaded with us to help them with Cubans first.

While our building crew worked to finish the first two refugee cabins, I went to Miami to help with the interviewing process, to be held at Krom Detention Center, about twenty miles west of the city. This was my first introduction to such Immigration and Naturalization Service (INS) facilities. I was shocked to find a thousand people sweltering behind a ten-foot, chain-link fence topped by coils of barbed concertina wire. There were no trees and little grass in the hot sand of the compound.

Most of the refugees were men, but there were also many women and children. All were crowded into a few large tents and some rusty, old World War II airplane hangars that had long since lost their doors.

Armed guards ushered me through the gate and pointed toward a small building. There I was to interview applicants for the Jubilee program. I decided to tour the camp first and talk with some of the people. My Spanish was poor, but soon a crowd collected and my language skills got a thorough workout. The people complained that the mosquitoes were a great problem every night, but an even greater concern was that poisonous snakes crawled from the surrounding swamp into the open tents where they slept.

"Most of all, *señor*, it is the waiting that is hard," one man said. "Many of us have been here for months. There is a limit to how long any man can lie in a hot tent with nothing to do!"

As I turned back toward the building to begin the interviews, my entourage grew. One man hurried across the yard and made his way determinedly through the crowd. He was about fifty and small, dark as ebony, and had a sad face. He introduced himself as Rodolfo Portillo, and said he must speak with me. As soon as he confirmed that I was a possible means of getting out of the compound, he ran ahead to get his name on the list for an interview.

After I was settled at a table with a CWS interpreter, the door opened. There was Rodolfo, at the head of the line. Soon I learned why he was so anxious to gain freedom. Rodolfo had come from Havana several months earlier after his wife became ill. She did not respond to the medicine available at the Cuban government clinic, but Rodolfo had no money to buy the more expensive medicine he was convinced she needed. There was barely enough money for food to feed their large family.

Rodolfo was growing desperate when he heard of the exodus from Cuba. He decided he must leave his family and try to reach the United States, where he might have some chance to earn money. Rodolfo's wife pleaded with him not to leave her and the children, but he insisted that he must go—for her sake most of all.

He managed to get a seat in a crowded fishing boat headed north. After a difficult trip he landed on the Florida shore. Rodolfo was almost immediately arrested by the Border Patrol and brought to this center. For three months he had begged the officials to let him go so he could help his wife and family, but he was trapped. As his eyes filled with tears, he told me, "Yesterday I received word that I am too late. My wife has died."

There was an awkward pause. I tried to express my sympathy. When he was able to speak again, Rodolfo insisted, "But now, you see, it is more important than ever for me to get out of here so I can help my children."

I assured Rodolfo Portillo that I would do all I could to see that his name was on the list to come to Jubilee. With calm dignity, he thanked me and left.

For the next several hours I listened to one plea for help after another. No doubt some of the stories were embellished a bit for dramatic effect, but the accounts were all so compelling that I knew more clearly than ever that we had to help all the refugees we could.

I left Miami with a list of the men who seemed most appropriate for the kind of program we would offer at Jubilee. All the way back to north Georgia, I felt like singing, grateful that my friends and I had been led to this work.

The big day came. Ed and I drove our vans to the Atlanta airport. We were feeling proud—after fifteen months of hard work, with more than a hundred helpers, we had finished the refugee cabins and other basic essentials with just hours to spare.

At last we were standing at the plate-glass window, watching the Delta Airlines DC-9 pull up to the entrance ramp and cut its engines. The passengers began to file into the waiting area, most of them obviously middle-class folks accustomed to this kind of travel.

Then a pause—and here they came, a crowd of men who instantly brought to mind Bluebeard's pirates. They were all shades of black, brown, and white, with a wild variety of mustaches and beards. Most wore big smiles. Two or three looked as though they needed a "sick sack" more than anything else at that moment.

Rodolfo proudly led the way, wearing a huge smile that revealed a serious shortage of teeth. Behind him came Ernesto, Rafael, Felipe, Maximo, Jesús, Julio. . . . They were fourteen real flesh-and-blood people emerging from the anonymous statistics of the news reports.

Two hours later we rounded the curve into the Jubilee parking lot and were met by a cheering crowd with a big

sign, "BIENVENIDOS—WELCOME." Someone was ringing the dining-room bell. In the warmth of the handshakes
and introductions any remaining nervousness faded away.

The next few days were filled with tours of the Jubilee
grounds, hours of volleyball, cake and ice-cream breaks,
and the first of many bilingual worship services in the
Koinonia House. After long weeks or months of miserable
imprisonment in the INS compound, our new guests were
ecstatic.

A few days later, we started English classes for the
men, eighteen hours a week of intensive study in small
groups. In addition to the formal classes we pushed them
to use English as much as possible in other everyday activities. Their opportunities after leaving Jubilee would de-
pend more than any other single factor on ability to speak
English. They were eager students.

We also had a lot to learn. We thought, for instance,
that it would be great for the fellows to have a night free
once or twice a week to walk around Athens. Twenty miles
from Comer, Athens is a city of about 100,000 residents,
many of them students and faculty of the University of
Georgia. We blithely dropped the men off at a corner and
asked them to meet us back there in two hours.

It was a disaster. Completely free to do whatever they
liked, they pulled out all the stops. Their activities that evening included drinking, arguing with local men who had
no idea what they were saying, and pinching female university students. And, of course, they were not all waiting
at the rendezvous point at the appointed time. We spent
hours hunting for some of them. One was delivered to Jubilee the next morning by the Athens police.

The following evening they were the picture of contri-
tion as we held a special meeting to talk about what had
happened. We invited two Cuban friends to join us, local
professional men who had been in the United States for

twenty years. The refugees were full of questions—such as, "If you can't pat a lady on the backside to show her you think she is nice, what can you do?" It was a learning experience for all of us.

We discovered that one of our most important tasks was to serve as buffers between cultures. We had done our best to prepare our Comer neighbors for what was coming, but we had only a limited understanding of it ourselves. To make matters more difficult, a national backlash had set in against the Cubans just about the time our guests arrived. The public resented the "dirty trick" Castro had pulled by emptying his prisons onto our shores. Every problem involving a Cuban refugee was magnified by the news media.

Many of our new arrivals had been imprisoned in Cuba. However, as far as we were ever able to tell, their offenses had been petty. In several cases, the men had apparently been jailed for political actions such as demonstrations or painting anti-Castro graffiti in public places. One man said he had become angry when the Cuban government raised the cost of telephone service, so he smashed several public pay phones in protest. He was caught in the act and sentenced to two years in prison.

Whatever initial anxiety we had about prison backgrounds was soon replaced with strong ties of friendship and affection. The men were convinced we were doing our best to help them find permanent homes and jobs in the United States. They applied themselves to the English lessons and participated eagerly in the educational field trips we set up.

We worked hard to find sponsors for them. We soon found we had an advantage over the refugee resettlement officers in the various national offices of church denominations. Working from lists of names and facts, they had to persuade congregations to sponsor people they themselves had never met. We, by contrast, could assure potential sponsors that we knew the refugees personally.

We sent packets of tape recordings, slides, and personalized information to prospective sponsoring churches. In some cases we even arranged for one or more representatives to meet the men in person. Invariably that resulted in sponsorship. Soon we were saying good-byes to our Cuban friends, usually two or three at a time, as they went to their new sponsors.

The system worked so well, despite the worsening backlash against Cuban refugees in general, that we were soon asked by CWS to take twenty-four more men. We agreed. With part of the first group still with us when the second arrived, our buildings were bursting at the seams. Refugees outnumbered our staff by almost two-to-one.

At that point the friendship of our neighbors in Comer underwent the most severe test to date. Cubans are generally gregarious people who love to "promenade" through town and meet people. We were determined not to make Jubilee into yet another prison for the men. So we pointed them toward the center of Comer a mile away, gave them a few pointers about how to get along with folks, and held our breaths.

Thirty swashbuckling Cuban men are enough to send shock waves through a little Georgia town. The refugees did their best not to offend anyone, but inevitably there were some complaints. Most of the concerns made their way back to us by way of the long-suffering staff of Comer's City Hall. We always tried to follow up on complaints and make peace with those who were upset.

It was during this time that we began to feel deeply grateful that we had been led to Comer. In particular, we were ready to nominate Mayor Cliff Yarborough for the Nobel Peace Prize. Cliff had already become an instant favorite of ours the previous year when he had driven the

Comer police car across the fields to our little cluster of tents to assure us we were welcome in his town. We soon found that Cliff's warmth was both genuine and consistent. He was a deacon in the First Baptist Church, and seemed to spend all his time trying to serve the people of Comer. How fortunate that Cliff himself was present at the biggest misunderstanding of all!

One night in mid-December, a Jubilee volunteer ran into the Koinonia House shouting, "Luis just tried to slug Mayor Yarborough and Marlin Carithers while they were on police duty!"

Luis was a friendly, easygoing man who had been in a Cuban jail several years for some petty crime. Tonight he had ridden a bicycle to town to buy something at the store. As he started back toward Jubilee, he found himself being followed by a car with a flashing blue light.

"I didn't know what that light meant," he told us later, "so I tried to beat them back to Jubilee. I thought it was some hoodlums following me."

The "hoodlums" were our part-time police force, Cliff Yarborough and Marlin Carithers, who was also a member of First Baptist Church. Cliff tells the story.

"This bicycle went whizzing by right in front of City Hall. And Marlin said, 'Let me stop him and tell him he needs to have some kind of lights on that bicycle at night like that.' So he put the blue lights on. The guy just went faster. I guess it scared him.

"We got down where you turn into Jubilee, and Marlin just kept edging him over. All at once, when he hit the grass, the bicycle shot out from under him. So we jumped out. We were just trying to talk to him.

"I reached for his arm just to tell him we were trying to be friends. We saw right off that he couldn't speak English. He thought I was getting ready to fight him, I guess, 'cause he swung at me but missed. Marlin still laughs about that every once in a while."

Cliff and Marlin brought Luis back to Jubilee. When I found out about it, I quickly drove into Comer and found Cliff parked in his accustomed place near Comer's only traffic light. He was cordial but still a little shaken. We talked for half an hour. About midnight he began to chuckle as he saw the humor of the incident.

At noon the following day, I was standing with Luis and several other Cubans in front of one of their cabins. Luis was still retelling the story and marveling that he had not been put in jail. Suddenly we looked up and saw the Comer police car coming down the winding road through the forest. The refugees became quiet as it approached.

Cliff and Marlin got out of the car. "Hello, fellows," Cliff said to the group. "We've got a little Christmas present for you." Then, while Luis and his friends looked on in utter astonishment, the two men opened the back of the car and took out two bushels of fresh fruit they had bought for the refugees. They set them on the ground and tried awkwardly for a few minutes to make conversation across the language barrier.

"Kind of a goodwill gesture," Cliff said later. "We said maybe that'll help make them understand we're not picking on them."

After they drove away, Luis kept repeating, "But that's the man I tried to hit last night. Now they are giving us this fruit?" Luis' confusion was understandable. What we had witnessed was a rare and beautiful act of genuine Christian peacemaking by two of our neighbors. They had given all of us something a lot more valuable than the fruit.

Not wanting to be outdone by the Baptists, our friends at the Comer United Methodist Church also did everything they could to make the refugees feel welcome. For a while the men attended Sunday services there. The pastor spoke hardly a word of Spanish, but he always arranged to have the text read in Spanish as well as English. That simple gesture was enough to bring the refugees back again and again.

Two weeks before Christmas, the church invited the Cubans and the Jubilee staff to a sumptuous covered-dish dinner. We decided to reciprocate by inviting the Methodist congregation to join us for what is now to be remembered as "The Great Christmas Pageant."

We built props and rehearsed for days. With eager refugees and Jubilee children playing the parts, we prepared to reenact each of the scenes in the Christmas story—out in the fields under the stars rather than in some old building.

We strung wires and set up sound systems. On a long bamboo pole, we lifted a tinsel star—brightly lit by a 100-watt bulb—above the topmost branch of a pecan tree beside a little goat barn. In the barn was the manger scene itself. The weather was mild and promising as we made our preparations.

We transformed our community dining room into a thing of beauty. Twenty candles were hung from the ceiling, each mounted in one of the glass telephone-line insulators we had found in an old dump on the property.

On the day of the big event the temperature plummeted, but most of our Methodist guests bundled up and bravely came ahead anyway. We assured them that the pageant itself would take only a few minutes, then we would be serving them hot chocolate in front of a warm fire. We didn't tell them about the dramatic lighting. When we had lit the candles, the effect was so beautiful we decided to save that as the evening's big surprise.

The Cubans had practiced their lines in class. The Jubilee kids did a fine job, and we parents swelled with pride as our cold audience moved from scene to scene. Finally the star came on in the tree above the little barn. We gathered around the manger to sing "Silent Night" and "Joy to the World."

Then we ran for the dining room. Everything had gone beautifully, but now we were all shivering and thinking of the chocolate and the fire. Sure enough, as we filed into the dining room—all the lights off except for the twenty stars flickering above—there were exclamations of admiration from our chilled guests.

We hurried to pass out the hot chocolate. Just then the first explosion took place.

The remains of a burning candle fell to the floor with a shattered glass insulator, the larger pieces of which shattered again on impact with the concrete. For a moment none of us was quite sure what had happened. Just as we began to catch on, the same thing happened at the other end of the dining room. It dawned on us that we had suspended twenty glass grenades above our heads. We returned just in time to stand under them as the candles burned down and broke the holders.

As quickly as possible, we cleared the dining room of guests, turned on the electric lights, and began rushing around with a step ladder to blow out the remaining candles. We won the race in all but one or two cases. Fortunately, no one was hurt. We swept up the remains, made some fresh hot chocolate free of broken glass, and enjoyed a good laugh together.

It was during those few days remaining before Christmas that things began to fall apart for us. In October we made the rash decision to send Ryan and Karen Karis to Thailand for two months to work in a refugee camp. We felt that this would give us more understanding when the time came to work with Southeast Asians. Next, even though short-handed, we welcomed another twenty-four Cubans. Consequently, we were working from early morning until all hours of the night. We had pushed ourselves so hard for so long that we ran out of reserves.

Then came a series of strange accidents and health

problems with the refugees, which caused us to make a dash to the hospital emergency room almost every day or night for a week. These included a chainsaw accident, a heart condition, and Jesús Torres' asthma attacks.

Jesús had coped with asthma successfully for years, but it had grown worse in the few months since his arrival in the United States. We moved him into the Koinonia House. Twice we had to rush him in the middle of the night to the emergency room in an Athens hospital twenty miles away. We also took him to our local doctor in Comer. Dr. Hshi Yung Hu, another member of the First Baptist Church, was monitoring his condition closely.

Early on Christmas morning, I awoke to the sound of rapid tapping on the wall downstairs. I knew at once that the sound was coming from Jesús. I opened his door and found the poor man struggling desperately for breath, a look of panic on his strained face. I gave him his medication and tried to calm him. Half an hour later he was breathing normally again. When I asked Jesús why he had not been taking the medicine on the table beside him, he told me that he had no faith in it; it had come from a Chinese doctor.

Three hours later, on a beautiful Christmas morning, Jesús Torres died of a heart attack, almost certainly brought on by the strain of his struggle during the night. Dr. Hu and the local EMS unit arrived quickly and did their best to revive him, but it was too late. I watched Dr. Hu working intently over the lifeless body and thought of how unnecessary this death had been, the result of Jesús' own prejudice toward the Chinese doctor who was now trying so hard to help his heart to beat again.

That afternoon Ed, Robbie Buller, and I walked over Jubilee's forested hills, searching for the best place to lay out a cemetery. When we had settled on one, we dug a grave for Jesús, not anticipating that there would soon be others added nearby or that this little clearing in the woods would become a focal point of public resentment in the years ahead.

The following Saturday night, a few hours after the funeral service for Jesús, we called an emergency meeting of Jubilee's community members, or partners. Ryan and Karen would not return from Thailand for another week. That left only five of us—Ed and Mary Ruth Weir, Carolyn and I, and Robbie, a six-foot, seven-inch Nebraska Mennonite who had become a partner in the fall.

As each of us looked around the room at the fatigue on the other faces, we sensed we had reached a crisis point. There was no question about the value of our work; we were as convinced as ever that it was right for us. But somehow we were not being replenished as rapidly as we were giving ourselves to others. Something had to change.

Each person took a turn commenting on our situation. We had no clear idea how to continue. We needed to find sponsors for the thirty refugees with us, but the list of prospects was getting shorter as public opposition to the Cubans rose. The longer the men stayed, the more restless they grew, and thus the problems multiplied.

The discussion grew long and tense as we considered one idea after another and discarded them all. We could not find the practical, commonsense key that would unlock the dilemma. No new technique came to mind.

It was Ed who made the comment that seemed at first to be off the subject, a distraction from the process at hand. "Back at Koinonia, I remember reading a statement by Mother Teresa. It was something about how when you're doing the kind of work they do in Calcutta and you get really tired, that's when you need to spend more time praying—every day an hour or two at least, even three, when the work really gets tough."

I answered impatiently, "That sounds great, of course,

but the main problem we have is that already there isn't enough time to do all we need to do. There just isn't time for all that praying."

So we continued talking for another hour, struggling not to fall asleep, feeling that we had to decide something before quitting. In the end, I came around, and more prayer was the one idea we all agreed on. The only way we could see to make time for it was to get up an hour earlier every morning. We agreed to gather every morning at 5:30 for an hour of prayer—beginning the next morning.

Morning after morning we met in the dark dining room, added logs to the fire to fight off the chill, and sat in chairs circled as close to the fireplace as we could get them. Mostly we were silent, each absorbed in private prayer. Sometimes someone would speak aloud with a prayer or a reflection. More than once there was snoring from someone who had fallen asleep. At the end of the hour we held hands and prayed the Lord's Prayer. Then we were off to get the kids ready for school and to start the day's work.

Something happened. At first there was only a mild sense of satisfaction that at least we were making a gesture that seemed right. Then we began to look to that hour together each morning as a sure sign that we were in this work together. Gradually the feeling grew that something greater than our combined strength was at work.

There was never a flash of lightning in our midst or miraculous writing on the wall. But something did change in the way we looked at our life together and tackled the work each day. We were still tired most of the time, but it didn't matter as much as before. The problems didn't come to an end, but we felt more confident as we faced them.

One of our refugees had what appeared to be a mental breakdown. He went for days without sleep, his eyes bloodshot with a wild look of suffering in them. He was tortured by thoughts of his wife and children back in Cuba. We knew that if we returned him to the authorities, he would almost certainly be locked away with the hundreds of other "problem Cubans" still in prison.

He became the object of much of our prayer, both in the morning sessions and at noon when we gathered for lunch. Carolyn and I had just moved into a newly built house, and decided to move the man in with us so we could give him more personal care. Once I found him in the middle of the night scrubbing everything in his room with soap, including the walls. I sat with him and talked until he was able to calm down and go back to sleep.

With a doctor's help, we tried to guide him back into a healthy pattern of thought and behavior. Meanwhile we prayed daily for wisdom and strength. Not only did the man find his way back to health, but we were able to find a sponsoring team in Texas that gave him professional counseling and a job. We heard later that he had earned a college degree and was coping well with life in the United States.

As the number of Cubans at Jubilee began to diminish early in 1981, all of us were agreed on one thing. The greatest miracle of all would be to find a sponsor for the two brothers Pablo and Ramon. While these two men were as sweet and harmless as a pair of turtledoves, we could not imagine any setting in North America where they could support themselves. They had lived most of their lives with their mother and siblings on a tiny farm outside Havana. Somehow they got caught up in the "freedom flotilla"—and ended up at Jubilee—utterly without any technical skills or aptitudes that we could discern.

Pablo had a weakness for alcohol, and Ramon was severely limited intellectually. They were faithful attenders at the daily English classes, but it was purely a social exercise. After months of effort they could hardly utter an intelligible phrase. We loved them both, but we hadn't intended for them to become permanent residents at Jubilee. It became common at lunch for our prayers to include the petition, "And, Lord, *please* help us find a sponsor for Pablo and Ramon."

One day I got a tip that I should contact a rancher who was looking for two men to live on his spread and take care of his breed bulls in a little town near Austin, Texas. My heart began to beat faster as I dialed his number. After we had talked a minute or two I said, "We may have the right men for you, but I want to be honest about their shortcomings."

"Yeah, such as what?" the rancher asked.

"Well, first of all, Pablo gets a little drunk now and then, and Ramon isn't overly bright even when he is sober."

"Long as they don't drink on the job I don't care, and this work sure won't call for any great intellect."

"They can't drive a car or a tractor. They have no mechanical skills that I've noticed."

"Heck, that doesn't matter. If they can carry hay and shovel cow manure, that's good enough."

I held my breath for a few seconds then added, "And one other thing: neither man speaks English."

"No problem there," the rancher answered. "My foreman's from Mexico and doesn't speak much English himself."

"I'll call you back as soon as I can book their flights!"

The Koinonia House witnessed a lot of celebrations, but never was there greater exuberance than that day. Even the most skeptical among us became believers in the power of prayer after that. We didn't claim to know how it worked, but we knew from then on that we needed it at Jubilee no less than Mother Teresa needed it in Calcutta.

A year later we had occasion to celebrate again when I

went by the Texas ranch to see Pablo and Ramon. They couldn't have been happier. Their boss was so pleased he was trying to help other members of their family come over from Cuba to join them.

As the last of the Cubans prepared to leave Jubilee, we found ourselves grieving to see them go. A real bond of affection had developed, perhaps in part because of the troubles we had shared. These men had been dismissed by Castro as *los escorrios*—the refuse of his country—and regarded by an uneasy U.S. public as criminals and deadbeats. We had found them to be men hungry for loving encouragement and eager to please their new friends.

Eduardo had been in jail for nine years, the longest stay of all. He was one of many who left Jubilee weeping. As we departed for the airport, he said, "I have not had a family like this for many years."

The good-byes were difficult for us as well. But we didn't have time to linger long on the sadness. Southeast Asians were already knocking on the door.

4

Acts 29

It was early 1981. We had word that six Laotian and Hmong families would be arriving soon, but no one knew exactly when. We were holding our breaths; we didn't have enough room for all of them yet.

Ryan and Karen returned from their work with the refugees in Thailand. For a while they had difficulty talking about the experience without tears coming to their eyes. Their stories made us even more eager to begin working with Asian refugees.

While the last of the Cubans waited for their sponsorships to be confirmed, they pitched in to help us prepare for the Southeast Asians. At just the right time, the national office of the Disciples of Christ sent a crew of seventeen volunteer construction workers. For three weeks in January we all worked at top speed. Together we finished two buildings and got a good start on our new school.

Calls from the refugee resettlement offices of several denominations assured us that we were going to need all the space we could provide. Refugees were collecting at huge camps all around Southeast Asia faster than they could be transferred to host countries, even at the accelerated rate that Jimmy Carter had ordered. Rosalynn Carter had gone to Thailand herself and visited the camps to help bring more public attention to the crisis.

As we worked on the living quarters in the second building, we listened to the radio report of the presidential inauguration of Ronald Reagan. We had no idea then what an impact the change at the White House would have on Jubilee Partners—or that Jimmy and Rosalynn Carter would later be guests in the very bedroom where we were working while we listened.

When the confirmation came that the first Laotian families were on their way to the Atlanta airport, we were ready. By this time the six Cuban men still with us considered themselves fully part of the Jubilee staff. They wanted to go to the airport as part of the welcoming party, but space in the vans was limited. We told them when to expect us back and suggested that they think of ways to make the Laotians feel welcome. "*Bueno*, no problem," they said.

As we drove toward Atlanta that evening, we met a storm with heavy rain. The refugees' flight was delayed two hours. Finally they arrived, tired after thirty-six hours of travel from Thailand to California, then to Georgia, but still smiling and gracious. One of our Jubilee staff had been a Peace Corps volunteer in Thailand and was able to communicate with them. He explained that we still had a two-hour drive to reach Jubilee Partners.

As we left Atlanta and drove into the dark countryside, we tried to explain more clearly to the new arrivals what Jubilee was all about. It was evident that they understood little of the explanation, but they communicated their trust with constant smiles. We told them about the Cubans waiting to greet them, although they probably had never even heard of Cuba.

Their cross-cultural training was about to begin in earnest. At midnight we turned the last corner and stopped before one of the cabins at the Welcome Center. Six exuberant Cubans came spilling out the front door shouting

"Welcome!" at the startled Laotians. The men had waited patiently, even though we were hours late, but at some point they decided that a few beers would help the time pass. The alcohol expanded their innate hospitality; now they all but carried the bewildered Laotians into their cabins.

The same rain that delayed the flight also left the yard covered with sticky mud. Each time a smiling Laotian entered a building, shoes were left at the front door. Each time a smiling Cuban followed, a new trail of mud was left across the floor.

Over the next few days we marveled at the way the goodwill of each group seemed to overcome the barriers of our three contrasting cultures. The children were the best at this, and the Laotian boys and girls spent hours each day playing with their big Cuban friends while parents looked on. When the time came for the last Cubans to depart, there were Laotian as well as North American tears.

Soon we lost count of the number of trips we made to the huge Atlanta airport to pick up more families arriving from Southeast Asia. It never ceased to be a privilege, however. Whether Laotian, Vietnamese, Chinese, Hmong, or Cambodian, these people were special. The simple fact that they had made it this far was proof that they were skilled at survival and adaptation.

Slowly we began to grasp what a huge cultural leap they were making. We were meeting them at the end of their first experience of air travel, from halfway around the world. Many had little, if any, exposure to amenities such as flush toilets and telephones. Yet they calmly followed us up and down escalators, along moving sidewalks, and through underground trains that moved from one concourse to another guided by computers instead of human drivers.

When one Laotian family discovered the fat field mice in the Jubilee forest, the refugees were thrilled. Here was a delicacy they had feared they would never enjoy again. Soon the forest was full of little shovel holes around the bases of trees, signs of energetic hunters. One day excitement swept the Welcome Center as word spread of a "very big mouse" that had fallen into an empty trash barrel. Ed went to the barrel and looked into the face of an angry, hissing opossum. Reluctantly, we had to put the rest of the wildlife off limits to the hunters.

Another reflection of Mother Teresa's came to us often as we worked with these beautiful people—they truly gave us much more than we could give them. We realized how wrong we had been at the outset to see ourselves as the ones with all the resources and the refugees as the ones with all the needs. Time and again we were deeply moved by their acts of gratitude and generosity.

Each week Jubilee provided the refugees with a modest living allowance. From this they bought food and other basic necessities during the weekly trip to the supermarket. We also provided a supply of used clothing, donated by friends and sold to the refugees for prices ranging from five to fifty cents per item.

In return, from time to time the refugees prepared elaborate feasts to express appreciation to the Jubilee staff. They worked for hours cooking delicious egg rolls, huge mounds of steamed and fried rice, and many special dishes from their respective traditions. We knew that they had paid for the food by limiting purchases for their own families. The evenings always ended with carefully prepared and rehearsed speeches in broken English, expressions of gratitude that came from the heart.

As with the Cubans, we invited the Asian refugees to join us in our worship services. The great majority always chose to do so, even if they were not Christians themselves. We hoped our lives would make Christianity attractive, but we put no pressure on anyone to convert. We found that many of the refugees were eager to learn more about Christian faith, requesting Bibles in their language and attending weekly Bible study led by Carolyn and others.

In these settings, too, we often learned humility. I will always remember one informal worship service in which each of us was given a sheet of paper and a pencil. We were then asked to spend five minutes drawing something for which we were thankful. It was October, so I quickly drew a leaf to illustrate my appreciation for the colorful foliage in the Jubilee woods.

When we were asked to share our pictures with the others around the table, I explained my little sketch. Then I waited to see what the woman across the table had drawn.

Slowly she turned the paper over for me to see. There was a crude drawing of one man shooting another, while a woman and two children ran away. With tears in her eyes, she explained, "When we try escape from Laos to Thailand a soldier catch us. He say he will kill all of us. My husband say, 'No! Kill me and let wife and children go.' The soldier kill my husband and let us run away. I thank God for my good husband."

Our first Cambodian refugees were the Vong and Ly families. Among them was Chou Ly, a young widow, with her parents, siblings, and small son, Sovath. When the Khmer Rouge communists took over Cambodia, Chou's husband, an army officer, was taken away and never seen again.

The Khmer Rouge seized the Ly family's home and forced them into the countryside. There Chou was forced to work long days in the rice paddies. For months at a time, she was separated from Sovath. "It was hard for both of us," she says of that time. "He was just two. He forgot me somehow. And every time I came to see him and to visit my family, he thought I was a stranger."

In December 1979, Chou's family fled to a refugee camp in Thailand. "It was empty ground," she says of the camp. "No tents. They gave us a piece of plastic to make a roof as a shade from the sun. Each family got one bucket to put water in. There were 29,000 people, and not enough water for everybody. Once a week they gave us food."

Through Church World Service, the Ly and Vong families left the camp and headed toward Jubilee. As their plane was making its way from California, Robbie and Ed were on a precarious journey of their own.

We had decided we needed a bus to transport our guests, so we had looked around for a bargain. We were thrilled to find a used school bus for just $5,000. It had appeared to be in fairly sound condition, but in a few weeks we realized it hadn't been much of a bargain. It usually survived the forty-mile round trip to Athens and back but seldom made the 200-mile round trip to Atlanta without trouble.

About sundown, Robbie and Ed set out for the airport. The fuel gauge was broken, and they misjudged how much gasoline they had. Halfway to Atlanta, Ed had to get out and push the bus while Robbie steered it into a service station—fortunately close by and downhill.

When they reached the airport, they rushed in and found their passengers. Chou Ly was among them. She remembered the evening vividly.

"When we were in the hotel in San Francisco the first night we got off the plane, we opened the paper to look where we're going. We're going to *Georgia*. Jubilee Partners. We wondered where this was. We had no idea.

"We were told this was a rich country. We were scared. When we got off the plane, we had these tags on our shirts with 'CWS,' so they would know who to pick up. Ed was motioning to us."

Church World Service had arranged for a Cambodian interpreter to meet the plane as well. Chou continued, "He just said, 'You will get on the bus and ride from here for two hours, go to a small town called Comer, and the house where your family will live will be in the woods. But do not worry—no tigers!' It was a brief orientation."

Everyone went out and took seats on the bus. Robbie closed the door and stepped on the starter. Nothing. The interpreter stood on the curb, still waving good-bye to the Cambodians. After some minutes of checking battery connections and beating on things, Ed sheepishly asked him to explain to the new arrivals that they would have to get off the bus and push to get it started. Chou laughed. "He just shook his head and said, 'Okay, everybody out. Can you help us push the bus?' *He* didn't laugh.

"We were so tired; we came directly from Thailand to California. But we pushed the bus."

If there were any complaints, they were spoken discreetly in Khmer. A few minutes later, the expedition was finally on its way to Jubilee.

Chou did not realize on that first night that a little over a year later she would be married to Robbie, or that a few years after that she would be in charge of the Welcome Center. She sometimes laughs with new refugees about her first impressions of Jubilee Partners.

"There was a twelve-hour difference from Thailand. We'd look at the watch and say, 'How come it's still Friday?' We had been traveling forever, and it was still Friday! I couldn't believe it.

"When we were pulling into Jubilee, it was getting dark and the people said, 'Oh my. There are so many trees here.' Where we lived it was open. Here we could not see much.

"Then the bus stopped again. It didn't make it up the last hill. So we got off the bus, got in an old pickup truck, and they took us to the Welcome Center.

"We didn't know where the other family was going, because we didn't know how to ask to find out. We began to worry, and we said good-bye to them. We said, 'Nice knowing you.' They told us not to worry, not to be afraid living in the woods. It was so quiet. We used to hear bullets and bombs and things.

"We didn't think we would see the other family again. But in the morning when we woke up, we came out, and we heard children. And we said, 'Somebody else lives here.' And somebody said, 'They speak Cambodian.'

"Then we realized, 'They are here!' We were happy to see each other again. It was kind of funny."

One hundred Cambodian refugees came through Jubilee in less than a year. Every one of them had lost relatives in the mass slaughter and starvation that had visited their country. For many the suffering had begun when U.S. bombs destroyed their farms and villages in rural Cambodia. Then when the brutal Khmer Rouge took over, Cambodia became one vast "killing field." The precise number of victims will never be known, but the world had seen nothing like it since the Holocaust of World War II.

I had particular admiration for Soum Sirk, forty-seven-year-old mother of the Kong family. In Cambodia Soum's husband had been a skilled military engineer, supervisor of a large construction project and a job-training program for soldiers who had lost arms or legs. They had eight children. The oldest son, Phamarith, was in college. Kary, the oldest daughter, was happily married and mother of the family's first grandchild, a little girl named Srey. She was due to give birth again soon.

Phamarith remembers very clearly the day their world fell apart.

"On April 17, 1975, our family and relatives were gathered at our house in Phnom Penh. We had just celebrated the Cambodian New Year, with the sounds of battle all around us. Then the shooting stopped, the Republic troops surrendered, and the Khmer Rouge marched into the city and took control. As soon as we saw the anger on their faces, we knew there would be much suffering."

The first order of the Khmer Rouge regime was that Phnom Penh, a city of more than two million people, was to be evacuated immediately. Many of the military men, including Kary's husband, were taken outside the city and shot. Kary was too near childbirth to be able to travel. She sent Srey with the rest of the family and remained in Phnom Penh, hoping somehow to rejoin them soon. The family never heard from her again.

The rest of the family joined the river of people moving out of the city. After ten days and nights on the road, they arrived at a small town near the Vietnamese border, an area covered by thousands of craters left by American bombs. Phamarith estimated that there was a large crater every fifty yards.

Hunger and hard labor dominated the lives of the Uong family for the next four years. They were moved to a village near the deserted city of Battambang, about fifty miles from the Thai border, where the family was divided—adults in one labor camp, older children in a second camp, younger children in a third. All were forced to work. Even two-year-old Srey spent several hours a day with a bucket, gathering dung into a central pile to be used as fertilizer.

Phamarith was assigned to a wrecking crew whose job it was to dismantle the buildings of Battambang and distribute the materials throughout the rice fields for new shelters. They worked from 5:00 in the morning until late in the evening. During the day they had only a few spoonfuls of rice and whatever edible vegetables they could find around the work sites. At night there was a small meal back at the camp.

Weak from hunger, Phamarith fell from a roof and broke his back. He was carried into a medical shelter and left to survive as best he could with little care. Somehow he did survive months of great pain and gradually regained ability to move and work again.

Soum's husband, however, suffered so much from illness and from the sight of his family's misery that he slowly lost his desire to live. When orders came from the Khmer Rouge for him to report for "special training," he and his family knew he would not return. He told them good-bye and went away quietly.

Vietnam took control of Cambodia in 1979. Conditions changed little for Soum's family, except that they were allowed to live together again. They had not been together long before they began planning their escape to Thailand.

The most dangerous part of the escape was the three-day walk from Battambang to a temporary camp on the Thai border. The family was too large to travel in a single group without being detected, so they decided to go in four groups. Saying good-bye to one another was very hard; the odds were great that some would never see the others again.

They divided and set out, walking at night through jungle paths and rice paddies. In the daylight hours they hid in the brush and tried to rest. During these tension-filled nights and days, they worried constantly about how many, if any, of the other members of the family would make it to the camp.

Incredibly, the whole family managed to get through to the Thai border. What a joyful reunion they had when seventeen-year-old Phamaret finally rode into the camp on a bicycle with his younger sister Pechmony on the back and little Srey bouncing in the basket on the front!

Two months later they were transferred by Red Cross trucks to the major Cambodian refugee camp in Thailand.

There they registered as refugees and began their two-year wait for an overseas sponsor. They put the time to good use, studying English and such trade skills as welding and carpentry.

By the time the good news came that they would soon be sponsored by Jubilee, their English was advanced enough that they were able to write a family letter to us.

"We do hope that you are very kind and always have a high willing to save the suffering people of all nations. We have a great aim to go and live quietly in your beautiful country. . . ."

After apologies for their "poor English," they closed with a promise. "We will try to learn more that will make us having the possibility to speak and be easy to live with."

If only the rest of the world were as easy to live with!

We exposed all of the refugees to a wide variety of experiences selected to give them a better understanding of life in the United States. Field trips were always adventures compounded by the uncertainties of travel on our old yellow school bus. We toured modern farms, sat in courtrooms to watch trials, climbed Atlanta's Stone Mountain, picnicked beside waterfalls in the north Georgia mountains, and visited local trade schools and colleges.

Early one morning we cooked breakfast for homeless people at the first such meal ever served by our friends at the Open Door Community in inner-city Atlanta. As dozens of ragged and hungry people filed through the line, the Cambodian refugees served them hot food, their eyes wide with wonder. At their first opportunity, two of the women drew me aside and one said, "We do not understand this. Who are these poor people? Are they really Americans, so poor in this rich country?"

The refugee children worked their way right into our hearts. With little obvious effort, they learned English at an amazing rate, as though they had little tape recorders in their heads. They followed their teachers around laughing and chattering incessantly.

One of young Sovath's favorite topics was the big leeches found in Cambodia's rice fields. He smiled proudly as he explained to me how to kill these tough creatures. "You cut them down the middle, turn them inside out, tie them around a stick, and dry them in the sun." I had to agree that would probably dispatch even a Southeast Asian leech.

At Christmas, Ryan, Karen, and Robbie passed out stockings filled with fruit, candy, and small gifts. The children received them with shining eyes and broad smiles. In their short lives, spent mostly in overcrowded refugee camps, they had enjoyed precious little of such "luxuries." As the Jubilee folks turned to walk back to their houses, a little girl followed them. She was soon joined by others. Then all the children began to empty their stockings and insist on sharing the contents with the givers. How could anyone help falling in love with such children?

Yet we began to find it increasingly difficult to persuade churches to sponsor the families. Under the Reagan administration, the refugee quota was quickly slashed to a fraction of what it had been during Carter's presidency. Instead of protesting, however, churches across the country withdrew their welcome to refugees.

I began to travel more frequently to appeal personally to people in the churches, trying to help them understand the needs of the refugees and our responsibility as Christians. I pointed out that, according to official estimates, the average per capita income in the United States was just about one hundred times greater than in Cambodia.

This comparison became more striking for us when we thought of the one hundred Cambodian men, women, and children we had hosted at Jubilee. I sometimes asked congregations to imagine saying to these Cambodians that, while the average Christian in the United States has an income equal to all one hundred of their combined incomes, "economic pressure" in the United States was the main excuse for lack of sponsorships. Should we be surprised if the refugees found that hard to comprehend, especially coming from people who claimed to be followers of a compassionate Lord who spoke frequently about sharing possessions with others?

My speaking efforts, combined with duties on the board of directors of Habitat for Humanity, took me one Sunday morning to the pulpit of Maranatha Baptist Church in Plains, Georgia, where Jimmy and Rosalynn Carter were in the congregation. I made the case as strongly as I could that if we claim to be disciples of Jesus Christ, we must stop spending our money on weapons designed to destroy other nations. We must turn our efforts instead toward welcoming victims of wars into our communities.

At the end of the sermon, the Carters approached me with warm smiles. Jimmy said, "We are so glad to meet someone who feels as we do about refugees!" The brief conversation that followed was the beginning of a friendship that has been enriching and challenging ever since.

Slowly, over time, we found sponsors for all our Southeast Asian families. Chou Ly's family moved near Atlanta. But before long Chou returned to Jubilee Partners as a volunteer.

"There were still some Cambodians here as refugees," Chou says, "so I felt that I could help. Jubilee helped me; now it's my turn to help others. I could tell the other refugees, 'I'm one who was you. I was afraid to be in this place the first time too.' It makes them feel better. I'm somebody who's had the same experience.

"It took me a long time to adjust to this culture and feel comfortable," Chou says. She adds with a smile, "And now I have to learn Jubilee culture—not even American culture!"

Adopting a new language was difficult. For a long time Chou missed her church. She and her family had become Christians at the refugee camp in Thailand, in a Baptist church without walls—to accommodate five hundred members.

But perhaps the biggest cultural difference of all had to do with relationships between the sexes. "In our culture, men and women didn't have much contact," she explains. "Just two sitting together and talking was considered a bad thing to do." Parents arranged marriages, and "a man and woman who were getting married didn't know each other at all."

So it was with some awkwardness that Chou and Robbie, her English teacher, developed their relationship. Their love for each other grew despite all the cultural differences. At Thanksgiving 1982, they were married at Jubilee. The grand wedding celebration was attended by 150 guests—mostly refugees who had lived for a time at the community.

As I looked out over the crowd of joyous people from so many different countries, I thought back to the days just three-and-a-half years earlier when the cattle had stampeded around our tents on this very spot. At that same time, most of the people in this celebration had been struggling desperately on the other side of the world to keep their families alive and together.

As I was pondering what a privilege it was to have been touched by these lives, the telephone rang. The familiar voice of an old friend boomed through the receiver. It was Harry Haines. He was calling to say that he would like to visit Jubilee Partners to see for himself what our "Hebrews 11 faith" had brought about.

When Harry arrived, he was accompanied by several United Methodist leaders of north Georgia. We gave them the grand tour of all the new buildings, introduced them to the refugees then in residence, and had a lively reception and discussion in the Koinonia House.

That night some of us from Jubilee went to the Athens First United Methodist Church for a regional meeting at which Harry was the featured speaker. The church was filled to capacity, with more than seven hundred people present. Toward the end of his sermon, Harry suddenly asked the congregation, "How many chapters are there in the book of Acts?"

After a few moments, a general consensus was reached that Acts has twenty-eight chapters.

"Well," Harry announced with vigor, "I have good news for you. Twenty miles from here, at a place called Jubilee Partners, the twenty-*ninth* chapter of Acts is being written!"

Then, while we squirmed self-consciously in our pew, Harry proceeded to hold Jubilee up before the assembled Methodists as a model of what the church should be doing. We were grateful that only a handful of those present knew that some of the reputed paragons of spiritual virtue were sitting in their midst.

As we drove back to Jubilee after the service, we discussed our reactions to Harry's comments. Some were more uneasy with the praise than others. But after a few minutes, we realized that in fact we all agreed with what he had said. Who could experience what we had seen and heard over the past months and not feel that God was indeed working among us? We were not the source of what was happening, but we were certainly privileged to have box seats at an amazing show—and to be actors in it as well.

It was good to be reminded that we Christians of the twentieth century should think of ourselves as participants in the work that was started by the early church—which was by no means intended to end when Luke finished his account. The exciting story *is* continuing to be written—not just at Jubilee, but all over the world where people make the claim that "Jesus is Lord," then set out to demonstrate that fact by their actions.

We were buoyed by these thoughts as we made our way back to Jubilee. We did not begin to realize how much we still had to learn about the unpredictable call of God or the difficulties just ahead.

5

Preparing the Way

"It has been a very hard trip, *señor*. The *coyotes* [refugee smugglers] took all of our money and abandoned us. Eight of us walked the rest of the way to the United States and crossed the river at night. We have been hiding here for three days. We have no money, no food, nothing. But at least we are alive. Back in our village many people have died."

The speaker was a young Guatemalan. Eric Drewry and I met him and his three friends at their hiding place in Brownsville, Texas, just a few minutes earlier. Now we were waiting nervously in an alley behind a church, where four more young men from the same village were soon to join us.

It was November 1982. Eric and I came to the Rio Grande Valley in response to calls from friends in south Texas. They insisted that Jubilee Partners should know what was happening there to thousands of Central American refugees. We rushed from one appointment to another to collect information from lawyers, social service workers, and pastors.

Our meeting with a Presbyterian pastor was interrupted by a telephone call. It was an urgent appeal from a priest fifty miles away in Brownsville. Eric and I could hear enough of the conversation to understand that there were four frightened refugees who had crossed the Rio Grande and were hiding from the Border Patrol. We had already learned enough to know their arrest would almost certainly lead to deportation back into extreme danger.

"Well, yes," we heard our pastor friend say, "I know of a place where they would be welcome and safe, if they could get there. I also know that four more of their friends are hiding in a different place not far from you; I got a call from the Lutheran church about them. But I don't know anyone who is available right now and who would be willing to risk transporting them."

Eric and I glanced at each other. We didn't even need to discuss it. The time had come for us to move our investigation beyond statistics and political analysis. We motioned to our host; he passed on the word with a smile. "Just a minute, Father. I think our transportation has just turned up."

All the way to Brownsville we wrestled with misgivings. Among other facts, we knew we could go to jail if we were caught transporting illegal aliens. We also knew the loss of our car would doubtless be automatic. As a lawyer, Eric had an additional fear—he would likely lose his law license.

We borrowed a second car from a sympathetic friend and went to meet the first four refugees. As soon as we met them we knew we had made the right decision.

"*Gracias, señores*, for helping us like this," said a young man still in his teens. "God will bless you."

When the second group of four arrived, there were joyful smiles and hugs all around. They had separated many miles to the south, and each group had been worried about the other. We quickly got the men into the cars and began the trip to the town, where they were to be given refuge in a vacant church.

As we drove along the highway, the men told of their ordeal. A bloody struggle was taking place in their province of El Quiché in central Guatemala. It was a story we would hear again and again in the years to come—of helpless peasants caught between the brutality of the Guatemalan military forces on one side and the local guerrilla fighters on the other.

They told of bombed villages, the shooting of whole families, torture and rape. These young men had been the objects of recruitment attempts from both sides. Finally they decided they should leave, both to save their own lives and to ease the pressure on their neighbors.

My attention strayed from time to time as Texas Highway Patrol cars came into view. To my horror, one fell in behind us. My heart pounded like a kettledrum. The car followed us as we exited from the main highway, but after another block or two, it dropped back and left us alone. It was several minutes before I could focus again on my passengers' story.

The refugees had been stopped repeatedly by Mexican police, who demanded bribes before letting them go on. A hundred miles from the Texas border they had pooled what remained of their money and hired a *coyote* to guide them into the United States. They had not gone far before the coyote disappeared, leaving them to make their way northward as best they could without money.

To be less conspicuous, they divided into two groups and agreed to rendezvous at a certain village they thought was near the Texas border. Neither group ever found the village. Finally, at about the same time, both groups managed to swim the Rio Grande and hide in Brownsville.

Night fell as we drove. Finally we parked in the shadows in front of a church. It was a small, white building on the edge of town, surrounded by a low chain-link fence. While Eric walked down the street to get the key from a neighbor, the rest of us crowded into the darkness on the front porch and waited quietly. I began to feel a deep sense of gratitude that I was being allowed to share this experience with these men.

The neighbor and Eric returned a few minutes later, bringing not only the key but also a big pot of beans and a stack of tortillas. Soon the famished men were eating the first food they had had in days. As Eric and I said our good-byes and drove away, we knew we had also found what we needed—a clear answer that there was a need here for the resources Jubilee Partners could offer. That answer had not been in the discovery of more facts—we had plenty of facts already—but in the experience of seeing and touching human beings who personalized the tragedy.

The most recent chapter of Guatemala's long history of repression began in 1954. Democratically elected President Jacobo Arbenz had launched a comprehensive program of land reform, specifically targeting the U.S.-owned United Fruit Company (now United Brands), whose vast landholdings dominated Guatemala's agriculture. Branding Arbenz a communist, United Fruit executives convinced the CIA to engineer and finance a right-wing coup. A U.S. embassy plane flew in the new military dictator Colonel Castillo Armas, who began his reign with a bloodbath that claimed the lives of 8,000 Guatemalans in two months.

Knowing that their interests would be protected, almost two hundred U.S.-based multinational corporations flooded Guatemala after the coup. They joined forces with the elite landholding minority, consigning Guatemala's landless majority to desperate poverty. Within a few years after the coup, 81 percent of the country's children were suffering from malnutrition, and more than half died before they reached age five.

Through the years, Guatemalan soldiers and police enforced the injustice with unspeakable brutality. In the decade before Jimmy Carter became U.S. president, the Guatemalan government presided over the slaughter of some 50,000 people. When President Carter publicly condemned the carnage and threatened to cut off the flow of U.S. military aid, Guatemalan officials told him just to keep the aid—and stay out of Guatemalan politics.

El Salvador presented a similarly tragic picture. In 1980, 2 percent of the population owned 60 percent of the land. Ninety percent of the people earned less than $100 per year. As church leaders, union organizers, students, and others began denouncing the injustice and organizing for change, they were targeted with systematic brutality. Government-sponsored death squads attempted to eliminate all popular leadership; corpses turned up bearing evidence of rape, torture, and mutilation.

In March of that year, as he concluded a Sunday sermon, San Salvador's Archbishop Oscar Romero thundered a defiant challenge to the government's National Guard, the army, and the death squads. "I beseech you, I beg you, I command you in the name of God: stop the repression!"

It was no surprise that those were among the archbishop's last words. A few days later, while celebrating a funeral Mass in the small chapel of a hospital where he ministered to the cancer-ridden poor, Romero was gunned down. Eight months after that, Ita Ford, Maura Clarke, Jean Donovan, and Dorothy Kazel—four U.S. churchwomen who were beloved missionaries among El Salvador's poor—were also murdered.

These were only the most visible victims of nationwide terror. According to the Human Rights Office of the Salvador Catholic Church, close to 10,000 political murders a year were being carried out in the late 1970s and into the

1980s. The vast majority of these murders were committed by the government or by right-wing death squads that operated with impunity.

President Carter struggled until the final days of his term with whether to give military aid to the Salvadoran government. President Reagan suffered from no such ambivalence. Ignoring the economic realities that drove Salvadorans to work and fight for justice, Reagan couched the struggle in East-West terms, declaring El Salvador the staging ground for a battle between Western freedom and Soviet-sponsored communism. He was determined to spend whatever it might take to help the Salvadoran government fight off the growing challenge from the predominantly Marxist FMLN guerrilla forces. He was equally anxious to resume the flow of military aid to Guatemala.

As we learned of the refugee exodus caused by the political crisis in Central America, we at Jubilee began to explore just how our facilities and our growing network of contacts might be useful in work with Central Americans. We knew enough about the politics of the situation to realize that U.S. Immigration officials were under great pressure from Washington to limit the influx of refugees from El Salvador and Guatemala. It wasn't difficult to understand why the U.S. would not welcome refugees fleeing from the very governments Washington was now supporting.

We had spirited debates about whether to get involved. I argued, "We need to recognize that if we throw ourselves into this, we could end up saving *many*—maybe a *hundred* people—from being deported back into the hands of the death squads!" All of us would have been astounded if we could have foreseen that in the next eight years more than 1,300 Central Americans would come through Jubilee.

In south Texas, Eric and I were discovering that the

Reagan administration policy toward Central Americans was resulting in a miscarriage of justice on a massive scale. Refugees were flooding across the border by the thousands, pleading to be allowed at least temporary political refuge. Instead of receiving protection, they were rounded up and crowded into jails and concentration camps. They were then herded in groups through rapid "hearings" before INS judges.

Frightened and totally bewildered by the procedures, usually without benefit of independent legal counsel, the refugees were almost universally denied political asylum. We found that men, women, and children were being deported at the rate of one thousand a month. They were flown directly back to national airports and into the hands of the very governments they had fled. They were now in greater danger than if they had never tried to escape.

The more we learned about the plight of the Central American refugees, the clearer it became that we had to do something. So far our refugee work had been with the full cooperation of the U.S. government. Now we realized we would have to take actions that would be controversial at best and perhaps even illegal.

"What would Jesus have us do?" became the question underlying all others. What would we do if we found ourselves having to choose between cooperation with U.S. policy and faithfulness to God? Were we willing to go to jail for our beliefs? If it came to it, were we willing to see Jubilee Partners taken over or shut down by the government?

After several long meetings and a lot of prayer, we decided we must help the refugees, whatever the risk. We felt that to put our own safety or the preservation of our community ahead of their lives would be wrong. We would do all we could to work within the law. But if we came to a point of conflict between human law and God's law, we knew which we would choose.

Eight months earlier, on the second anniversary of the assassination of Archbishop Romero, several congregations had declared their churches public "sanctuaries" for Central American refugees. They were using that church term in its most fundamental sense: they were defying the authorities by harboring people labeled "illegal aliens" by the U.S. government.

They became involved the same way we did—by touching the suffering and being unable to ignore it. When a group of refugees was found dead in the Arizona desert, Jim Corbett, a Quaker rancher with a Harvard degree in philosophy, and John Fife, pastor of Tucson's Southside Presbyterian Church, began asking what they could do. Before long they discovered other concerned people across the country and launched the "sanctuary movement."

Within three years that movement became well known throughout the United States—largely because of the arrests of Fife, Corbett, and others on charges of conspiracy and harboring and transporting illegal aliens. Corbett was acquitted; Fife and others were sentenced to years on probation. In Texas, another sanctuary worker, Stacey Lynn Merkt, served seventy-eight days of a 179-day jail sentence and was released to house arrest three months before she gave birth to her first child. Stacey became involved with the refugees after spending several months with us in Georgia.

We also had many friends in Canada who we thought would be willing to help in our effort. We began to talk about reviving the old "Underground Railroad" that had once helped thousands of fugitive slaves go from the South to Canada. Remains of small cabins in our woods reminded us that the land where Jubilee is located was cotton country in the nineteenth century. Slaves might very well have waited here in the darkness long ago, listening for the signal that another "freedom train" was passing by on its way north.

Surrounded by that heritage, we began to have a new vision for our work. After two years of helping refugees come into the United States, it was time to reverse that process and help people leave.

Canadian friends were enthusiastic, but they said it would work only if we had the full cooperation of the Canadian government. Carolyn and I were chosen to approach the Canadian consul in Atlanta. We knew the success of the plan depended on the consul's response, so we carefully rehearsed how we would present our argument.

Just as we were driving away from the Jubilee parking lot, Ed Weir ran to intercept us. It was clear he was upset about something. "I hate to dump this on you at the last minute," he said, "but I've been thinking a lot about this meeting with the consul. I think you'd better try to get him to meet with you away from his office. I believe there is a pretty good chance his office is bugged."

Carolyn and I looked at each other. If anyone else had suggested to us that the United States might spy on a Canadian consulate, we might have dismissed the idea as paranoid. But Ed had spent thirteen years working at the headquarters of the National Security Agency (NSA) just outside Washington, D.C.

The NSA specializes in electronic spying around the world. Ed's specialty had been deciphering encoded messages. Just before they were married, Ed's wife, Mary Ruth, was a librarian at the CIA. Most of the time the couple's unusual background for life at Jubilee was the material for humorous skits at our parties; now it was suddenly relevant.

All the way to Atlanta, Carolyn and I wondered what we should do. We knew that if we tipped off the INS at this stage, we could endanger the whole effort. It was one thing to risk jail ourselves, but we had to take every precaution to safeguard the refugees who would be putting their lives in our hands.

At the consulate we introduced ourselves to the receptionist and took seats to wait. I wrote rapidly on a legal pad: "We want to talk with you about a sensitive matter but have reason to think that your office may be bugged. Would it be possible for us to meet away from your office?"

Just as I finished, a dignified gentleman in his early sixties came through the steel security entrance, greeted us warmly, and introduced himself as Leslie Scott, the consul. He led us down a hall to his office. Before we sat, I handed him the note. He stood behind his desk and read it, looked carefully at us for a few seconds, then read the note again. Suddenly I felt like a fool. I was afraid we had ruined our credibility by playing spy games before even getting a chance to explain why we were there.

Carolyn and I looked as straight and proper as possible and waited. "Fine," he said after a long silence. "Let's go across the street and get a cup of coffee." Thus began the first of hundreds of conversations with Canadian officials and staff.

Within a few minutes we felt like we were talking with an old friend. Scott quickly agreed to work with us on behalf of the refugees. He said he would be pleased to come out to Jubilee to interview them in groups each time we indicated we were ready for him. Here was a foreign service officer, with decades of experience, who seemed genuinely concerned about the plight of the refugees and eager to help. It was the best cup of coffee we ever had.

Scott and his successors would come to Jubilee Partners scores of times over the next eight years. Both the United States and Canada supposedly applied the same criteria for admission of immigrants, based on the United Nations Convention on Refugees to which both nations were signatories. But the Canadian officials accepted 98 percent of the refugees we brought before them. The acceptance rate by U.S. officials was consistently 3 percent or less for Salvadorans and less than one percent for Guatemalans!

Year after year through the 1980s, the White House solemnly certified that democracy was "making progress" in these countries. As hundreds of thousands of civilians fled northward from the spiraling violence, they were rejected by U.S. officials as being not bona fide political refugees. They were deemed merely "economic opportunists" who, as one official put it, had come north seeking "a welfare card and a Cadillac."

With Canada's help, our *Año de Jubileo*—Year of Jubilee— program was rolling. What we offered that appealed to the Canadians was a flow of refugees preselected by us in the Rio Grande Valley, already started in English training and cultural orientation, gathered at one central place where the Canadian consul could interview them.

We soon realized that we would be transporting a lot of people—first from the Rio Grande Valley to Jubilee, more than 1,200 miles away, then from Jubilee to Canada, another 1,000 miles. Like it or not, we were going to have to set up our own bus service.

After a few weeks of shopping around—and fervent prayers that we would make a better choice this time around—we found a thirty-passenger bus. It was almost new and equipped with reclining seats and a special engine that gave good fuel economy. But the thing we liked best about it was the paint job. Red, orange, blue, and white—it looked like it had been painted in a Mexican souvenir factory! We fell in love with it at once.

One problem—it cost $31,000. That was very nearly all

the money we had. An even greater concern—we didn't yet have INS cooperation or approval to haul busloads of refugees out of the Rio Grande Valley. After months of exploration, we stood on the bank of the Rubicon. If we bought the bus, we would have little money to feed the refugees (or ourselves) once they arrived at Jubilee. We prayed constantly to know what to do. Jubilee's fate hung in the balance—but so did that of the refugees. The time had come to take a leap of faith or forget the whole thing.

We jumped. We bought the bus and brought it to Jubilee. There we immediately began preparing it for long trips. We installed a bathroom, a bunk for a relief driver, and overhead storage racks for baggage.

We sent word to our friends in south Texas to start assembling the first group of refugees. "Be ready to leave for Georgia early in January." Then, having committed ourselves thoroughly, we did something we had never done before. We sent out 1,200 letters asking for additional financial help from our friends.

Not knowing how things were going to turn out but in great need of rest, Carolyn and I took the kids to north Texas to spend a few days of our Christmas vacation with relatives there. I was so keyed up about the whole venture that I found it impossible to relax and celebrate Christmas with the others. I spent a lot of time jogging to dissipate my nervous energy.

As I ran along a road beside Eagle Mountain Lake, I prayed nonstop about our predicament. Despite my best efforts, I could not relax. "God," I finally prayed, "I know Jesus had some hard things to say to people who asked for signs from you, but I sure would appreciate *some* indication that we are on the right track. I can't take this tension much longer."

As clearly as if I had actually heard a voice, I felt the answer. "Stop running. Look up into the sky." I stopped right in the middle of the pavement, feeling foolish.

Then I saw something that made me gasp. There had been a sky full of rain clouds when I had set out from the house half an hour earlier. Now there was one single cloud. It was a long slender cloud directly above me that stretched all the way from the southern to the northern horizon, where it disappeared in the direction of Canada! The rest of the sky was completely clear.

I had never felt more positively that God had spoken to me. I stared at the cloud, trying to absorb the fact that this was real—not a scene from a Cecil B. De Mille movie. If I could have grasped fully the implications of it, I probably would have fainted in the middle of the road. Instead, a surge of relief and joy ran through me. I laughed aloud and starting running as fast as I could down the center line of the road, saying over and over, "Thank you, God! Thank you, God!"

The next few days were a blur as I went to the Rio Grande Valley for a meeting with the first group of Año de Jubileo refugees. We met in the same little abandoned church where Eric and I had brought the eight Guatemalan refugees a few months earlier. Now there were five families gathered there, including five beautiful children.

This was their first meeting with one another. I sensed that they were as nervous about each other as about the proposed Jubilee program. For years their lives had been plagued by *orejas* (ears)—neighborhood spies. Now they were making themselves particularly vulnerable as they sought to become the pioneers in this mysterious new program.

But soon we were singing lively hymns and praying for God's help. By the time I showed them slides of Jubilee Partners and explained what we were proposing to do, their nervousness was visibly giving way to trust. Before the evening was over, the kids were sitting in my lap, spilling hot chocolate as they laughed at my funny Spanish.

When I left that night, I was full of joy. All the months of talk and planning had finally led to real people! I already felt deeply bonded to this little group of twenty-four courageous people. Whatever it took, we were going to get them safely to Canada.

A few days later I met with the INS district director, Hal Boldin, a man who held tremendous power over the lives of thousands of people in the Rio Grande Valley. He now presided, in fact, over the deportation of a thousand each month. I was accompanied by Jim Rausch, a lawyer whose legal skills were matched by his faith as a Christian and a deep love for the people he was helping.

As we were led into the office of the director, I wondered what this local potentate would be like. To my amazement, Jim walked up to him, put his arm around his shoulders and said warmly, "Hal, it's good of you to take time for us this morning. Have you had time lately to do any fishing in the Gulf?"

"Well no, Jim, as a matter of fact. I've just been too busy, you know. . . ." And for the next several minutes I watched as this feared official responded openly and gratefully to Jim's concern for him. As the meeting progressed, it seemed clear he didn't really enjoy the role he was playing. He saw himself as an instrument of government policies far beyond his reach. Part of his job was evidently to absorb the criticism brought on by a policy that was ugly in practice but silently affirmed by many, if not most, U.S. citizens.

By the time Jim brought up our proposal, Hal Boldin seemed ready to help us save at least a few families from deportation. He was openly skeptical, however, about our ability to "control" them at Jubilee. "You'll never get them to Canada. As soon as they get a chance, they'll break and scatter like a bunch of rabbits," he said. "All these Central

Americans want just one thing—to come to America and make a lot of money. It's really not an efficient use of our time. But I'll go along with it once anyway. Then you'll see."

An hour later we had made all the arrangements to bring our first group of refugees to the INS office, where they would be documented, fingerprinted, and furnished with papers allowing them to travel in the United States as long as they were part of the Año de Jubileo program. That meeting opened the door a crack. In the months following, we were able to wedge it open so a river of refugees was able to escape to new life in Canada.

Back at Jubilee we had a great celebration. Not only had we passed an important legal hurdle with the INS, but to our astonishment the answer to our financial problems was coming in a stream of generous gifts from people all over the United States. By the time our new bus left for Texas in mid-January, more than five hundred contributions had come in—and were still coming! Before it returned, enough money had arrived to pay for the bus and meet all the needs of the program for months to come.

Whatever doubts we might have had about God's hand in this had long since vanished. We had called out for help, and God had answered, "Here I am!"

Two visitors from Wisconsin, Max and Nancy Rice, helped us paint "Año de Jubileo" in bold letters on each side of the bus—with bonfires nearby to warm both us and the surface we were painting in the cold January weather. Less than three years later, Max and Nancy moved to Jubilee to become deeply involved in the work.

Before the paint was completely dry, the engine was started and the crew climbed aboard. While our big bell rang loudly, the bus began to roll down the drive toward Texas. All of us waved until it was out of sight.

At last the way was prepared for Año de Jubileo.

6

Año de Jubileo

Five days later the bell rang again to welcome the first arrivals from Central America—twenty-four men, women, and children from El Salvador. The Jubilee folks spilled out of the Koinonia House and ran down the hill to welcome them. After thirty hours on the road, passengers and crew were all very tired, but the Salvadorans clapped and cheered in response to their welcomers.

We looked on their arrival as a miracle long in the making. For them the miracle was a profoundly personal reality. Some of them had begun their escape from the terrible events back home as much as three years earlier and had been enduring great hardship since. Most had been facing likely arrest and deportation until they boarded the Año de Jubileo bus.

Now they were safe, traveling through the Jubilee program with documents guaranteeing their safe passage through the United States. They could finally relax, and their weary smiles showed they were ready to do so.

A few days later, our new guests began to tell us their personal stories. They recounted cruel murders of helpless people, torture, mutilation, and an atmosphere of unrelieved fear. They told of disappearing relatives, arrests at night, and pitched battles in their neighborhoods.

One young woman in the group had been abandoned by her foreign husband two years earlier when the fighting became too dangerous. Six months later she set out with her infant daughter to reach safety in the north. After months of dangerous traveling, she was caught in northern Mexico by the police and thrown into jail. There she was raped repeatedly by the guards before she was taken back south and forced across the Guatemalan border.

Somehow she found the courage to try again. She was now pregnant with the child of one of the guards. Several more months of furtive travel brought her to a home in northern Mexico, where she was allowed to hide and rest for a few weeks in return for working as a maid. Finally she waded the Rio Grande River, carrying her small daughter above her head. Someone took pity on her and directed her to a nearby convent. A short time later she gave birth to her second daughter. The nuns hid the little family for several months until they were picked up by our bus.

As the mother told us her story, the signs of strain on her face made her look years older than she was. But in her lap sat Melisa, smiling and chortling, with her fingers in her mouth, blissfully unaware of the suffering her mother had undergone to bring her and her older sister to safety.

In the days that followed, we became close to these brave people as they struggled in our English classes to learn their new language, as our children played together, and as we raised our voices together in worship, thanking God for all we were seeing. Others might have been amused by our accents as we alternated between verses of *"Resucitó"* and "He Lives," but they could never doubt that the songs were from our hearts.

We were heartened that, just two months later, friends from Reba Place Fellowship, a Christian community in Evanston, Illinois, launched the "Overground Railroad" program to complement the refugee work that we had started.

They set up a network involving hundreds of churches all across the United States. A steady stream of volunteer drivers went to south Texas and brought "legal" refugees back to their communities, hosting them while the refugees' entry into Canada was being negotiated.

Overseeing the project was David Janzen, a creative and committed man who did the work out of a tiny basement office. He echoed the feelings of many of us after his first visit to south Texas. "It was like falling through a hole in the kitchen floor and discovering that our basement is full of people huddled in the shadows. . . . It is no longer possible to return to the main floor and live our lives as if no one is down there. Either we must harden our hearts and drive them out or invite them to our table and somehow become the family God meant us to be."

The Jubilee table was enriched beyond measure by the flow of gracious and courageous people who shared it with us. Many had faced obstacles and anguish of a sort that we could barely comprehend.

The Martell family had had a particularly dramatic crossing into the United States. Medardo, a construction supervisor, and his wife, Ana, had lived comfortably in El Salvador with their five children. They were active in church and blessed with many friends.

They were swept into El Salvador's torrent of violence when a union was organized at a company where Medardo had been chief supervisor. The National Police reacted by attacking the workers with machine guns, killing dozens of them. Medardo was pressured to join the Salvadoran military forces but resisted.

Medardo lost his job and began working as a taxi driver. A cache of machine guns and other military materials were discovered hidden in the house next to the Martells'. A few days later, two men armed with military pistols climbed into Medardo's taxi and forced him to drive from one lonely place to another. Miraculously, there were people at each place. Medardo was convinced he would have been shot if they had found an isolated place.

Life became a deadly game of hide and seek. Six armed men narrowly missed him as he fled from one hiding place to another. In May 1983, he and Ana fled with their children to Belize. Medardo took odd jobs. Ana cooked tortillas for the children to sell on the street. They received reports of the torture and murder of other taxi drivers with whom Medardo had worked. The Belize government stepped up pressure to get the family to leave the country.

Finally they decided they must try to reach the United States and apply for political asylum. They felt their chances would be best if they divided into two groups, with Ana and two of the children leaving first. One of the hardest moments of their lives was saying good-bye.

Four days later, Medardo received word that Ana had made it to the United States. He left with the other children for a journey by bus up through Mexico. The following days and nights were such a nightmare that, three months later when they arrived at Jubilee, the family still had difficulty talking about it without breaking into tears.

In Matamoros, Mexico, ten-year-old Salvador became separated from the others. He ran wildly up and down the streets looking for them, while they, fighting panic, searched the city. Again and again Medardo thought he spied Salvador and ran toward him, shouting his name—only to discover that it was not Salvador at all. After eight terrible hours, they found him at the bus terminal.

When night fell, Medardo waded across the Rio Grande River. He signaled to thirteen-year-old Douglas to push his younger brother and sister across on an inner tube. On the other riverbank, as they stumbled through debris, Salvador fell and cut a deep gash in his leg. He began to bleed so profusely Medardo had to apply a makeshift tourniquet above his knee.

"What could I do, without medicine or anything?" Medardo said as he recounted it. "I begged God to help us, and the Lord healed it right then and there! The bleeding stopped immediately."

Weakened by fatigue, Medardo and the children rested for a while among the weeds at the edge of the river. U.S. Border Patrol searchlights swept back and forth just above them and clouds of mosquitoes tormented them. The terrified children struggled to remain motionless and not cry out.

They set off again, dodging searchlights and crawling through snake-infested fields—only to discover that another river barred their passage. They crossed it and fell asleep until daybreak. Medardo cautiously set out to get his bearings.

"I was surprised to see that all the signs were in Spanish, then to find a cemetery where all the stones had Latin-American names on them," he recounted.

Gradually the horrible realization dawned on him that there had not been two rivers the night before. They had recrossed the Rio Grande and were back in Mexico! Moreover, the river had risen during the night and was much too fast and turbulent for another crossing.

Nearly overcome by despair, Medardo kept praying. He knew Ana would be frantic when they did not show up on schedule. She was in fact at that moment fighting the temptation to cross back over into Mexico to look for her husband and children.

Eventually Medardo found an old man in a field who took pity on them and gave them food and a place to sleep. His son-in-law was a *coyote*. He was willing to help the family cross the river when the waters receded. His price—every peso Medardo had.

Finally they made it into Texas. A few hours later the entire Martell family was reunited—the most joyful event of their lives.

Rosa also had a dramatic story to tell. She was a tall, slim woman, with eyes that signaled a very lively mind at work behind them. From our first meeting, I was moved by her intelligence and strength, a sense of humor that protected her from despair, and a powerful faith in God.

"When I left El Salvador, the first thing I did was to put myself into God's hands" was the way she began her story. Her crime in El Salvador was that she was a teacher. Her father's participation in ANDES, the teachers' union, had marked him as a subversive in the eyes of the Salvadoran government and the right-wing death squads. He and several other professors were arrested by the National Guard and held in prison for about a month. He was tortured and questioned; some of the others were shot.

After his release, he continued to receive death threats by phone and letter from the National Guard. One night about 1:00 a.m. came the dreaded pounding on the door. A group of soldiers wearing camouflage clothes and bandana masks were outside, beating on the door and windows. Rosa finally went to the door and insisted that her father was not in the house, but they burst inside and found him hiding in a bedroom. They dragged him away, along with several neighbors they had also arrested.

After daylight someone reported that he had seen many bodies on the shore of Lake Ilopango, a few miles outside of San Salvador. Rosa and her neighbors went and identified their relatives. Her father had been tortured severely, then choked to death with a cord.

Almost immediately Rosa began to receive anonymous death threats herself, some painted on the outside of the house where she and her husband were staying with relatives after her father's murder. A man in a military jeep came to the house one day and told Rosa there was an investigation into her activities. He left behind this threat: "Rosa, we're going to keep an eye on you."

Rosa's husband was injured in an automobile accident, and an earthquake destroyed much of San Salvador, including the house where they had been living. They had to live separately for a while, in the limited space their relatives could offer them. Rosa moved in with a cousin.

Her pursuers tracked her down again. Rosa barely managed to escape by climbing through a back window with her small daughter as soldiers came through the front of the house. She was eight months' pregnant with their second child. She knew she could not delay her escape from El Salvador.

Rosa managed to rendezvous with her husband to plan their escape, but the next day he had to go to the hospital for emergency surgery. Rosa tried to hide until he could recover enough strength to travel, but a government spy tracked her down again, forcing her to leave their small daughter with her husband and set out alone.

"I didn't know exactly where I was going," she recounted. "I just pointed my nose and followed it. I had to leave my two loved ones without knowing how or whether I would see them again—or if I would lose myself along the way. On the whole trip, from the moment I left El Salvador, I prayed for God to accompany me."

After many days she came to the Rio Grande River. "I was very afraid," she recounted, "because I can't swim, and I was so pregnant I thought I would sink."

She waded across about thirty miles upstream from Brownsville. She scrambled up the steep bank on the north side. Fortunately, there were no Border Patrol cars in sight. Soaked to the skin and muddy, she hid in a grove of mesquite trees and watched the traffic. It was tempting to step out to the side of the road and try to flag down a sympathetic helper, but she knew she couldn't trust that she would find one.

She crossed the highway and set out across wide, irrigated fields of vegetables. She could just make out in the distance a water tower and the buildings of the small town of Weslaco. She headed for them, but her body could no longer wait. Labor began as she plodded toward the town.

"Oh, please, God. Let me have just a few more hours to find a safe place," she prayed, but the pains quickly became stronger and more frequent. She tried not to panic amd kept walking until she came to a grove of palm trees two miles from the Rio Grande River. Finally pain forced her to stop there in the trees beside the dirt road.

"I couldn't go on. I put myself in God's hands," she said. "A car came to a stop, and a woman got out. She helped me. About 8:00 p.m. I gave birth there beside the road in that grove of trees. I was praying for my life and my baby's. Then the woman told me, 'It's a girl, and she's all right.' I thanked God."

The kind woman who had served as midwife took care of Rosa and the new baby that night. In the morning she found a farm family willing to give them shelter for a while. Then a church in a neighboring town took her in for several weeks while Rosa regained her strength.

People at the church knew of Jubilee. Rosa decided she would like to try to come through our program and apply to go to Canada. A sympathetic lawyer explained to her that she probably would be able to immigrate to Canada, but that it might take another three years to get her husband and older daughter admitted as well.

"I became very depressed," she recalled, "because in El Salvador so much was happening that three days was a long time—and three years were like an eternity. I prayed for a miracle, and it happened. My husband and daughter managed to escape to the U.S. and find us again with the help of other people who help refugees."

While Rosa and her family were at Jubilee, the Canadian consul gave them permission to move to Canada. Rosa declared, "I thank God for so much, for the ones who helped me, for Jubilee—and for the baby!"

Things went amazingly well overall for the first six months of the Año de Jubileo program. The first three groups who came to us spent their time at Jubilee and were accepted by the Canadian consul. As the time came to take them to Canada, there were many good-bye parties—and lots of late-night guitar playing on the porches and sad songs sung about leaving friends once again. Romances glowed briefly here and there as lonely young people far from home were befriended by our young volunteers.

The departures for Canada were an emotional mixture of sorrow and the thrill of knowing that the long journey to safety was finally about to end. At last the families could truly live without fear of death squads or deportation. The children could talk with new friends without worrying whether their parents might be informers eager to pass along any hint of "subversion."

We delivered the first three groups, seventy-two people in all, to the Toronto International Airport. From there most flew to Edmonton, Alberta—closer to the North Pole than to their homeland. One insisted, "It is very cold here, but we can survive the cold better than the bullets back in El Salvador. Don't worry about us."

Our Canadian consul friend Scott brought his supervisor from Ottawa to see Jubilee Partners. The two of them assured us Canada was enthusiastic about the program. "Carry on, friends," the supervisor said. "We will cooperate with you any way we can."

It was too good to last.

7

Showdown and Deliverance

Near the end of July 1983, we returned to Jubilee after driving nonstop for three days to deliver the third group to Canada. The telephone rang late that night. I picked it up so groggy from fatigue I could barely talk. On the line were our new representatives in south Texas, Richard and Ruth Anne Friesen. They had bad news. I got Ed and Ryan on other extensions.

The fear in Richard's and Ruth Anne's voices came through and collected down inside me, my own weariness making that easier. I was trembling as I listened to them. I couldn't stop.

The Friesens had gone to the Rio Grande Valley only a few days before, from Reba Place Fellowship. They were brand new at this work and had arrived hoping to be able to keep a friendly relationship with everyone—including INS officials. It was not to be.

The INS had given us a strong hint that a break with their past cooperation was coming. When I had tried a few days earlier to call the district director, who had agreed in January to work with us, he would not talk to me. "Too busy," said his secretary.

Then a junior officer delivered the bad news. "We are under increased pressure from Washington to deter the flow of Central Americans into the United States. Your program gives them hope and encourages more to come north." He hung up without agreeing to a time for our usual appointment to get travel papers for the refugees.

Now the Friesens reported that their first meeting with INS officials in Harlingen was a disaster. They had taken three Salvadoran families in for a prearranged interview. Then they had to watch helplessly as the INS arrested five of them and took them away to prepare them for deportation.

Ruth Anne was crying as she described the two young wives, both several months' pregnant, in the process of being separated from their husbands. The women were taken to one prison compound, and the men were placed in another down the road. We could picture the scene easily, since we had already visited the place several times.

The refugees call it *el Corralón*, the Corral. It was well named; people were herded about in it like cattle. High fences topped by concertina wire surrounded several dormitories, each of which contained row upon row of steel cots. Men moved around the main compound slowly, listless in the south Texas heat. Sometimes there were so many they spilled over into large tents, unbearably hot during the afternoons. Some crowded into the narrow strips of shade along the northern sides of the buildings. Waiting.

A few hundred yards away, the women were similarly herded together in a smaller pen, most separated from husbands and children with no way to contact them or even to know if they might already have been deported. Often part of the INS strategy for persuading families to cooperate with quick "voluntary" departures was to lead the men and women to believe that spouses or children had already decided to board the deportation plane.

Children were kept in numerous places along the Rio Grande Valley. Some of the valley towns contracted with the INS to keep children in their spare cells in local jails. Their plight was one of the first things that drew the attention and protest of local churches and refugee support groups. In a few cases, religious workers themselves provided homes for the prison children, so more humane conditions could be assured for them. It was in such a home a few days later that we found the youngest of the prisoners we went to collect, a sad and scared sixteen-year-old boy.

The Friesens told us that a $5,000 bond had been set on each of the arrested refugees. We decided that somehow we would raise the money and get our friends back.

"Hang on, we're coming to Texas as soon as we can get there," I said. "Just don't lose track of the Salvadorans. Tell the INS we're on the way with the bail money."

By the time we hung up, we had crossed another important threshold in our work—though its implications would not be clear for many months. Step by step, our lives were becoming more deeply intertwined with those of the refugees.

Soon we were back in the Jubilee bus and on our way to south Texas. Ed and I were joined by Eric Drewry, whose skills as a lawyer were certain to be needed over the next few days. All the way we talked over one scenario after another, exploring how far we were willing to go in defense of the refugees.

Our friends in south Texas and in Arizona were under growing pressure from the INS to stop their work with the refugees. Arrests were just around the corner. The U.S. public was becoming increasingly aware of the tragic struggle in Central America. Momentum was building on behalf of the refugees, whose desperate search for safety was beginning to draw attention. The INS reflected the determination of the Reagan administration to treat the whole matter as a political struggle in which, ultimately, our nation's future as the great bulwark against Soviet communism was somehow at stake.

While global geopolitical calculations guided the policies being made in Washington, we arrived in south Texas to work with the individual human beings whose lives were being affected most directly by them. We headed straight for the Corralón to see how the prisoners were doing. After arguing with the INS officials there, some of us were finally able to meet with the women in a guarded room.

We found that both of them had been so sick all week from their pregnancies that they had been unable to eat the prison food, except for a little rice now and then. They were also frightened that their families had already been sent back to El Salvador. We assured them their husbands were in the prison just a hundred yards away and that we were working to get all of them out immediately.

Eric went to work at once and managed by early afternoon to persuade the local INS judge to lower the bonds from $5,000 to $1,000 apiece. The rest of us rushed from office to office, filling out forms and arguing with officials. Just before the end of the day, we had the great pleasure of leading all the prisoners out past the guards to a joyful reunion in the INS parking lot. The sixteen-year-old had been released a couple of hours earlier and was waiting there with a huge smile.

The young husbands and wives embraced with tears of joy and relief. I felt another wave of deep satisfaction, and the words of the Jubilee text took on deeper meaning than ever. "The spirit of the Lord is upon me . . . to proclaim release for prisoners . . . to let the oppressed go free. . . ." Then I became aware that hundreds of other prisoners were watching silently from behind the high fence beyond the parking lot.

"Hey, I know a good Mexican restaurant in Harlingen," Ed suggested, as the sun began to set. "Let's go get these people some real food to eat!"

All of us had to crowd into two small cars for the drive into town. We just managed to force the door shut, trying not to crush the pregnant wives any more than necessary. Packed into the cars with our new friends, all of us in need of a good shower, we were acutely aware of our shared humanity. As we drove past the miles of dark mesquite and prickly pear thickets toward the lights of Harlingen, I kept hearing those beautiful words—". . . spirit of the Lord . . . release for prisoners . . . oppressed go free. . . ."

The next two days were as long and busy as the first had been. Thirty-five refugees in the valley wanted to go to Jubilee, with another family of four waiting to be picked up in Houston on the way there. We were going to fill the bus to capacity, and then some.

All the while, the great problem loomed over us. The INS was making it clear they did not want this to go further. We had spent many hours in their waiting rooms and on the telephone, trying to persuade them to cooperate with us. We argued that, after all, we were simply trying to help them get the refugees out of the United States.

The INS district director, would not talk to me anymore. When I finally managed to see his second in command, I reminded him of their earlier concerns that the refugees would "break and run" before we could get them to Canada. This would not be an "efficient" use of INS time. Every refugee so far had gone to Canada. Releasing them to Jubilee took less INS time and money than complicated deportation procedures.

"The problem, Mr. Mosley, as we now see it," he told me, "is that your Jubilee operation is *too* efficient. If we let

you take these people to Canada, it will give encouragement to the others—and we cannot allow that!"

Our attempts at persuasion went nowhere. But our
dogged insistence on gaining every right the law allowed
for the refugees slowly wore the officials down. We would
not run the risk of bringing the refugees to the INS office
for personal interviews anymore. But we filled out piles of
forms—applications for political asylum in the United
States—and brought these into the office. Thanks to the
lawyers on our side, we knew that the law required the
INS officials to accept these applications from our hands
on behalf of the refugees. The anger grew in their faces as
we gave them one set after another.

The day before our scheduled departure, we gathered
at the Friesens' home and took stock of the situation. We
were at a critical point. The INS was threatening constantly
in the newspapers, as well as to our faces, that the people
who got involved on behalf of the refugees might end up
in jail. And the threat would soon prove not to be an empty one in south Texas and Arizona, where our sanctuary
friends were also hard at work.

We spent several hours praying and going over the situation. Aside from our own safety, were we foolishly exposing the refugees to greater danger? Would those who
had chosen to join our program now be targeted in a way
that would bring them harsher treatment, in order to make
them a public example for others? And always the linger-
ing doubt: were we truly following God's leading in all of
this? Or were we being led by less pure motives than we
would admit even to ourselves, such as the temptation to
be seen as brave heroes? Finally, if it came to it, were we
really ready to go to prison on behalf of these refugees?

We decided to go ahead. Some of us called the refugee
families and arranged for a rendezvous the next morning.
Others laid mattresses down the aisle of the bus to make a

place for the overflow crowd to lie down.

The next morning dawned with dark thunderclouds overhead, which added to our tension. We began zigzagging through the Rio Grande Valley, meeting one family after another as they emerged from their hiding places. By midmorning we had everyone aboard—thirty in the seats, seven lying in the aisle, and the driver. One last time we explained the situation to everyone and gave them a chance to drop out. No one did. So, with the Friesens waving good-bye from the curb, we moved out onto the highway and headed north.

We were aware that Texas really has two southern borders. The Rio Grande River is the official border, but for most of its length it is relatively easy to cross without detection. Just north of the fertile valley, however, lies a wide band of inhospitable wilderness. Much of it lies in the boundaries of King Ranch, largest ranch in the world. It is rattlesnake and cactus country. Clumps of thorny mesquite trees alternate with huge expanses of brush and prickly pears so dense even a person on foot has great difficulty finding a way through.

This natural barrier makes it easier for the U.S. Border Patrol to operate the second "border," a line of highway checkpoints about a hundred miles north of the Rio Grande. All northbound traffic must pass through these checkpoints and account for the citizenship of every passenger. According to newspaper reports, there is also a zone of electronic sensors sprinkled across the region to prevent people from walking around the checkpoints. We never bothered to test whether that was fact or deliberate rumor.

We knew that, for better or worse, the showdown was waiting up ahead at the checkpoint five miles south of Sarita. As we drove up Highway 77, the tension grew. Conversation stopped.

From the driver's seat, I had the best view. I began to notice that the thunderclouds were getting darker and more turbulent. I spent my boyhood in Texas, and so I recognized that this was tornado weather.

Sure enough, when we were about ten miles from the dreaded checkpoint, I saw funnels descending one after another from the huge cloud up ahead, just to the west of the highway. I called to the others. All of us watched as four funnels extended downward, swinging slowly from side to side like great fingers searching blindly for the earth. I kept driving, but I was ready to make a U-turn to try to outrun the tornadoes if they reached the ground in our path.

The checkpoint came into view. It was clearly open for business. All the yellow lights were flashing and barricades were in place to channel traffic through a single lane beside the Border Patrol building. As we came closer I drew in my breath. I had never seen so many Border Patrol vehicles in one place! At least a dozen of their green cars were gathered there, as well as a Border Patrol bus with bars on the windows—obviously waiting to haul people to the Corralón.

One last time there was a brief temptation to turn around, take our passengers back to their hiding places, and call this whole effort off. But we kept going, with the tornadoes dangling high above us and to our left, like observers from another world.

There was no other traffic near us, but I began to slow the bus as we came near the barricade. With all the official vehicles parked around us, I expected a small army of armed Border Patrol officers to swarm around the bus. They never showed up.

The checkpoint building was lined with windows so the officers could have a panoramic view of the approaching traffic. All the lights were on inside, but there was no sign of a human anywhere!

We didn't stop to investigate. A few seconds later we were past the barricade and moving on up the open highway to freedom. *"Gloria a Dios!"* Suddenly our silent passengers exploded into laughter and spontaneous thanks to God. We weren't sure what was going on, but we were starting to like it very much.

"Señor," said one of the Salvadorans, "now I know what the children of Israel felt like when they were coming out of the Red Sea!"

As I accelerated away, I kept watching the rearview mirrors for a clue. There was nothing but cactus and scrubby trees for miles around. Where were all the people who had come in all those vehicles?

We never found out. In the months that followed, we returned again and again, filled our bus with refugees, and drove north through that same checkpoint. Often we would be behind vehicles that were the objects of thorough searches, with the Border Patrol checking every possible hiding place for undocumented passengers. But when our turn came—our bus packed with plainly visible Central Americans—there would often be no more than a frown from a solemn officer, then a quick wave of a hand indicating we were cleared to move on.

Occasionally we were boarded and there was a quick check of documents, but that was rare. At such times we might get a brief lecture. "You people are doing a lot more harm than good. You ought to wake up and see the problems you're causing by helping all these Central Americans." But at least one time an officer managed to sneak a private wink and say softly, "Thanks for what you are doing."

In the years that followed, we almost never had anyone taken from our bus. The few who were arrested were quickly bonded out and brought to Jubilee to rejoin the others. Not one person accepted into the Año de Jubileo program was ever deported.

And so the passage through the checkpoint became a regular part of our life, sixty busloads of refugees over an eight-year period. It was a time of remembering that God was indeed with us, as we put our own security on the line with that of these beautiful families—*our* family—who had put their trust in God and in us as God's agents.

8

Release to the Captives

Months passed like strong heartbeats as we worked constantly to save as many people as we could. We made trips from Jubilee Partners to the Rio Grande Valley every few weeks. The five refugees we had first bailed out made it safely to Canada, but we kept finding more and more people in grave danger for whom we could not afford to pay bond.

Our brightly colored Jubilee bus became a symbol of hope, even to the many prisoners who could not actually come through our program. Until the INS authorities barred us from doing so, we took pleasure in parking the bus in a conspicuous location just outside the Corralón's high fence, to assure the prisoners inside that friends were nearby. Word passed quickly among them that the Año de Jubileo people were near, hope was lifted, and our resolve was strengthened to keep struggling to make their claims heard by the courts.

The INS judges routinely set bond requirements so high that few of the refugees could meet them—a few thousand dollars in most cases. It might as well have been a few million. Few of the refugees had any money at all or any friends on whom they could call for such amounts.

A race of life against death went on constantly at the

Corralón. Refugees were herded through formal hearings that pretended to determine whether their appeals for political asylum were genuinely based on "well-founded fear of persecution," as required by U.S. law. We began to sit in on as many of these hearings as possible. While the INS machine ground refugees through its gears, filling one deportation plane after another, we worked frantically outside the fences to rescue those most likely to be tortured or killed on their return.

Mario was a young man who seemed to us almost certain to be killed by the death squads in El Salvador if deported. He had been a labor union leader there and had narrowly escaped several assassination attempts. His bond was set at $4,000. The judge refused to reduce it—ironically, precisely because Mario was so afraid and was therefore thought more likely to jump bond and make a dash for freedom. We had appealed to our friends at Koinonia Partners for help, feeling somehow that Mario deserved even more than the usual effort.

On the critical day for Mario—his legal appeals exhausted—the public-address system blared out the list of sixty men who were to assemble that morning for deportation. Tension mounted as the men counted the names. After the sixtieth, there was a moment of relief for those who had escaped the list.

But then, to Mario's horror, his name was also called out—the sixty-first. He thought his battle for survival had finally been lost, and he presented himself at the gate— and found Ryan and the Friesens standing there with the necessary $4,000! Koinonia had come through just in time.

Our fears about what could happen to the deported were confirmed by the story of Roberto. Roberto was a gentle young man—tall, lean, and handsome. He smiled often, but it was easy to look into his eyes and see that he had suffered.

When Roberto was in high school, he became acquainted with students at the University of San Carlos in Guatemala City who worked with indigenous people. Intrigued by their work, he soon began to help them in their literacy work, distribute medicine and food, and run a farm produce cooperative.

The work began to draw the suspicion of wealthy landowners nearby, who falsely accused the students of doing political work that was "communist-inspired." Warnings were issued. At first they were fairly subtle, but soon they became more blunt and threatening.

One day two student leaders of the group disappeared. A few days later, their disfigured bodies were dumped in a public place, with signs pinned to them bearing the black imprint of a hand and the words *"Escuadrón de la Muerte"* (Death Squad). The other students were terrified, but most, including Roberto, decided to continue their work.

A few months later, Roberto was in a meeting of the group when the door burst open and masked men with machine guns seized two more leaders. All the rest were forced to sit still as tear gas was thrown into the room and the door locked.

Now the remaining students in the group were, in fact, becoming very "political" in their determination to keep the work going on behalf of the poor. Roberto began to spend practically all his time working with an agricultural project outside the village of San Mateo, near Lake Atitlán. Several times he was stopped by police along the highway. Once he was beaten so badly that his thumb was broken and his back injured from a hard kick.

The army attacked the village where Roberto had been working. Soldiers shot several villagers and burned homes. Soldiers came several times to Roberto's house looking for him, but each time he was away or managed to escape. He knew he must flee to the United States or be killed.

Roberto's mother was a North American, the daughter of United Fruit employees. She abandoned him when he was five, leaving him to be raised by a Guatemalan foster family. She returned to the United States. Roberto found it relatively easy to make his way in the United States. He spent nine years working at various odd jobs and trying to become a U.S. citizen. His mother gave him some help, but his application for citizenship was denied.

Despite his insistence that he would be in danger if deported, the INS flew Roberto back to Guatemala City. At the airport he was seized at once by the police of Interpol Guatemala, part of an internationally coordinated police system supported by the U.S. government.

Like those of all deportees, Roberto's documents declared that he was being deported after a stay in the United States. This was an alarm signal to the Guatemalan authorities. They fingerprinted and photographed him, questioned him for hours, then held him at the airport until the next morning.

As Roberto headed through the customs room and toward the exit, he looked up at the balcony above, where dozens of people stared down at him. Any one might be an agent waiting for him to step outside. He went through the glass doors and the crowd of waiting relatives and hawkers outside, then down the steps to the street. He walked briskly away from the airport but was not fast enough to escape the Escuadrón de la Muerte waiting for him.

A Ford Bronco swerved to the curb beside him. Several armed men jumped out and seized Roberto; his worst fears were coming true. The days and nights that followed —about two weeks, as nearly as Roberto could reconstruct it—were horrible. He was taken to a room where he was held incommunicado, given no food, and seldom allowed sleep.

As he weakened, the questioning intensified. "Who are you working with? What have you been doing in the United States? Why did you run from Guatemala? Are you a communist?"

He was taken to a remote place, thumbs tied to his toes behind his back, and threatened with a machine gun. When his answers still failed to satisfy the torturers, they beat him until he was unconscious. They thought he was dead. The death squad then tossed Roberto's body into the huge city dump in Guatemala City.

The dump is perhaps the most grotesque symbol of the social problems underlying Guatemala's violent system. Guatemala City is sliced into sectors by several deep canyons, each of which drains down toward the Pacific. One canyon serves as the central garbage dump. An endless stream of yellow collection trucks hauls refuse past high walls to the edge of the canyon.

Within these walls live and work thousands of the poorest of Guatemala's people, most of them women and children. Hundreds of buzzards circle overhead and emaciated dogs watch for a chance to dart in for food. These people unload the trucks by hand. As they work, they watch constantly for edible garbage. If they are too slow, the buzzards or the dogs beat them to it. If the food is not too rotten, they can salvage it by frying it on a piece of scrap metal over a fire of burning plastic or broken furniture. Bits of recyclable metal or plastic are carefully separated out to be sold to men who come with trucks from local businesses every afternoon.

The garbage workers have their own subculture and techniques of survival in a stinking, ugly compound in the middle of this large, modern city. Much of Guatemalan society considers them as disposable as the garbage with which they live twenty-four hours a day. Most of them, including the children, endure the misery by sniffing glue or finding other ways to dull their senses. They live in tiny shacks that hang precariously on the brink of the canyon. The shacks are sometimes washed loose by rains or shaken by earthquakes. They occasionally plummet into the abyss with their occupants, who then literally become part of the slowly moving, filthy glacier of garbage.

The dump has always been a popular place for the death squads to dispose of the bodies of their victims. Their Ford Broncos and Jeep Cherokees with tinted glass windows wheel into the area, and the men toss bloody bodies over the edge of the canyon. No one dares question or approach them. But after the dreaded vehicles leave, the garbage workers—experts on living death—usually make it a point to see if there is any life left in the bodies.

In Roberto's case there was.

When he regained consciousness, he found himself in a garbage worker's shack. His body was a mass of bruises and cuts. The worker gave him water to drink. When he was able to eat, the family shared their meager food supply with him.

Though Roberto was still weak, after some time he left to find the home of his foster parents. The police had arrived some days earlier. According to neighbors, they had broken into the house and beaten Roberto's foster father so severely the family had gone into hiding.

Though fearing for their own safety, the neighbors gave Roberto shelter and food for a few days to help him regain his strength. Then they gave him money for a bus ticket and urged him to get out of Guatemala quickly. Almost three months later, Roberto waded the Rio Grande River into Texas.

He was discovered and arrested by the U.S. Border Patrol within twenty-four hours. The deportation hearings began immediately, in spite of Roberto's frantic protests that deportation would mean certain death for him this time. That was when the Friesens found him.

Ruth Anne and Richard Friesen had the difficult job of interviewing hundreds of refugees in order to decide which were most likely to be killed if deported. They always had a list of many more urgent cases than we could help. Ryan Karis had the heavy responsibility of making decisions on Jubilee's behalf. Often it came down to a painful choice based simply on the size of bonds. Over and over, one group of frightened men and women were rounded up and flown back to likely deaths—while we drove in the opposite direction with a handful of those we had managed to save.

It took several months for the implications of our experience with bailing out refugees to become clear. We had thousands of dollars of Jubilee operating funds tied up in their bonds. The basic requirement of bond was that the refugees leave the United States. Of course the INS judges intended for the refugees to return to Central America; we took them instead to safety in the North. As we crossed into Canada each time, we got documents to prove that the refugees were indeed out of the United States, which we sent on to the INS. We were somewhat surprised when our bond money was returned in a few weeks.

One evening at a Jubilee worship service, we read the familiar story of Paul and Silas in jail: "About midnight Paul and Silas were praying and singing hymns to God, and the prisoners were listening to them. Suddenly there was an earthquake, so violent that the foundations of the prison were shaken; and immediately all the doors were opened and everyone's chains were unfastened" (Acts 16:25-26, NRSV).

For us the story was alive and relevant, because of our constant trips to the Corralón and the thrill of helping prisoners to freedom. A new idea began to take shape among us. We decided to see if we could organize a large-scale "prison break."

We announced that we were setting up the "Paul and Silas Revolving Bail Fund." Supporters were invited to make noninterest loans to us. We proposed to use the money to bail out a steady stream of refugees. Once they were in Canada, the bond money would be refunded to us. We would use it as quickly as possible to bail out more prisoners.

The loans began to roll in, along with dozens of letters full of excitement about the idea. Before long we had more than $100,000 in the fund. After some weeks of negotiation on Roberto's behalf, Jubilee was able to post bond of $7,500 for him from the Paul and Silas funds.

We worked as fast as we could to keep the funds in use, bailing out scores of prisoners and moving them on to Canada. When the money came in faster than we could put the refugees through the Año de Jubileo program, we began to furnish bail for a flow of others through the broader Overground Railroad network.

Eventually INS officials found a way to slow the process. They simply took longer to repay the money once the refugees reached Canada. Instead of a turn-around time of a few weeks, it lengthened to several months. Some bond money was returned only after we wrote letters and made phone calls over a period of years, trying to get the paperwork moved through the necessary bureaucratic channels. Still, "release to the captives" had become a daily and exciting reality in our work.

The program brought Pablo to safety. An itinerant preacher from Guatemala, Pablo drew strength from the story of Paul and Silas long before he had heard of our fund. Pablo was of Mayan ancestry, a man with great faith and energy.

He and another man set out to preach to the people of the remote villages and countryside of El Quiché, an area where government troops had massacred many people in the previous few years. Then there was something of a lull in the violence. Pablo took that as a God-sent opportunity to preach the gospel. His father told him he was a fool and would not be able to make a living from preaching to people. Pablo responded, "You don't understand, Father. I am not asking them for money. I am preaching because I love them and because I think this is what God wants me to do."

In a short time, however, it became obvious the preachers were not welcomed by everyone. As Pablo and his co-worker walked from village to village, giving spiritual education and conducting services, they began to notice that propaganda fliers from local guerrillas showed up frequently in the paths they followed.

Soon the guerrillas became more pointed in their communication. One flier had a handwritten note: "Be careful. You might run into problems if you keep preaching. If you continue, you will reap the consequences of your stubbornness—EGP" (an acronym for the Guerrilla Army of the Poor).

Other notes followed, each becoming more adamant. Even though Pablo and his co-worker tried to avoid saying anything that might be understood as political, the guerrillas believed their preaching would weaken the resolve of the people in the area to resist the government. They thought the people would become less interested in armed struggle as they became Christians.

The itinerant preachers prayed and strengthened their resolve by reminding themselves of the persecution suffered by Paul and Silas and others in the book of Acts. They became more determined than ever not to be stopped by such threats.

Then the two local men who had served as guides were seized by members of the local Civil Patrol, men organized by the army to guard villagers against the guerrillas. The guides were interrogated roughly and beaten severely. The interrogators accused them of helping the evangelists prepare the people to overthrow the army and enter the guerrilla forces.

One guide returned, badly injured, but the other never did. He likely died from the brutal interrogation. The surviving guide urged Pablo and his friend to leave the area immediately. They realized they were now being pursued by both the guerrillas and the army, and so they went into hiding.

Pablo had a hard decision to make. He knew he would be in danger even if he returned to his home near Guatemala City. He decided he had to leave the country. He judged that his wife and three small children, ages one to five, would be safe while they waited to join him when he got established in the North. He sent a letter to them, urging them to be brave and to pray for him. He promised to call as soon as he reached the United States.

After a month of travel, Pablo managed to cross into south Texas, where he was given shelter. He eagerly called back home. To his horror, he found that his decision to leave his family behind had been a tragic mistake. His wife had "disappeared," and her mother had the three children in her home. She appealed to Pablo to come back for them quickly before someone harmed them as well. She had already received anonymous notes threatening the children if Pablo did not turn himself in.

Pablo set out at once to rescue his children. He had barely gotten across the Rio Grande when he was caught by Mexican authorities in Matamoros and severely beaten. One official seemed convinced that Pablo had been involved in an attack on him, even though Pablo protested that he knew nothing about it. The official refused to believe him and launched what became an extended persecution of Pablo. First the official held Pablo in a house in

Matamoros, then he transferred him to a jail in Tampico and finally to another jail in the little town of Papantla, four hundred miles south of the Rio Grande.

There Pablo was locked up and apparently forgotten. Month after month passed, as Pablo waited and worried about his family. The jailers often struck him (once breaking a finger). As time went by they brought him less and less food. He was held incommunicado for almost seven months, the last three of which he was given nothing except water and an occasional tortilla. He was close to starvation.

"I prayed constantly for my children and for strength to survive this ordeal," Pablo told us at Jubilee. "But I was afraid I was losing my mind. I cried more and more as I begged God for help.

"One day as I was praying, I looked up and saw I had a visitor. He was a tall man with long hair and white clothes. He told me, 'Pablo, don't cry anymore. You don't have much longer to stay here.' Then he simply disappeared.

"I called the guards and asked them, 'Who was that who came to see me?'

" 'You are losing your mind,' they answered. 'No one can even get into this hall without coming through the locked door at the front, and there has been no one here to see you.'

"I decided I really was going crazy.

"But one week later, two men really did come into the jail and to the door of my cell. They were Christians from Poza Rica de Hidalgo, a small town a few miles northwest of Papantla. They said they had heard of me and asked to visit earlier but had been refused. They had prayed more and tried again. Finally the guards agreed to let them in.

"When they found me I was in very bad condition, almost dead from hunger. One arm was infected where the guards had stabbed me with a needle while torturing me.

"The Christians told me, 'Don't worry. We are praying for you, and we will have you free very soon.' A few days later they came back with official papers ordering my release. I think they had paid a bribe to someone to save me."

Pablo's new Mexican friends took him to Poza Rica de Hidalgo. They gave him a place to live for several months while they nursed him back to health. While he was recovering, they went to Guatemala and brought Pablo's three young children to join him.

When he and the children tried to cross the Rio Grande near Brownsville, they were immediately caught by the Border Patrol. The children were taken to a shelter and Pablo was put in the Corralón. He knew he was in danger of deportation, and so Pablo was thrilled when his prayers were answered again. This time the "angel" was Richard Friesen. A few weeks later, beaming from ear to ear and praising God, this determined evangelist arrived at Jubilee—freed from prison by bond money from the Paul and Silas Revolving Bail Fund.

But his joy was short-lived. While Pablo was waiting for final clearance to go to Canada, his father was having pangs of conscience in Guatemala. Apparently inspired by Pablo's love for the people in the villages, he started taking baskets of fruit from the orchards where he worked and delivering them as gifts. He was noticed by the military police in a station that he often passed.

One day his body was found beside the road. Near it was a military belt that had apparently been dropped by one of the murderers. Pablo's grieving sister took the belt and ran straight to the military post. She Waved the belt in front of a crowd of people. She screamed at the soldiers, "You murderers! You are the ones who killed my innocent father!"

The soldiers made no reply at the time, but two weeks

later her body was found several miles away at the edge of Lake Atitlán. When this news reached Pablo in Chicago, he became so ill he had to be hospitalized briefly.

After he was settled in Canada, Pablo continued the search for his wife. He appealed to Amnesty International for help, and to Ramiro de León Carpio, then head of the Guatemalan Human Rights Commission and later president of Guatemala. De León Carpio responded that she was probably dead; nothing more could be done.

Still Pablo has held onto hope. In a recent phone conversation, he told me he had been fasting for four weeks, praying that God would give him some word about his wife.

Pablo was only one of many pastors persecuted in Central America. Almost a decade earlier, in the spring of 1977, an intensive campaign against Catholic priests had been launched in El Salvador by the Salvadoran government. Eight priests were expelled, two killed, and several others tortured. An infamous flier was circulated with this message: "Be a patriot—kill a priest."

Church World Service later published a poster that was displayed for years in churches all over the United States. It pictured a young Central American man with a tired smile on his face, holding his son in his arms. Under the picture was the caption "A REFUGEE WOULD LIKE TO HAVE YOUR PROBLEMS." Few of the thousands of people who saw it could have guessed what an understatement that really was in the particular case of the man in the picture.

Francisco, the man pictured, came through Jubilee with his family in the spring of 1985. He had been a bright, young priest in El Salvador who quickly caught the attention of his local bishop, Oscar Romero. In the summer of 1976, he became Romero's personal secretary and served as parish priest in several locations. At the very time when tension was rising most rapidly between the wealthy families of El Salvador and the Catholic Church, Francisco was taking an increasingly public role, often traveling with Romero.

Romero was named archbishop by the Vatican on February 3, 1977. Three weeks later a national election was held in El Salvador and subsequently declared fraudulent. Ten thousand people gathered in Plaza Libertad in San Salvador on the evening of February 27 to protest the fraud. Just after midnight the National Guard attacked the crowd, murdering more than one hundred people and wounding many others.

Before daybreak, Francisco drove the archbishop to San Salvador to assume his new role. They went straight to Plaza Libertad, where they could still see evidence of the massacre that had taken place a few hours earlier, despite frantic efforts by the National Guard to wash away the blood.

Francisco returned to Santiago de María, the parish from which Romero had just come, and conducted a Mass in which he spoke out passionately against the massacre. Step by step he was drawn into a crescendo of events, among them a public victory against Señora Del Peck, a wealthy landowner trying to monopolize the water of the area and keep it from the poor people.

Concurrent with this struggle was one being waged in Aguilares by Fr. Rutilio Grande, a mutual friend of Romero and Francisco. On the afternoon of March 12, two weeks after the Plaza Libertad massacre, Grande was ambushed and murdered. As the new archbishop grieved for his dead friend, he began in earnest his transformation from a restrained, relatively conservative church leader to the powerful spokesman for the poor who was to become known around the world for his eloquence and courage.

Francisco's jeopardy continued to increase in proportion to Romero's rise and his own intensifying activities. He began to live a life of constant danger, often dodging ambushes on remote roads as his loyal parishioners slipped tips to him about them. Even so he was stopped countless times by the police on public streets, searched, threatened, and sometimes beaten.

Early in May, the National Guardsmen who watched over the properties of Señora Del Peck beat him so severely he was hospitalized for fifteen days. The soldiers told him that if he continued to speak out for the poor, he would be "erased from the map."

A wealthy doctor, chief of a death squad, was assigned by the right-wing paramilitary group ORDEN to "check Francisco out"—to see if he was actually a member of the guerrilla forces. The doctor became a friend of Francisco instead, convinced he was not connected to the guerrillas. Rather than marking him for assassination, the doctor convinced Francisco he had to leave the country.

Francisco spent eight months in the United States. Then he decided to return to El Salvador, hoping the threat against him had subsided. Throughout 1978 he continued his work as a priest. He organized Bible studies, job training, used clothing distribution, and classes on health, as well as forums in which the people talked about current social issues.

He worked with CARITAS, the Catholic relief organization, distributing wheat, oil, and milk to those in need. He heard reports through friends that once again he had been labeled "subversive" because of his parish work with the poor and for teaching a philosophy course at the university.

Several times in 1978, Francisco asked for permission to leave the diocese and go to another country because of the risk. Requests were denied by his local bishop. In December, because of the danger of his work, Francisco left the priesthood, hoping to slip out of the public eye and thus avoid problems. However, his popularity with the people was such that leaders on both sides of the conflict began to try to recruit him to their causes.

In May 1980, Francisco married Silvia, a woman from a wealthy family in Usulutan. One of her relatives was chief of security at the Presidential Palace. Another was married to Roberto D'Aubisson, the unofficial leader of the death squads. Silvia was already the political renegade of her family. Her marriage to Francisco was the last straw. In late 1980, D'Aubisson sent word that Francisco had until December 10 to get out of El Salvador or be killed. Francisco flew to Houston and was joined a month later by Silvia.

It was now clear that they would not be able to return to El Salvador, so Francisco and Silvia brought their children to Jubilee. Months later they were finally settled safely in Canada.

9

Faith to Keep Going

At Jubilee Partners, what often kept us going was the courage and faith of the refugees who came to us. Always we were inspired by the deep trust in God that the refugees carried with them. Armando, who had taken on more risks than we were ever likely to face, challenged us by his example to go further in our acts of compassion.

As a young man, Armando had enjoyed the privileges of membership in the wealthy elite of Guatemala. The twelve children of his family all received university educations and became professional people of one type or another.

Armando was a doctor. While still an intern, he was assigned to work with the Mayan people of the mountains north of Guatemala City. His interest in these gentle people, who make up the majority of Guatemala's population, deepened into a real love for them. After he became a licensed physician, he and his wife returned to the mountains to serve the Mayans rather than establish a more lucrative (and safer) practice in a major city, as most doctors did.

Despite warnings from his patrician family, Armando became more and more concerned about the Guatemalan government's persecution of the indigenous people. He expressed that concern through his medical services to them rather than through outspoken political activities, yet even that was enough to arouse suspicions of the local Guatemalan authorities.

Armando served the people vigorously. He often walked steep trails for hours to reach remote villages and hold clinics. He traveled with an assistant who helped him carry his little stock of medicine and equipment. As time passed, his patients recognized his genuine concern for them and increasingly took him into their confidence. Armando and his assistant became the most knowledgeable outsiders in the region about the activities in the area.

Predictably, that did not escape the notice of the Guatemalan military leaders. Casually at first, then with increasing persistence, they pried into Armando's store of knowledge. They sought the names of the young men in the villages and information about any who might be sympathetic to, or active supporters of, the guerrillas in the nearby jungle. Pleading professional privilege, Armando refused to give any information.

One day Armando and his assistant were met by several soldiers, who bluntly told them that the local army officer had run out of patience and wanted information immediately. Armando was afraid but responded unequivocally that he would not divulge information.

The soldiers grabbed Armando's assistant. One put a gun to his head. "This will show you what we will do to you if you do not cooperate!" he shouted.

Armando threw his arms around his assistant and tried to wrestle him away from the soldiers, but they fired point-blank toward the assistant's head, killing him instantly. The man's body convulsed and went limp in Armando's arms.

"Think what will happen to you and your family if you don't cooperate," the soldier continued. "We'll be back soon for that information." The soldiers left Armando standing in the middle of the road, holding the bloody body of his friend.

The next few days were agony for Armando and his wife as they debated whether they should abandon the people to whom they had grown so close and run to save their own lives. Most of all, they feared for the safety of their three children, two beautiful young daughters and a small son, Armando Jr. They were a close, loving family. Armando loved to have his son walk with him on short medical trips.

Armando was with a patient in his office when someone burst through the door and shouted, "They've taken Armando Jr.! A man has picked him up and is running with him down the street!"

Instantly, Armando ran out of his office in the direction of the kidnapping. He ran at full speed up and down the streets until he heard his son's screams. Armando caught up with the kidnapper and, with desperate strength, ripped his son from the man's arms. The unarmed man ran in the opposite direction and disappeared around a corner.

Crying with tears of relief, Armando held his son close to him and walked back to his office, a crowd of curious people following. His indecision was ended. He dismissed the waiting patients. He took his medical records into a small courtyard and burned them. Then he closed his office and went home. In hours he and his family were on their way to Guatemala City.

Whatever relief from danger they might have felt was short-lived, however. Guatemalan soldiers soon began to visit his relatives' homes searching for Armando. Until then Armando had not realized that he might actually have to leave his country to find safety.

Armando and his family moved furtively from one

home to another, grateful that he had many relatives willing to take risks on their behalf. One day Armando took a taxi from one hiding place back to a brother's house, to pick up some things they had left behind. As he approached the house, Armando was terrified. A military truck was parked in front of it and a group of soldiers surrounded the building.

He told the taxi driver to keep moving. As the taxi passed the house, Armando slumped down in the back seat. He raised his head just high enough to peek through the window as the soldiers broke into the house. Then he rushed back to his family and began preparing to leave Guatemala.

With his credentials as a doctor, he managed to escape to California, pretending to be on his way to a medical conference. Friends helped his family leave by way of Mexico City, and after what seemed like an eternity, they were reunited and directed to Jubilee.

Armando was a poet, a sensitive man who often got tears in his eyes when he told stories about his country. He and his family went on to Ontario. When I last heard from him, he was still trying to get permission to practice medicine in Canada.

Pedro demonstrated that a commitment to nonviolence is more than just words. He had paid a heavy price at a young age for his belief.

Most of those coming to us were families and adults. Pedro was by himself, a sad young man of sixteen. When he was not in class, he was usually out under a tree alone, strumming his guitar and singing softly. One day I sat beside him and drew him out about his experiences in El Salvador.

"My mother is a very holy person," he said, eyes moistening instantly at the thought. "She always read the Bible and prayed with us every night. She loved the Sermon on the Mount. She read to us many times where Jesus taught us that we should love our neighbors—even our enemies."

Pedro told me how he had been drafted into the army by the Salvadoran government when he was just fifteen. His younger brother had been drafted not long after and ended up serving with Pedro.

"My brother and I were put through a few months of training. Then we were sent out on patrols in mountain areas where there were guerrillas," he explained. "If we didn't cooperate and try to kill the guerrillas, the army would kill us.

"After about a year I was sent out as the leader of one patrol, and the other guys were all younger than I! My brother was one of them. We were walking as quietly as we could up a little valley full of trees and bushes. When I looked up ahead I saw a guerrilla soldier standing in full view with his back turned to me. He was no farther away than there." He pointed to the top of a nearby tree.

"I aimed my rifle at him and tried to squeeze the trigger, but just then I thought about my mother reading to us that we should love our enemies. I could not shoot! I lowered my rifle and motioned to the others to go back.

"Then the guerrilla heard us. He whirled around and started shooting at us. I think my brother was the first to die.

"Some of us escaped, but one bullet had gone through my foot, and I was having a hard time running. Other men started shooting. Everything was confusing. After a few minutes I got down to a road, but my foot was hurting so bad I couldn't stand it. I decided to kill myself with a hand grenade, but just then my officer came up in a jeep and yelled at me not to do it. I saw he had been hit in the chest himself. He was bleeding badly.

"I jumped into the jeep, and he started driving fast down to where we could be picked up by a helicopter.

When we got there, he stopped the jeep and just leaned against the steering wheel and died."

Pedro sat quietly for a few minutes, trying to control his emotions. Then he continued softly, "After a while they let me leave the army. But after I had been at home about three weeks, I started getting notes saying somebody was going to kill me for serving in the army. I didn't want to be in the army in the first place, but now the guerrillas were after me.

"After I got two warnings, I left El Salvador for a few months. I made it all the way to the United States, then got deported back to El Salvador. I was discouraged but also so homesick I decided to try to stay in El Salvador in a different place, just a few miles from my mother's home. In a few days I found another note telling me I would be killed if I didn't get out of El Salvador in twenty-four hours.

"I went to my mother again late at night and told her about it. She told me I had no choice, I must leave at once. So I left."

There was a long pause. Then Pedro said softly, "I wish I could be home again with her."

When I finally left him, Pedro was strumming and singing softly again. After hearing his story, I understood the great sadness of this young man. And I was humbled by the way he had already been true to the same teachings of Jesus I had embraced without such cost.

Another young man tested our belief in "love for enemies" in a very different way. The Canadian consul was unlikely to approve anyone on either extreme of the political spectrum, so we tried to screen refugees carefully for the Año program. But we couldn't always trust that we were getting the whole picture. Once refugees were at Jubilee, part of our job was to prepare them for interviews with the consul, to enable them to make the most of their chances of acceptance into Canada.

Robbie Buller describes his experience. "One of the Canadian consul's favorite questions was 'Did you experience more persecution than other people who lived around you?'

"When I asked this of refugees, over and over they said, 'No, we were all in danger.' If you gave that kind of answer to the Canadian consul, he was likely to say, 'Well, then, you're not a refugee—there's nothing more compelling about your reasons for leaving your country than all the other hundreds of thousands of people who are out there.'

"When we would question the refugees a little more, asking, 'What was life like for you?' we'd find out that people had been sleeping under the beds because bullets kept going through the house.

"And we'd say, 'Well, then, what do you mean you weren't in more danger?'

"They'd answer, 'Well, the neighbors all slept under the bed, too.'

"One of the men I was helping to prepare explained in vivid detail everything he had done in El Salvador. Every Saturday night, he would get a list. He told me, 'We were to go and knock on the door [of the people on the list]. If they let us in, we were simply to take them away and turn them over to our superiors. But if they would not let us in, we were to break in. If we found them, we were to execute them.' It became clear he had been a member of a death squad.

"I kept wondering, why is he admitting all this? When I asked, he said, 'I've got more reason to go to Canada than anybody else, because I've done all of these things, and now I've left. If I ever go back, they'll kill me for sure.' He was saying, 'That's why my case is more compelling than other people's.'

"I had heard all these terrible stories about what happened to people who had been on a death list. But sitting face to face with somebody who had actually carried out those orders and explained in great detail how he had done it was shocking.

"We walked back to the school after one of our sessions. They were at break time between English classes. There were some small children running around with their parents. And some of the adults in the group were doing what adults always do with small children—picking them up, making little silly games to play with them, laughing. This fellow who had just bared his soul to me looked at this. I saw him all of a sudden look away and wipe a tear from his eye.

"There was recognition there that 'Yes, I've done awful things.' He never verbalized it, but there was something going on inside him.

"I'm sure that went on for a lot of people here at Jubilee, while they were here with people from the opposite side. They knew that back in their own country they would have loved to have had the chance to kill each other, simply because they believed in what they were fighting for. That's not true for most of the people who were here, because most were caught in the crossfire and not actively involved on either side.

"But I think a few people had told enough lies along the way to be able to get in here at Jubilee. And I think while they were here they had to see those people whom they had been against for so long in a slightly different way. They sat in the same English classes with them, ate at table together when the whole community gathered, and worshiped together. I think people had twinges of conscience about what they had done in their own country."

Late in 1989 the war in El Salvador became more violent. San Salvador exploded into a city-wide battle between the guerrillas and the army. In one week more than

1,000 people were killed.

The event that especially caught the world's attention was the murder of six Jesuit priests on the campus of the Central American University. Three years earlier, after an earthquake, Jubilee had collected and delivered relief supplies to some of these priests and talked to them just yards from where they were later murdered. When we heard of their deaths, we felt the loss personally.

The "November Offensive" by the guerrillas was overcome by the Salvadoran military, with the help of massive aid from the United States. Predictably, a great surge of new refugees ran for their lives. At one point it was estimated that between 300,000 and 400,000 Central American refugees were in Mexico, many attempting to reach safety in the United States.

A few months earlier, the U.S. Border Patrol and the INS had launched an effort to build their forces to a new level along the Rio Grande River. They called it the "3-D Program"—"Detect, Detain, and Deport."

The program worked well. Arrests and deportations soared. Almost no Salvadorans were given political asylum, however strong their appeals for protection. Even so, the numbers of desperate refugees who successfully ran the gauntlet into the United States continued to climb.

The United States was sending the equivalent of $50,000 per guerrilla each year to the corrupt Salvadoran government in an effort to solve the crisis militarily. Surely if we were not so blindly confident in the power of violence to bring peace, a less costly and more humane resolution to the conflict could have been found—especially when the average income of the fighters on both sides was no more than one or 2 percent of $50,000.

Jubilee Partners responded by increasing the size of our staff in the Rio Grande Valley and opening a second house in which to process applicants. In 1990 we interviewed far more refugees than ever before in one year. Inquiries were coming so fast that we could accept only about one out of twenty-five who appealed for help.

As we worked with this river of people, we noticed a change from the earlier years. An increasing number of the applicants were men who had left wives and children behind. We were puzzled at first. The situation was no less dangerous for the families in Central America; certainly these men loved their families no less than the men who had come earlier to Jubilee.

Gradually we learned why. First, we found out that arrests of refugees in Mexico were soaring. There had been more arrests right across the Rio Grande in Matamoros in January and February alone than in all the previous year. Then we also began to notice an increase in the number of stories about human rights abuses against Central Americans by Mexican authorities. Amnesty International and Human Rights Watch reported the increase, and soon the topic made the U.S. newspapers on a regular basis.

Central Americans in Matamoros caught by the Mexican Border Patrol, the *Migra*, were packed into small rooms. Up to one hundred men at a time were forced into cells so small none could sit. Women and children were sometimes locked in a windowless storage room. Some were reportedly held in these tiny spaces for up to two weeks before deportation.

Many men were still desperate enough to risk the journey north, but it was more difficult to imagine bringing families along. Most men expected to send for wives and children as soon as the situation settled down.

It was also becoming evident that greater pressure was being applied by Mexico on the refugees because of the Mexican government's desire for a trade agreement. One of the prices the U.S. government exacted for the North American Free Trade Agreement (NAFTA) was better

Mexican blocking of the northward flow of refugees.

At first U.S. authorities denied putting pressure on the Mexican government to do their dirty work. But eventually it became public knowledge that a team of INS officials had been working in Mexico City to develop "Operation Hold the Line." This included the training of Mexican Federal Judicial Police and immigration officers. Intelligence-gathering operations were merged, with several INS agents working in Mexico and Central America.

All the while our refugees, and many other sources, told of the rapid increase in abuses by the Migra—everything from theft and rape to murder. It was clear at least that the Migra felt themselves to have more freedom to commit such abuses, whether or not they received any actual encouragement from U.S. officials to do so.

In the spring of 1990, we could see that the Año de Jubileo program was nearing its end. The surge of refugees after the November Offensive in El Salvador had peaked and began to diminish. Death-squad activity and military operations had waned somewhat in El Salvador and Guatemala. "Operation Hold the Line" was working: fewer refugees were getting through Mexico to the U.S. border. In Canada the mood was turning conservative, manifesting itself in less hospitality toward refugees.

We became increasingly concerned about the many families left behind by the men who had come through our program. The families had refugee status by virtue of the men's status, and the men were anxious to get them to Canada. But in reality the women had an almost impossible (and dangerous) task of getting from their scattered locations in El Salvador and Guatemala to Canada with their children. And Canada had essentially pulled in the welcome mat.

In May we at Jubilee decided we should try to bring up the 250-plus wives and children. Otherwise, the chances of the families ever being reunited were dim. Jim Corbett and David Janzen came to Jubilee for an all-day consultation, and we pondered how to go about a task that seemed overwhelming.

Although in Canada funds that were to be used for family reunification had dried up, the Canadian consul in Atlanta remained sympathetic. We went to his office and secured his promise to help in every way he could.

Meanwhile, we made another trip to the Rio Grande Valley. I argued that we should raise our caseload of refugees from the proposed fifteen to twenty-five cases, in hopes of getting as many people as possible through Jubilee before the Canadian doors closed completely.

This was a lot to ask of the Jubilee staff. Some of us were already putting in seventy-hour work weeks. I felt so strongly about it that I offered to take on the extra ten cases myself. Intake interviews typically took several hours—in some cases a day or two—but we finished them all. When the Canadian consul conducted his interviews, all twenty-five cases were approved.

That night I had a dream in which the extra ten men we had helped to save from probable deportation were all standing in a room. They were smiling their shy Central American smiles at me and saying, "Gracias, Mr. Don!" I felt overcome with love and gratitude to God for this work.

But then, in my dream, I turned and looked out the upstairs window of our house. I was amazed to see wives and children camping in little groups all over the field out front. Each family was standing or sitting beside a small campfire, with little bundles of clothing alongside them. All were perfectly quiet, looking up at my window. They were waiting, trusting the time soon would come when they could rejoin husbands and fathers.

Two hundred and fifty women and children. That

dream stayed with me through the next fourteen months as we fought doggedly to bring all the families up.

We sent out letters to dozens of refugee men in Canada or still with Overground Railroad hosts in the United States about our proposed family reunification program. We mentioned that danger might be involved, particularly if the Salvadoran or Guatemalan governments—or guerrillas, in some cases—discovered families trying to leave. But we emphasized that we expected cooperation from the Mexican, U.S., and Canadian governments. We asked for their permission to move ahead. The list of "yeses" grew quickly.

In September I met Jimmy and Rosalynn Carter at their home in Plains and went for a long run with them. As we ran along the dirt roads between the peanut fields, I described the family reunification plans. Jimmy was enthusiastic about the idea. He sent a letter of support to INS director Gene McNary in Washington.

In November I met with the INS regional director in San Antonio, Richard Casillas. He gave a very different reaction. He said he "wouldn't touch it without the full cooperation of the Mexicans and clear instructions from the INS in Washington." I assured him confidently that I would soon have both.

Four days later I went to Mexico City and El Salvador to set up safe houses and to find someone in San Salvador willing to risk helping the women and children get out of the country. Only the Jesuits (God bless them!) were willing to do so. They literally agreed to it while the bells were ringing on the Central American University campus a few hundred yards away, commemorating the first anniversary of the murder of the Jesuit priests there.

In early December, through a network of contacts, I secured a meeting with the *Secretario de Gubernación* (roughly equivalent to a prime minister) of Mexico. In his huge, walnut-paneled office, he exuded boundless graciousness while ignoring the ringing of numerous telephones on his desk.

Secretario Gutierrez Barrios assured me that Jubilee Partners would get red-carpet treatment and be welcome anytime to drive our bus through Mexico to the southern border to collect the women and children. He assigned his chief aide to the project, saying, "Anything we can do to help."

When I called the INS in Washington to tell them all was on track, the representative told me, "Not until we are sure Canada will agree."

"No problem at all," I answered. "I've been working closely with the Canadian consul on this—and he with Ottawa—from the beginning."

"Just the same," the INS official insisted, "we want to have a joint meeting with you and the Canadian consul in Washington about it."

In mid-December INS Director McNary finally answered Jimmy Carter's letter, but only after a reminder from Carter's office. After apologies about taking so long to respond to a former president, he expressed concern about whether the Canadians would be fully supportive. But his ending was encouraging. "However, the work of Jubilee Partners has been excellent and their track record speaks for itself. . . . Please set up a joint meeting."

On December 19 I met with the first rude Canadian official I had yet encountered, in the Canadian Embassy in Washington. He lectured me for twenty minutes before even letting me speak. It was obvious he had no intention of cooperating with us.

All the while the INS director of deportations, representing Director McNary, sat to one side, studying a spot high on the opposite wall. The bottom line came from him. "So you see, Mr. Mosley, if the Canadian government does not want this program, there is nothing the INS can do about it."

I discovered later that this official had come to his Washington post from the Atlanta INS office. Though he never betrayed the fact, he undoubtedly knew about Jubilee's work, including our public opposition to INS policies.

It was plain that this was a setup in which Canada had played the "bad guy." Thus the INS would not have to say "no" to a former U.S. president.

Jimmy Carter insisted on writing to Canadian Prime Minister Brian Mulroney to try to overcome the problem. But Mulroney's political fortunes were declining just as refugees were becoming unpopular with the Canadian public. In April 1991, he sent Carter a polite letter, the gist of which was "no." He did end, however, by saying, "If Jubilee Partners is aware of any Central American families in particular danger in their home countries, they should advise Canadian officials in the region who would be prepared to review their situation."

The following months we did exactly that. The results were disappointing. The Canadian consul in Mexico City, whose region included Guatemala, insisted that the people could come to him safely for an interview, at which point he could process them and fly the bona fide political refugees to Canada. On his next trip to Guatemala, a refugee who had come to him for such an interview was murdered. His body was dumped in front of the Canadian consul's office in Guatemala City.

We spent months trying to get the most desperate families to Canada. Without Canadian cooperation three families had to be smuggled out of Central America and all the way into Canada. Friends in Mexico City took great risks and received warnings from the Mexican government. The fourth family had such a classic history of persecution that we decided to play the game exactly by Canadian rules, certain they would receive quick attention.

No such luck. Even after the family was smuggled out of El Salvador at great risk and given thirty-day visas to remain in Mexico City, the Canadian officials failed to process their papers so they could move on to Vancouver. The Mexican officials complained but extended the visas for another thirty days.

There was still no action by the Canadians, despite a constant stream of faxes and telephone calls from our office. Angrily, the Mexicans gave one more extension. The Canadians waited right up to the third deadline before they finally allowed the family to move north.

A few months later the family sent me a photograph of themselves, standing against a backdrop of flowers and mountains in British Columbia. The happy father had his arms around his wife and his oldest daughter. On the back, above all their signatures, are the words *"Con amor y recuerdo"* (With love and remembrance).

But the message from the authorities was equally clear. We were defeated in our effort to reunite the rest of the families. We had run out of avenues for helping them. Most of the women and children I pictured in my dream are still waiting. In at least two cases, the wives have already lost their lives.

After fifty-eight round trips to Texas and many others to Canada, our faithful old Año de Jubileo bus was showing the wear and tear of the quarter-million miles we had put on it. A generous supporter in Maine named Charlie Brown donated a newer, forty-passenger coach to Jubilee, which made our final two trips to the Rio Grande.

It was time to send our old bus on to a new mission. But first we decided that all the Jubilee folks should board one last time and share a time of singing and storytelling.

We recalled the tornado miracle and many confronta-

tions with Border Patrol officers. We remembered sweltering picnics along the road, long cold winter nights of driving, and the time a refugee pulled out a guitar and got everyone singing at a Louisiana rest stop. There were lots of
stories about breakdowns—including one that had become the stuff of legend.

On a trip returning from south Texas in early July
1987, the bus's electrical system began malfunctioning. We
took it to shops in Harlingen and Houston. Repairs were
made, but new problems kept developing. I opened the
battery compartment and discovered that the batteries
were blown up like balloons, about to explode. There were
more repairs while thirty people waited.

We took off again, hoping that all would be well. But
soon after dark, the charging system went out completely.
For the rest of what seemed like an endless night, we had
to charge the batteries at service stations. We would drive
until the headlights started going dim—every thirty to fifty
miles—and find a place to stop again and recharge the batteries.

Meanwhile, all the Jubilee staff except two had contracted a serious stomach ailment. That added to our need
to make frequent stops. Ryan almost turned green. He was
so weak at one point that he actually crawled part of the
way across the grass at a Mississippi rest stop toward the
men's room.

The next day was July 4. Terry Conway was driving as
we passed through Montgomery, Alabama, and headed
up I-85 toward Georgia. She decided to exit to buy some
fuel. When she slowed down and turned up the exit ramp,
the faulty electrical system apparently caused the engine
to die. Without power steering or power brakes, Terry
wasn't strong enough to control the bus. I heard her call
for help. I grabbed the steering wheel with her to help
steer the fast-moving bus while she pressed the brake ped-

al with all her strength.

We barely missed a line of cars, bounced over a traffic island, and swerved through traffic while cars scrambled to get out of our way. We narrowly avoided the opposite ditch and went hurtling down the left lane of the road toward oncoming traffic. Leaving many a startled driver behind us, we finally coasted into a truck stop.

One blessing of the stomach ailment—Ryan had been too sick to notice the excitement. While the rest of us tried to catch our breath and calm our racing hearts, he sat up groggily and asked, "Is it time to get off and throw up again?"

The sharing of stories was an emotional time. The bus had become a mascot of sorts. We had become attached to that old piece of metal, which had served us faithfully and become such a sign of hope to so many.

It was hard to let go, but the bus was headed off to do more good work. We donated it to friends in Nicaragua, where they know how to keep a vehicle running for years after we have given up on it. Two former Jubilee volunteers drove it there for us. It was an appropriate destination for our old flagship.

10

Witnessing for Peace in Nicaragua

A large truck bumped its way over an isolated dirt road toward Jalapa, Nicaragua. I stood in the seat beside the driver with the upper part of my body extended through an opening in the roof of the cab. I scanned the road ahead for signs of recent digging.

All of us were uncomfortably aware of how often in recent months land mines had been placed on this road. The driver was prepared to come to a screeching halt if I pounded on the roof. The rich valley we were crossing was bordered by Honduran territory, which provided safe haven for the U.S.-supported "contras" who had planted the mines. Contra forces had been trying for months to "liberate" the Jalapa Valley and establish a foothold on Nicaraguan soil, with hopes that they (and their supporters in Washington) could make a convincing claim to be an indigenous uprising against an oppressive government.

The truth was far different. Events that began almost a century before had led up to this critical moment in Nicaragua's history.

In the early 1900s, the United States forced out Nicaragua's president and established a puppet government. This safeguarded the interests of U.S. fruit and mining companies and insured Nicaragua's availability as a base for U.S. military campaigns in the region. U.S. marines occupied Nicaragua from 1911 to 1933. Before withdrawing, the United States established a National Guard in Nicaragua, headed by Anastasio Somoza Garcia. The Somoza dynasty became one of the cruelest in the history of the Western Hemisphere.

The third and last Somoza to rule Nicaragua, Anastasio Somoza Debayle, came to power in 1967. While most of the country lived in extreme poverty, he amassed a personal fortune worth half a billion dollars. Owning half of Nicaragua's arable land and 40 percent of its industry, he created a climate that enabled U.S. companies to appropriate still more land and exploit Nicaraguan labor.

The injustice was enforced with brutality and terror. Torture and massacres by the National Guard were widespread. For years the Somoza regime, backed by U.S. power and money, felt unshakable.

But in July 1979 dramatic change came. The broadly supported Sandinista Front for National Liberation (FSLN) marched triumphant into Managua, dethroning Somoza. It was named for Augusto César Sandino, who had fought against the marines and U.S. imperialism in the 1930s. The FSLN orchestrated a campaign that included an armed struggle as well as nonviolent marches and general strikes. President Jimmy Carter's concern for human rights contributed to a climate that helped topple Somoza, but the triumph was rightly claimed as a victory for the Nicaraguan people.

The Sandinistas reversed the decades-long priority of catering to the appetites of a small elite. They committed themselves to improving life for Nicaragua's majority. They embraced their namesake Sandino's concern for literacy. They launched a highly successful campaign that raised the national literacy rate in the first six months from 40 percent to 88 percent. They made great strides in health care. They brought a rapid decline in infant mortality and virtually eradicated polio.

All of this was only vaguely familiar to us at Jubilee Partners. Carolyn and I had arrived at Jubilee just seventeen days before the Sandinistas marched into Managua. We had heard reports over our little transistor radio. But we were so busy building our first house, investigating the situation of the Vietnamese boat people, and repairing tents cattle had knocked down that we hardly noticed the event that would affect our lives for years to come.

In Washington, the fall of Somoza was seen as a serious blow to U.S. dominance in Central America. When Ronald Reagan took over the presidency in January 1981, Jimmy Carter's diplomatic overtures toward the Sandinistas were quickly replaced with an unequivocal campaign against them. One of Reagan's first actions was to cut off all U.S. aid to Nicaragua.

Reagan had entered state and then national politics by way of union politics in Hollywood. Anti-communism was the heart of his vision there, and as president he defined his foreign policy agenda around the same issue. He called the Sandinistas a "cancer" that posed a direct threat to the United States, and made "stopping communism and international terrorism" there a critical test of his presidency.

Reagan and his advisers decided even before he took office that the Nicaraguan revolution had to be reversed as soon as possible. A paper popularly known as the "Sante Fe Document" referred to Central America and the Caribbean as "the soft underbelly of the United States." The paper propounded Reagan's simplistic view that the Nicaraguan conflict was an attempt by the Soviet Union to breach U.S. defenses and spread worldwide communism.

The smoke had barely cleared from Nicaragua's revolutionary war when U.S. interests began looking for a way to unseat the Sandinistas. They found their answer in the National Guard, most of whom had fled to Honduras after Somoza's fall. U.S. money and equipment transformed the defeated troops into a force that could pose a serious threat to the Sandinista government. CIA and U.S. military personnel, as well as Argentine torture experts, provided training. Using the same methods of terror they had employed under Somoza, the "counterrevolutionaries," or contras, began launching raids into Nicaragua.

President Reagan insisted that covert operations against Nicaragua were limited to halting an "arms flow" from Nicaragua to guerrillas in El Salvador. In December 1982 the U.S. Congress passed the Boland Amendment, and seven months later the Boland-Zablocki Act, prohibiting use of U.S. funds for overthrowing the Sandinistas. Insisting that the contras were "freedom fighters," Reagan flouted the law—to an extent which became public only when the Iran-contra scandal broke several years later.

At Jubilee Partners, our introduction to Nicaraguans came in the fourth busload out of the Rio Grande Valley, the same one that had the dramatic encounter with the tornado funnels. We developed a liking for the Nicaraguan refugees as quickly as we had for the others. One family was especially appealing, with a gregarious father, an engaging mother, and four attractive children. They came to Jubilee like all the other Central Americans, with only the clothes they wore and a small suitcase or two of possessions.

One day I complimented the father on the beautifully embroidered traditional Nicaraguan shirt, or *guayabera*, he was wearing. He smiled broadly and took the shirt off. "It is yours," he said graciously. "I am happy I have something I can give in return for your kindness to my family."

As much as we liked this family and the other Nicara-

guans, we soon realized that there were substantial differences between their situation and that of the Salvadorans
and Guatemalans with us. As it turned out, the man who
gave me the shirt off his back had been an officer in the
National Guard. It is likely that he had commanded some
of the very troops who were slaughtering civilians in the
last months before Somoza was overthrown.

Even though immigration laws mandated that all applicants for political asylum be considered on the merits of
their individual cases without regard for the political lean-
ings of the countries from which they came, the Nicaraguans were proof that the reality was different. During the
early and mid-1980s Salvadoran applicants were successful only from 2 to 3 percent of the time nationwide (with
virtually none in the Rio Grande Valley courts) and Guatemalans less than half of one percent. Meanwhile, Nicaraguan applicants were approved about one third of the
time. More important, it was rare for any of the other two
thirds to be deported.

INS officials knew that they were faithfully reflecting
the attitude in the White House, and they openly defied
the law and refused to deport the Nicaraguans. They insisted that the people would be slaughtered by the
Sandinistas if deported back into Nicaragua. All the while,
thousands of men, women, and children were being deported back into El Salvador and Guatemala where—as we
could document abundantly—they were in far greater
danger of losing their lives to the forces supported by the
United States.

In reaction to President Carter's emphasis on human
rights, Reagan's foreign policy transition team had recommended that questions of human rights not be allowed to
"paralyze or unduly delay" decisions on "other vital U.S.
interests." Reagan's choice to head the State Department's
Human Rights Bureau was Elliot Abrams, who frequently

expressed in public his contempt for all those "lousy countries" around the world from which people were scrambling to escape and crowd into the United States.

The official line from Washington was that human rights abuses in El Salvador and Guatemala were being exaggerated. Abrams' view was that the revolutionary activity in El Salvador was imported from the Sandinistas. Precisely as we were faced with a growing number of victims of torture and other abuses carried out by people our own government was training and funding, we were hearing a constant stream of White House and State Department assurances that the opposite was true. We were confronted with massive amounts of evidence—we literally held it in our hands—that our president and some of his top advisers were lying to us about what was happening in Central America.

At one point Elliot Abrams declared, "I have asked a lot of human rights groups for information and . . . I think it is quite persuasive evidence that no one produces anything." In truth the Reagan administration had been given massive amounts of such documentation—from Amnesty International, Americans Watch, the American Civil Liberties Union, and our own friends and co-workers in south Texas.

Jubilee became a source of solid and voluminous documentation that refuted the administration's version of the situation. We had a team of Spanish-speaking interviewers working in the Rio Grande Valley for eight years, talking with thousands of refugees. We accumulated literally thousands of pages of detailed chronologies of the refugees' stories, collected in private interviews, cross-checked and verified whenever possible, supported by private and public documents.

Still the Reagan administration's defense of El Salvador and Guatemala continued and its attacks on Nicaragua intensified. At Jubilee we felt a growing need to get a firsthand look at Central America.

In June 1983 we sent Ed Weir to Nicaragua as part of a large delegation organized by friends in North Carolina. Before leaving Nicaragua, the delegation made a visit to the small town of Jalapa. It was situated on an isolated point of land that juts into Honduras and was an easy target for the contras.

The delegation spent only four days in Nicaragua. They saw enough, however, to resolve that an effort needed to be launched to correct the official version of what was happening there.

Witness for Peace was born out of late-night discussions by these tired travelers on their way home. No one could have foreseen at that time what an extraordinary role this organization—which kept a sustained, prayerful, nonviolent presence in Nicaragua's war zones—would play as a buffer against the Reagan administration's vendetta against Nicaragua.

Eight months later, in February 1984, I was making my own journey to Jalapa, as coleader of a fact-finding delegation cosponsored by Witness for Peace and the Fellowship of Reconciliation. The FOR, an international religious pacifist organization, was founded in 1915 and includes about 15,000 members in the United States. At the time, I was national vice-chairman (then became chairman 1984-1986).

I responded to the invitation to help lead the delegation with an immediate "yes," but the decision brought deep wrestlings in the days that followed. These were days when my old blinders were starting to come off and the reality of evil in this world was becoming clearer to me than ever before. One memorable September night in Nyack, New York—after a long day of FOR Executive Committee meetings—I walked down to a park bench at the edge of the Hudson River with Sister Mary Evelyn Jegen, S.N.D., then FOR chairwoman.

A large moon shone on the water and the scene was beautiful, but we were in the most serious of discussions. We were asking ourselves whether we were genuinely ready to die if necessary for our belief in Jesus Christ and the way of peace he demonstrated and died for.

Since the beginning of time, people going off to war have had to face the possibility of giving up their lives. I was preparing to go to a war zone to "wage peace" and knew the question had to be mine as well. Mary Evelyn and I agreed that we could not be sure what we would actually do at a crisis moment, but we hoped we would give our lives readily if called to.

I was still struggling with these thoughts a few weeks later, at a retreat for peacemakers at the Kirkridge Retreat and Study Center in Pennsylvania's Pocono Mountains. The group gathered there received a phone call from Gustavo Parajón, Nicaraguan physician and Baptist pastor. Days before, the United States had invaded Grenada.

"We are anticipating an invasion at any time now," Parajón said of the situation in Nicaragua. "For God's sake, please try to help us!" At that gathering, we launched the Pledge of Resistance—a promise that in the event of a U.S. invasion of Nicaragua, we would participate in and encourage massive public resistance, including occupation of local congressional offices and a large demonstration in Washington, D.C. In the days that followed, we put an extensive contingency plan into place through our networks across the country.

While at Kirkridge, I wrote in my journal, " 'No one who does not carry his cross and come with me can be a disciple of mine' (Luke 14:27, NEB) meets me exactly where I am—on the road to Jerusalem, afraid of what lies ahead and even more afraid of what I might do when the test comes.

"I know that the evil I deplore so much cannot be overcome without great sacrifice, and I cannot stand back while *others* make that sacrifice in my place. But, God help me, I have not yet fully 'died to myself.' I keep looking for the loophole. . . . I don't want to be shot in Nicaragua. Becoming a martyr holds no attraction for me. But being a disciple of Jesus *does*, being given wholly to the pursuit of God's will in my life *does.*

"Whatever suffering that brings, even death, is in God's hands. I am stubbornly determined to try to do God's will as well as I can discern it in this time of great crisis."

On February 4, 1984, I landed with seventeen others in Managua, Nicaragua. Even as we drove from the Managua airport to our hotel, we saw evidence on every side that people expected an invasion by the United States. There were AK-47s and other weapons being carried by people everywhere.

We had made a brief stop in San Salvador, El Salvador, on our way to Managua, where we saw plenty of weapons. But there every gun was in the hands of visibly tense Salvadoran soldiers. It was clear that the enemy they feared was all around them—namely, the Salvadoran people. In Managua the weapons were carried by civilians and soldiers alike. The casual way they were handled, often held by the barrel and balanced across the shoulder, made it clear the enemy was farther away.

The thing that struck us most, however, was that the city was honeycombed with trenches in every available yard and vacant lot. Sandbags were piled in front of windows and makeshift barricades were erected at key places all over the city.

As we made our way from meeting to meeting, traveling freely wherever we wanted to go, we found the Nicaraguan people anything but hesitant to state their political views, whether for or against the Sandinistas. We found far more people supportive of their new government than opposed to it. It was clear to us that we were not seeing an "enslaved people," as Reagan put it. To the contrary, the most common emotions we found were pride in the accomplishments of the revolution and bewilderment about why the United States was so determined to crush it.

Near the end of our visit, we decided to go to the battle line in the north, to Jalapa. After a truck ride that was fortunately uneventful, we pulled into the little town just before dark. Primitive as it was, it was a sight for sore eyes—and mine ached with the strain of being the road mine watchman.

The next day some of us decided to take our appeal for peace all the way to the front. We hitchhiked the few miles to the little village of Teotecacinte, a settlement no more than a few hundred yards from the Honduran border. Evidence of the town's extremely vulnerable position was everywhere. Almost every house was pockmarked with bullet holes or damaged from mortar blasts. Yet the village was fully occupied by its resolute residents.

With our hearts beating faster than usual, we talked our way past the Sandinista soldiers at the last barricade, climbed through a barbed-wire fence, and walked out into the open field that lay between the opposing sides. There we unfurled a banner that read *"ORAMOS POR LA PAZ"* ("We pray for peace"). For half an hour we stood in the middle of that field, facing first one side then the other as we read Scriptures, sang songs, and took turns praying aloud. It was marvelous to discover how genuine our petitions can become under such circumstances.

From time to time we scanned the deep jungle growth on the contra side of the field, trying to detect signs of activity. As we continued our service, I found I was feeling sympathy toward the people on both sides of the conflict, the vast majority of them caught up in something far beyond their control. I became uncomfortably aware of the fact that, as a U.S. citizen, I had much more power than they to affect the international forces that pitted them against one another.

I had come to Nicaragua a committed Christian pacifist, but knew I had not yet had to pay much of a price for that belief. The Nicaraguan revolution was successful in part because of the widespread participation of Christians in the resistance. Part of my reason for coming had been to probe the question of nonviolence, to find out how people caught up in this conflict could reconcile armed struggle with the teachings of Jesus.

But as I stood under the tropical sun between the ragged men on either side of the field—many no more than teenagers—it struck me with great force that I was asking the wrong question—and the wrong people. The real question with which I should be struggling was, what could *I* do to change the awful circumstances that promoted this mutual slaughter?

After awhile, our group rolled up our banner and walked back toward the battered little houses of Teotecacinte. As we climbed through the fence, a small woman walked quickly toward us and invited us to step into her yard for a few minutes. We followed her and soon found ourselves standing behind her simple house. Like most backyards in Nicaragua, hers had a bomb shelter in it. Several small children watched silently as we inspected it.

"I am Carmen Gutierrez," the woman began. "I saw you praying in the field. I want to thank you for coming to do that."

"No," one of our party responded. "We should be asking your forgiveness for the suffering our country has brought to you."

Carmen waved that suggestion aside, saying, "I understand the difference between you and your leaders. You do not have to apologize to me." Then, with tears running down her cheeks, Carmen told us of the tragedy that had occurred a few months earlier where we were standing.

Carmen and her children were in this yard when the contras launched a mortar attack across the field. The first mortar exploded at the edge of the yard, knocking Carmen and the children to the ground. As soon as they could, they plunged into the safety of the bomb shelter, but Carmen found that her four-year-old daughter, Suyapa, was missing.

Carmen emerged from the shelter and found Suyapa's body, all but decapitated by the shrapnel. Weeping, Carmen returned to the other children and huddled with them in the shelter for three endless days, while the attack continued and Suyapa's little body lay on the ground above them. As Carmen finished her story, she pointed out a tiny plot of flowers she had planted on the spot where Suyapa's body had lain.

Each of us stood silent, tears on our faces. There was nothing adequate to say. But inside me something profound was happening.

11

Justice Rebuffed

What happened to me that day in Nicaragua was something as dramatic as it was private. Until then, my concern about the conflict in Central America had been that of a somewhat distant onlooker. Now, as I stood grieving with this mother, I suddenly felt that Suyapa—and all of these beautiful wide-eyed children—were *my* children, too. Their suffering was becoming my suffering as well.

Suddenly the words came to me strong and clear from a passage of Isaiah that I had not read in several years.

> Justice is rebuffed and flouted.
> while righteousness stands aloof;
> truth stumbles in the market-place
> and honesty is kept out of court,
> so truth is lost to sight,
> and whoever shuns evil is thought a madman.
> Isaiah 59:14-15a (NEB)

I was surprised to "hear" this text as clearly in my mind as if it had been broadcast from huge speakers. I was struck by how well it described what I was observing. Moreover, I suddenly realized that I myself——not Ronald Reagan, the CIA, the contras—was the one to whom it most applied. *I* had been a perfect example of "righteousness" standing aloof.

The Scripture echoed in my thoughts all the way back to our little hotel in Jalapa. There I quickly found my Bible and looked up the verses. Then I was struck by the next few lines as well:

> The Lord saw, and in his eyes it was an evil thing,
>> that there was no justice;
> he saw that there was no man to help
> and was outraged that no one intervened. . . .
>
> Isaiah 59:15b-16a (NEB)

That experience in a little backyard in Teotecacinte became one of the most important turning points in my life. In the following years, I returned to Nicaragua again and again. Between trips to Central America, I spoke over five hundred times in more than a hundred cities in the United States, trying to awaken people to the terrible consequences of our government's misguided policies in Nicaragua.

After two weeks in Nicaragua, our delegation flew to Tegucigalpa, Honduras. There we were treated to a special briefing by a whole panel of U.S. officials. Among them was the military attaché on Ambassador John Negroponte's staff. Negroponte and some of these officials had been in service together as a team in South Vietnam. The panel was presided over by a disarmingly friendly woman, who served as the chief public relations officer for the embassy.

For all of the casual friendliness exuding from our hosts, it soon became obvious that we were being given a party line so out of touch with the truth it was insulting. For a while we quietly took notes as though we were grateful to be privy to such information. As one fabrication followed another, however, we found it impossible to remain silent.

As politely as we could manage, first one and then another of us began to protest when the speakers strained credulity too far. The PR officer never lost her smile, as though confident we were just momentarily confused and would get it right in a moment.

"You folks have to realize that what we're up against here is a beachhead in Nicaragua manned by the communists, with the intent of taking over all of Central America by force," said one official. "Why, not long ago the Nicaraguans were preparing to launch a massive tank attack on Honduras, until we made clear that the United States would not tolerate that."

"I never heard of such a threat," I protested. "What do you mean by 'massive'?"

"Oh, lots of tanks. They've got enough military hardware from the Russians to sweep right across any border they choose to, if we let them."

"But how many tanks were gathered at the border?" I persisted. "A hundred?"

"Well, maybe not that many."

"Ten?"

"Yeah, probably close to that," the speaker said lamely.

It was clear to everyone in the room that "sweeping across the border" into the mountains of Honduras with fewer than ten tanks would be such an idiotic move that— well, we dropped that topic and moved to another one.

The attaché changed his approach a bit. "Well, the main threat all along, you know, has been the huge supply of Soviet equipment the 'Nicas' are moving up to the communist rebels in Salvador."

Our attention picked up—this had been President Reagan's chief justification before Congress for military action against the Sandinistas. We pressed for details.

"We know some of that was happening briefly in the months after the Nicaraguan revolution," said a member of our delegation. "But we were under the impression that the Nicaraguans had pretty well stopped that under pressure from the Carter administration. Since all such shipments would either have to come across fifty miles of open water—easy to prevent with all the U.S. hardware that is now in place in El Salvador—or through Honduran territory, maybe you could provide hard evidence of such shipments."

"Darn right!" exclaimed the attaché. "In fact, just the other day we caught one truck headed across Honduras from Nicaragua with over one hundred rifles hidden in the walls of the truck, bound for El Salvador."

Something clicked in my memory. I remembered seeing such a report in the *New York Times*, but it had been about two years before. Once again we forced the attaché to back up step by step, until finally he had to admit there had been no such discovery since that incident two years earlier. "Boy, time sure flies, doesn't it?" he said to one of the other panelists.

So it went for an hour. On one topic after another, the panel—led by the inept attaché—made statements that were patently inaccurate, inane, or irrelevant. All the while, the PR officer in charge of the session leaned casually against a table at our left, appearing to be enjoying this conversation with these fine people from back in the U.S. of A. Then the final blow fell.

The military attaché had just painted us a cheerful picture of how much the Hondurans loved and appreciated the U.S. military presence in their country. We had responded that we had heard quite the opposite expressed by several Hondurans we had met. Without missing a beat, he brushed that aside as inconsequential.

"Sure, you'll find a few complainers anywhere. But listen, this place is just like Nam. When we first got there, the Viets didn't think much of us. But once they saw what we were really like, they learned to love us."

The woman at our left motioned to the attaché to step out into the hall with her. Before they were ten feet away from the room, still within easy hearing of some of our group, she began to tongue-lash him. "Don't you *ever* make such a stupid remark to one of my groups again. . . ."

A few days after my return, I wrote to Millard Fuller, head of Habitat for Humanity (HFH), to suggest that a housing project be started in Nicaragua. As founding board member of HFH, I had already helped start projects at several other sites. I offered to go back immediately to Nicaragua to help set the stage for the new venture.

Jimmy Carter had recently expressed an interest in learning more about HFH, so I added that such a project might even help entice Carter to visit Nicaragua. As it happened, my letter to Millard coincided with a surprise visit by Carter to the HFH work site in Americus, Georgia. At lunch Millard handed my letter to Carter and asked him what he thought.

"Go for it!" responded Carter with a big smile. "I'm interested. And I'd like to talk to Don about his observations in Nicaragua as soon as he gets back."

At the end of March 1984, Bob Stevens, HFH executive vice-president, and I spent a rigorous week in Nicaragua. We explored possible project sites in several locations, met dozens of people, and talked at length with Gustavo Parajón.

In consultation with Parajón, we chose the poverty-stricken village of German Pomares in the westernmost part of Nicaragua for the first project. The existing houses were little more than thatched shelters with a primitive mud or stick wall here and there. Animals ran in and out at will, and the interiors of many of the houses were blackened by smoke from cooking fires.

People slept on homemade cots made of feed bags wrapped around poles, raised just high enough off the ground to discourage snakes from climbing in with the sleepers at night. I was asleep on one of these primitive beds one night when a fight broke out directly beneath me between a small pig and a goose. The bed and I were knocked about in the dark as the pig screeched and the goose honked. I was so unnerved it took me a long time to go back to sleep.

In early April, Carolyn, Bob, and I went to Plains, Georgia, to meet Jimmy and Rosalynn Carter at their home. I had a stack of barely dry photographs and a lot of stories to tell them. What impressed me most about the meeting was the open humility of the Carters and their intense desire to learn all they could about what was happening in Nicaragua. When I pulled out the photographs, Rosalynn went to the bedroom to get her glasses, then got down on her knees with me on the living-room floor and studied each picture carefully.

"Let me be sure I have this right," she interjected at one point. "The contras—they're ours, right?"

"Not *mine!*" Jimmy responded quickly. "They're Mr. Reagan's."

Near the end of the meeting, Jimmy asked, "What would you like for me to do to help?"

I was completely unprepared to answer. I suggested awkwardly that maybe he could call a press conference to criticize Reagan's policies.

"It wouldn't make page ten of the newspaper," he answered with a bitter smile, well aware of how eroded was his influence since his unsuccessful reelection bid.

Instead, Carter offered to join the HFH board of directors. He emphasized that he wanted to be an active member, not just an honorary figure. Millard had been working on him, and this meeting seemed to tip the balance. That offer helped to turn Habitat for Humanity into one of the nation's best-known charitable organizations. In addition, to a degree I doubt even Carter could foresee at that time, the decision contributed to the rehabilitation of Carter's image and influence around the world.

The following week I was pleased to see a lengthy interview in the *Atlanta Constitution* that grew out of our meeting. Without a single error, Rosalynn had related many of the stories I had told her, expanding on them effectively. She and Jimmy were on their way to becoming experts on Nicaragua. Their future lessons came from the Nicaraguans themselves during the Carters' periodic trips there.

In the fall of 1985, Jimmy Carter suggested that the HFH board of directors and staff have a two-day retreat at Jubilee Partners. The goal would be to reexamine the organization's basic objectives and principles in the ambiance the Jubilee community could provide. The meeting was set for early January 1986. We spent the weeks prior to it working feverishly to prepare for fifty special guests.

The Secret Service sent an advance agent to check out security details. They asked us to lay a new telephone cable down the road to the Welcome Center where the Carters would be staying. In the process of laying the cable, we inadvertently cut the main Jubilee water line in several places.

Meanwhile members of the building crew were rushing to complete our new library and office building for the meetings. They were running into problems as well. Among other things, they broke a plate-glass window in the library just hours before the guests were to arrive. We sent someone to the building supply store twenty-five miles away to buy a replacement. As it was being lifted into place a nervous worker slipped—and it too ended up shattered.

We decided that the decor was going to be rustic, whatever we might have intended. The buildings had jury-rigged emergency water systems, the picture window was covered with a sheet of polyethylene, and some lighting fixtures were merely bulbs hanging on the end of wires. The HFH folks took it all in good humor—insisting this was the perfect backdrop for the kind of discussion they needed about building low-cost houses around the world.

The second evening I was asked to tell the gathering about our work with Central American refugees. About sixty people crowded into the library. Jimmy sat on the floor over in one corner of the room. As I warmed to my favorite topic, I launched into a vigorous defense of the many Christians who had declared their church buildings sanctuaries for refugees denied their right of asylum.

"It is not the church members who are breaking the law," I declared, "but the United States government. The Refugee Act of 1980 clearly states that these people should have a genuine opportunity to make their case for political asylum in this country."

"You're exactly right!" interrupted Carter suddenly from his corner. "When I signed that act into law, I intended it to provide protection for bona fide refugees such as these. Now the present administration is breaking both the letter and the spirit of this important law!"

I rested my case and moved on to my next point. I wondered what some lawyers would give for such a confirmation of their arguments.

The next day, at the end of the conference, Carter told a local newspaper reporter that he firmly supported the sanctuary movement. To act according to their religious beliefs and conscience, even when it meant defying U.S. authorities, he said, is "a very wonderful thing for Christians to do."

Throughout the following year, Carter and I talked several times about the dilemma he felt himself in. He felt caught between the promise he had made in his presidential swearing-in ceremony to uphold the laws of the United States and his conviction that duty to God must take precedence when the two conflict. By the end of the year, he had resolved the matter enough to fly to Houston and present a $10,000 human rights award to Rev. John Fife on behalf of the sanctuary movement.

While at Jubilee, Carter told me he was ready to go to Nicaragua. Over the next few days, I put together files on more than a dozen key people and organizations in Nicaragua. Jimmy and Rosalynn extended their February 1986 visit by several days to allow time to see every one of them.

After their return, Jimmy told me privately the dramatic story of what he had almost achieved behind the scenes—a cease-fire that could have changed the course of history in Nicaragua and the surrounding region and saved many thousands of lives.

The U.S. Congress was preparing to make its largest appropriation yet for the contras—$100 million, in June 1986. Arturo Cruz had emerged as the chief spokesperson for the contras. Carter contacted Cruz, and the two met secretly in Costa Rica. Carter persuaded Cruz to agree to call publicly for an end to U.S. aid to the contras if the Sandinistas agreed to a list of demands. These included permission for Cruz and other legitimate opposition leaders to be allowed to participate in the democratic process in Nicaragua, as well as a lessening of the restrictive measures the Sandinistas had put into place against the press and the church. Carter and the contras would then call for an immediate cease-fire. They would be backed by Mexico, Panama, Venezuela, and Colombia—the so-called Contadora Group, which had formed in an effort to find a negotiated solution to the crises in Central America.

Carter spent most of that night drawing up a list of specific demands the Sandinistas would need to meet. He flew to Managua and met with Nicaraguan President Daniel Ortega for several hours. Ortega agreed to every point on Carter's list but wanted the other eight *comandantes* on the country's National Directorate to meet with Carter as well. The comandantes gave the full list of demands unanimous but tentative approval, asking for a few more hours to ponder the matter before publicizing it.

After a private dinner with Parajón and his family, the Carters set out to see the first Habitat for Humanity project in Nicaragua, two hours northwest of Managua. All the while, they were secretly elated that the cease-fire process seemed to be on track. In a caravan that included President Daniel Ortega, Vice-President Sergio Ramirez, Foreign Minister Miguel d'Escoto, and several other Nicaraguan officials, they toured the fifty-house project under a blazing sun.

HFH staff members Julie Knop and Jim and Sarah Hornsby joined the villagers in hosting the biggest group of dignitaries ever to come to their part of Nicaragua. Julie and the Hornsbys are longtime friends of mine, whom I had helped recruit to Nicaragua. All three are inspiring Christian disciples and splendid examples of "living in scorn of the consequences."

After the speeches, Jimmy Carter helped the villagers saw some wood and lay a few bricks. Then the party returned to Managua, with Carter hoping and praying the Sandinista leaders were ready to agree to the cease-fire proposal. But the comandantes were waiting with disappointing news. They were having second thoughts and needed more time to think about the matter.

Carter returned to the United States, still hoping for a breakthrough. He knew the Sandinistas feared that it would be a fatal mistake if they let down their guard without enough support to help them counter Reagan.

Instead of returning home to Plains, Jimmy Carter flew from Atlanta to New York City. He met secretly with United Nations Secretary General Javier Pérez de Cuéllar. Carter proposed that the secretary general take the initiative to recruit the presidents of the Contadora nations to come out publicly in support of the cease-fire. This would offer some protection to the hesitant Sandinistas against Reagan's possible reactions. Pérez de Cuéllar agreed to contact the various heads of state, then let Carter know the reaction.

Several days later the secretary general called Carter. "I have not gotten the approval of the Contadora leaders for such an arrangement." Carter suspected that he meant he had decided not to call them at all, possibly out of fear of Reagan's reaction—the United States was the largest financial supporter of the U.N. and already far behind in payments.

Carter then invited me to work discreetly through any contacts I had to encourage a reexamination of a cease-fire by the Sandinistas. He said he would be willing to interrupt any other work he was doing and go anywhere to help with negotiations. But the near-success never went further. Instead, there were at least 10,000 more unnecessary deaths and years of destruction in Nicaragua.

Meanwhile President Reagan seemed daily to become more obsessed with the Sandinistas. At one press conference he pointed out that Harlingen, Texas, is only a two-day drive from Nicaragua. He raised the absurd specter of a possible Nicaraguan invasion of the United States.

What I found even more disturbing was the way some Christian leaders joined the conflict. When Reagan wanted to lend credence to his invective, he could always find plenty of "documentation" from groups such as the Institute for Religion and Democracy, where people like Richard Neuhaus and Michael Novak poured forth a stream of politically conservative exaggerations and misinformation.

TV evangelist Pat Robertson went to the contra camps in Honduras and encouraged the contras in their enterprise, preaching to them, then returning to the United States to raise funds for them. Even Oliver North, whose central role in the conflict was just beginning to become public, would be protesting self-righteously within a year that his "persecution" by the U.S. Congress was an example of what Jesus predicted for his followers.

We did our best to keep following the Jesus who proclaimed hope for the poor, justice for the oppressed, peace for the brokenhearted. Helping "the lame to walk" had never been a central image of faith for me. Not until the Pantasma tragedy in the fall of 1986.

12

Explosion of Concern

Early on the morning of October 20, 1986, seventeen reporters, pastors, and leaders of Habitat for Humanity met at the Atlanta airport. I was leading another delegation to Nicaragua. As we watched Atlanta drop away below our Delta Whisper jet and I ordered orange juice from the flight attendant, an old truck lumbered along a dirt road 1,500 miles to the south of us. It was headed for the little town of Jinotega in north central Nicaragua.

Fifty-one people had somehow crowded into the truck —so many most of them had to stand. Some were perched dangerously on top of the cab and the framework built over the bed of the truck. Children and some older women were seated on bags of grain and other products headed for the market. But most of the passengers were swaying precariously with each bump while they stood and hung on to the framework of pipes that arched over their heads, there to carry a tarpaulin on rainy days.

Everyone on the truck knew there were bands of contras in the area. That reality had been a regular part of their lives for half a decade. Just three months earlier, a truck similar to theirs had run over a mine about thirty miles north of where they were now traveling. Thirty-four people had died, including many children. Every trip on these roads was a calculated risk, but one could not simply hide.

One person on the truck was especially inclined to look beyond the present ugliness of war to the promise of the future. Carmen Picado, nineteen, was a shy young woman from the village of Pantasma. Her face beamed with a beautiful smile when she talked about the marriage which was to happen soon. She was riding into Jinotega that day to make preparations for the wedding.

Crowded into the truck beside Carmen was her married sister, Cristina. Cristina's husband, Amancio Sanchez, was a thirty-year-old pastor of the Protestant church in Pantasma, a man of strong faith and body. Amancio was on his way into Jinotega to help plan a prayer vigil for peace. Several of the Sanchez children were also in the truck, including seven-year-old Elda—a lively little girl with big brown eyes, a mischievous smile, and an irrepressible spirit.

Night gave way to dawn as the truck bounced along the road. Amancio was talking to a fellow pastor, Juan Riso, about the earlier land mine tragedy. They were standing above the right rear wheel as they talked. At 6:45 that wheel hit a powerful road mine. The world exploded for those on board the truck. The explosion blew a hole a yard deep in the road as it destroyed the truck above, hurling people and debris everywhere.

"It happened so quickly I didn't even feel pain at first," Amancio said later. "But Juan made a pained face and went down. I started to fall and grabbed the side of the truck. My legs weren't working."

Somehow Amancio crawled out of the truck and lay on the ground. Still unaware of how badly he had been hurt, he tried again to stand up. "I couldn't," he explained later. "I looked down and saw that my right leg was missing from the knee down."

Four of the passengers were killed almost instantly by

the blast. Two more died before they reached the hospital in Jinotega. Forty-three others were seriously injured, twelve of them losing one or both legs.

Slowly grasping the scope of the tragedy, Amancio lay back on the ground and prayed, "Oh, God, please help us. Please help us!"

He told me about it a few weeks later. He recalled, "At that moment something beautiful happened. I suddenly felt a great sense of peace. I felt God's love all around me, like a little bird in a nest in a strong tree during a fierce storm!"

Amancio would need that inner peace in the days ahead. His family was scattered in two hospitals. Elda lay unconscious for almost two weeks. One of her legs had been blown off at the knee, and the other was broken in eight places.

Carmen lost both of her legs. Her wedding never took place. Her fiancé never came to see her again.

When our delegation arrived in Nicaragua, the front pages of all the newspapers were covered with reports of the tragedy. The explosion would shape not only the rest of our trip but much of Jubilee's work for years to come.

Some from our delegation visited Amancio. One got permission to photograph Elda's broken little body, and that picture became the grim motif for our trip.

A few days later, our group was sitting around a long table in an open-air restaurant, the Mirador Tiscapa. The restaurant sits dramatically on the rim of a volcanic crater near the center of Managua. Straight across the crater is the highest point in the city, long occupied by the Nicaraguan military. From there a helicopter lifted Somoza away from Nicaragua after his defeat in 1979. Somoza's infamous prison, El Chipote, a subterranean place of torture and despair, was also there.

We had in front of us on the table a large print of the

picture of Elda in her hospital bed, in a coma and stretched out in traction. We were in a somber mood, feeling a mixture of rage, frustration, and embarrassment at the thought that our tax dollars were providing the weapons that did this kind of work every day and paid the contras to carry it out.

"Look, there's Tomás Borge!" someone exclaimed. Sure enough, Nicaragua's minister of the interior was striding into the restaurant to the table next to ours. We were aware of Borge's near-mythical fame in Nicaragua as the only surviving founder of the Sandinista party. He was also the most enigmatic of Nicaragua's leaders, a man whose words and deeds seemed to demonstrate a profound sense of Christian compassion one day and a harsh, doctrinaire Marxism the next.

Most of all he was known for fiery, eloquent speeches in the style of his friend Fidel Castro. When he spotted seventeen gringos around one table, he could not pass up the opportunity. He smiled graciously and expressed his thanks that we had come to see with our own eyes the suffering of the Nicaraguan people. With dramatic gestures he poured out words like a fountain.

Borge was standing beside the eldest member of our group, Fran Warren from Koinonia. As he paused from time to time to allow our interpreter to do his part, Borge would gently kiss Fran's white hair and murmur, "Oh, you are so much like my mother. I love you." Suddenly Comandante Borge's gaze fell on the picture of Elda Sanchez in her hospital bed. At once his eyes began to flash and his gestures became angry slashes above our heads.

"You must return to the United States and tell your people that *this* is what Reagan's obsession is causing— horrible suffering and death for thousands of our innocent villagers! What is it that your president fears so much about our tiny little country? All of us together are not so many people as one of your great cities. We are poorer than any of you! What madness makes your people listen when President Reagan says that Harlingen, Texas, is in danger of an invasion from Nicaragua? How can they possibly believe such things are true?

"Yet he is right! We *are* going to invade the United States. Not with tanks and weapons, for you could crush us at once militarily. No, we are going to invade your country with *love*. Go home and tell what you have seen, that our people are much better at loving than at fighting."

Borge spoke with such passion that all the people in the restaurant forgot their food and were mesmerized by his oratory. Suddenly he threw up his hands, as if to say "What is the use?" and turned to leave. He paused, stooped once more to kiss Fran's hair, and repeated, "I love you."

Our final night in Nicaragua, I tossed about restlessly on my bed with images of all we had seen running through my mind. At 4:00 a.m. I had a strong urge to get up and pray. Feeling very tired, I tried to dismiss it and go back to sleep, but words ran through my mind. "Get up now and pray and something wonderful will happen. Go back to sleep and you'll miss a great opportunity." I got up.

As I fumbled to dress in the dark, I realized that my roommate, Ray Rockwell from Koinonia Partners, was doing the same thing. We said nothing to each other. I felt my way out of the room and downstairs to the living room of the little building. Silently Ray followed and took a seat across the room. Both of us prayed quietly as the darkness slowly gave way to dawn.

During those moments the Walk in Peace campaign was born. By the time it was light enough to see, thoughts were pouring through my mind faster than I could write them down in my notebook. My fatigue gave way to excitement, as the outlines of the program came to me. All this time Ray sat praying silently. Neither of us had yet said a word to the other. As the sun began to rise, I started telling Ray what I was writing. Both of us were soon laughing and thanking God for an answer to our prayers.

I found a telephone and called the home of Gustavo Parajón. In addition to being a physician and pastor, Parajón was the leader of CEPAD, the Council of Evangelical Churches of Nicaragua. CEPAD was also the main service arm of most Protestant denominations in Nicaragua. Founded after the severe Managua earthquake in 1972, CEPAD had an excellent reputation worldwide for its work.

"Dr. Parajón," I began excitedly, "if Elda Sanchez comes out of this coma—and I believe she will—I want to arrange for her to come to the United States, both to get a new leg and to show people there what our government is doing to the Nicaraguan people."

"Excellent!" he responded. "But would you be willing to take her whole family? I came back late last night from visiting them in their hospitals in Jinotega and Matagalpa. It would be wonderful if Amancio and Carmen could be there too."

After the rest of our party came down to breakfast, we talked excitedly about the new plans. We shared a sense of relief that we had found a concrete way to respond to the tragedy taking place all around us.

On our way home, we stopped in Honduras. We were filled with firsthand observations of what the war was doing to the people inside Nicaragua, but I was eager to give the group a chance to talk directly with the people on the other side of the battle line.

I had arranged to meet some of the contra leaders at one of their headquarters in Honduras. Our rendezvous had an unreal air about it, given the fact that the official line from Washington and from the contras themselves was still to insist that they were not in Honduras. Rather, they had "liberated" a part of Nicaragua and were operating entirely on Nicaraguan soil.

Everyone knew this was pure fiction. Nonetheless, the first thing one contra host said was, "We must ask that you not tell anyone where we are meeting, okay?" One of our writers later accommodated by datelining her newspaper article "SOMEWHERE IN CENTRAL AMERICA."

At a prearranged time, a shiny new Suzuki jeep met us at the front door of our hotel, La Ronda. Eight of us managed to squeeze into it with the driver, and eight more followed in taxis. For a long time we wound around through the streets of Tegucigalpa, some distance out into the countryside, and finally into a heavily guarded compound.

Night was falling. Floodlights beamed down on concertina wire atop high fences. As the perimeter guards waved us through the gate, I remembered this was Halloween night in the United States. None of the games back home could match the eeriness of what we were doing.

For the next two hours, we met with Carlos and Adela Icasa. Carlos was the attorney general of the Democratic National Front, largest branch of the contras. Adela was the official public relations officer for the FDN. Chain-smoking and intense throughout the session, they did their best to present every action of the contras as just, heroic, and successful.

"The time is not far off when our troops will liberate our country from the communists," said Adela. "Our people will be welcomed with open arms by the Nicaraguan people."

Earnest as they appeared, the Icasas struck out time and again as they tried to persuade us to accept their version of recent events in Nicaragua. We had the advantage of having just come from some of the battle sites and having talked to eyewitnesses of recent contra activities. The contras didn't sound nearly so good there as when being described by PR folks in another country.

"We don't mine roads in Nicaragua," Carlos said flatly in response to our description of the tragedy near Pantasma a few days earlier. As we pressed them, they made contradictory statements, insisting one minute that they only mined military roads in Nicaragua, the next that they didn't use mines at all because mines were too heavy for their foot soldiers to carry. Then they insisted the Nicaraguan army probably planted the mines in the roads to kill their own people and thus "discredit the contras."

The U.S. Embassy officer in Managua, T. J. Rose, had angrily made a similar charge. He insisted the Sandinistas probably mined their roads to stop contra vehicles. In truth, there were few if any contra vehicles on the roads. As almost everyone knew, the contras were operating on foot in the jungles.

Adela described her childhood in Nicaragua, as one of nine children of a wealthy cotton grower. Her father had come from the United States and was a strong supporter of Somoza. The family was loving and deeply religious. "Now we are scattered throughout Central America and the United States," she said sadly.

In his eagerness to assure us that the contras were getting a lot of bad press they didn't deserve, Carlos contradicted the bipartisan U.S. Senate report which stated that forty-six of the forty-eight contra leaders were former Somoza National Guard officers.

"There are less than 3 percent," he insisted. Then he went further, determined to impress us. "At one time there were such men in the FDN ranks," he told us earnestly, "but we trailed and shot them."

When the interview ended, the Icasas arranged for their jeep to take half of our group to the edge of Tegucigalpa. There we could hail taxis for the rest of the trip to the hotel. I waited out on the cool porch for the second trip. I found an opening to talk privately for a few minutes with Adela as we waited.

"Adela," I began, "there are two things I would like to say to you in response to your comments tonight. The first is that I have been to Nicaragua several times since you were last there. I can assure you that you are wrong when you insist that the people of Nicaragua are waiting to welcome the contras as their liberators. A few are, no doubt, but the great majority are terrified of your fighters—and every new atrocity committed by them makes you less welcome there.

"But more important, I want to tell you that I sensed your pain tonight as you described your childhood and the scattering of your family by this awful war. I have seen the suffering on both sides of the conflict. I believe *all* of you Nicaraguans are, to a large extent, the victims of a power struggle between my country and the Soviet Union. I want you to know that I feel very sad about that tonight. I apologize to you for my country's part in it."

Adela Icasa stood silent for a long minute, looking at me. I wasn't sure what response to expect from the contra's main public relations officer.

Suddenly her eyes filled with tears. After a long, awkward silence, she finally managed to say, "Pray for me, and I will pray for you." Then she turned and rushed into her house.

I had not expected that my chief emotion of the evening would be pity for the people causing such horrible suffering just across the border. Ephesians 6:12 came to mind: "For we are not contending against flesh and blood, but against the principalities, against the powers, against the world rulers of this present darkness, against the spiritual hosts of wickedness in the heavenly places" (RSV).

Two weeks before Amancio and his family hit the road

mine, another dramatic event took place. This one received far wider publicity and started a chain of events that finally turned even Ronald Reagan back from his crusade against Nicaragua.

It was common knowledge in Nicaragua that planes flew frequently from the north and dropped supplies to contras inside the country. The Neutrality Act makes it a crime to initiate or organize on U.S. soil military attacks against a country with which the United States is not formally at war.

President Reagan and his officials repeatedly assured the U.S. public that no such thing was happening. It had been well known for at least a year already that Oliver North, deputy director for political-military affairs on the National Security Council and a principal adviser to the president, had free rein to do whatever he felt he needed to do to get aid to the contras. He had been overseeing the contra program since sometime in 1984, when Congress stopped CIA aid to the rebels.

Until a ragged, teenage Nicaraguan soldier managed to hit C-123 cargo plane over southern Nicaragua with a surface-to-air missile, the Nicaraguans had little tangible proof to offer of U.S. involvement. Three U.S. airmen were killed as the missile exploded and the plane crashed. Eugene Hasenfus floated down by parachute into the arms of Nicaraguan troops and onto the front pages of the world's newspapers for weeks to come.

The Hasenfus trial began the same day we decided to bring the Sanchez family to the United States. Hasenfus proved a voluble witness, seemingly almost eager to tell all he knew about the supply operation. He said he had flown ten such supply missions. He "thought" he was working for the CIA. His employment was with Corporate Air Services, which had the same Miami address as Southern Air Transport, a CIA front that had shown up in clandestine operations from Central America to Southeast Asia.

"We would be flying into Honduras to an air base called Aguacate, and we would be loading up on small arms and ammunition, and this would be flown to Nicaragua," Hasenfus related. "These we would drop to the contras."

In Washington, Assistant Secretary of State Elliot Abrams insisted these were all lies told because of threats and intimidation by the Nicaraguans. As the weeks passed, however, it became clear that Hasenfus was indeed telling the truth—at least as much as he knew of it. Reagan's Nicaragua operation was in serious danger of unraveling.

On November 15, Hasenfus was sentenced in a Nicaraguan court to thirty years in prison. I returned to Nicaragua a month later with a small delegation of reporters to interview the Sanchez family and make arrangements for their trip north.

After we interviewed them in Jinotega, I strolled to the little plaza in the center of town to relax for a few minutes. A bent little Nicaraguan woman gave me a big smile that revealed the absence of most of her teeth. She was probably fifty but appeared much older.

We began to chat. Soon she was telling me about how her husband had been kidnapped by the contras and taken "across the mountains" six months earlier. Three weeks before this conversation, just when she had decided that he must be dead, he had escaped and returned home.

"Life was very hard while he was gone," the woman said. "But now I thank God for his great mercy to my husband. He is a good man."

While we were speaking, a man walked up to us and asked, "You are from the United States, aren't you?" When I confirmed that I was, he continued, "How do you feel about the announcement today that Hasenfus is to be set free, released to go home immediately?"

"I hadn't heard any such thing," I said. "But I must say, I am amazed! I can understand why the Nicaraguan government might choose to release him—for public relations purposes in the United States—but I'll bet this will make a lot of the Nicaraguan people furious. How many of them would approve of letting a man go who has admitted making many flights over your country to drop supplies to the contras?"

"Oh, I think almost everyone will like it," answered the woman. The man nodded in agreement.

"But I honestly don't understand," I continued. "*Why* would Nicaraguans agree to it at all?"

With a look of patient amusement, the woman said, "Well, of course, it is almost Christmas, don't you see? It is a good time for him to be home with his family."

Of course! But the truth is, I had never seen compassion for one's enemy expressed in such a natural, matter-of-fact way. I tried to imagine whether our people in the United States might agree to such a thing if the situation were reversed. It was unthinkable.

A few days later, a *New York Times* article reported, "Mr. Ortega and other officials generally sought to portray Mr. Hasenfus as a victim of American policy rather than a true enemy of the Nicaraguan people. Nonetheless, it was startling for many to see the president shake the American's hand during the release ceremony Wednesday."

On Saturday night, February 7, 1987, the Sanchez family arrived in Atlanta. Jimmy Carter helped us get visas for them. Otherwise, the Sanchezes might never have made it to the United States.

They were among the last ones on the plane when I entered it to help them up the exit ramp. The crew and a few sympathetic passengers were gathered around them. They looked so small and vulnerable. I could have carried Elda and Carmen both at the same time. As soon as he saw me,

Amancio broke into a big smile and called out, "Hello, brother!"

We had been assured by friends in Atlanta that they would take care of medical matters. I got word just before the Sanchez family arrived that the intended doctor had decided this was too controversial a job. "I suggest they get help in Mexico," he said. So the Sanchezes arrived without medical support waiting for them.

The next day over breakfast, we prayed together for help. I set out for Atlanta and the Emory University Health Sciences Center. I asked around for someone who might help us. I was told of one man who might be interested, a professor with a special interest in Central America.

When I knocked on his door, he invited me in but told me at once he was preparing for a lecture he was to deliver in just minutes. I quickly explained my problem.

"Don Mosley," he said. "Where have I heard your name before?"

It turned out that he was a member of the Fellowship of Reconciliation, of which I was then the national chairman.

"Call me tomorrow," he said. "I may have good news for you."

He did. He had made arrangements at the Emory Center for Rehabilitative Medicine for our three amputees to get a full examination. I passed the good news to Jimmy Carter's office.

At the appointed time, I took the Sanchez family to the Emory Center. We were met graciously by Dr. Ashok Bhoomkar, a specialist in rehabilitation. While he was examining Amancio, I looked up and saw a tall man with a "hearing aid" walk into the office. By now I was getting pretty good at spotting Secret Service men.

Sure enough, about two minutes later Jimmy Carter came striding into the room with a great smile. He gave

Amancio and his family a warm welcome, then chatted with them in Spanish for a few minutes. Amancio described the mine catastrophe. Carter responded that we had to keep working and praying to bring this war to an end as soon as possible.

The director of the center and some of his senior staff appeared. Soon we were being assured that everything would be taken care of at no cost. A husband and wife prosthetics team, Gerald and Betty Ferland, agreed to furnish the four prostheses free of charge.

Carmen had to undergo additional surgery on both legs, but again all expenses were waived. Moreover, all the medical people urged me to bring additional Nicaraguan war victims to them, promising to help at little or no cost. Dr. Bhoomkar and the Ferlands even offered to make periodic trips to Nicaragua if needed.

Meanwhile, the members of the Sanchez family were rapidly endearing themselves to everyone they met. Carolyn and I doubled up with our kids upstairs and turned our bedroom over to our visitors. Everything was a new adventure for them—hot water right out of the wall, flush toilets, gas stoves, refrigerators—suddenly we felt wealthy.

I received a call from a Spanish-speaking friend who asked to speak to Carmen. She held the phone in front of her face in both hands, hearing the faint voice coming from it but not sure how to respond. A look of wonder spread over her face as she began to speak to another woman in far-off Washington, D.C.

While the prostheses were being constructed, we set out for a week of political work in Washington. The timing was perfect. The Hasenfus debacle led to the establishment of a special commission that included Senator John Tower, former Senator Edmund Muskie, and former National Security Adviser Brent Scowcroft. They conducted an investigation into the Iran-contra affair and prepared a detailed report. For weeks the public was teased by tidbits released in advance by the commission. The Tower Commission report was to be published in full on February 26.

Our press conference was set for February 25. It was sponsored by Representative David Bonior of Michigan. He and Bishop Thomas Gumbleton of Detroit released a new report from Witness for Peace that detailed the killing of seventy-nine civilians and the rape, kidnapping, and wounding of many more in the previous six months. Carmen's picture was on the cover of that report—a graceful young woman propped up against pillows, an IV line in her right arm, two large bundles of gauze where her legs should have been. Her face was blank, expressionless.

The press conference took place in a room in the Capitol building, across the hall from the chamber of the House of Representatives. A dozen television crews crowded in, and there were many more reporters representing North American and foreign newspapers and magazines.

I told of the estimated two thousand amputees in Nicaragua, nearly one third of whom had lost arms or legs in just the previous year. After announcing the launching of the Walk in Peace campaign to help these amputees, I introduced Amancio and his family.

While the rest of us spoke, Cristina sat on a couch over to our right, holding baby Marjuri in her lap and clasping Elda beside her. Carmen sat stolidly next to them in her wheelchair, an afghan hiding the pitiful remains of what had so recently been the strong legs of a beautiful young woman. As the phalanx of reporters flashed away with their cameras at the little group, Elda crawled into her mother's lap beside Marjuri. The little stump of her destroyed leg protruded from her skirt, setting up the photograph that millions saw on the front page of their newspaper the next day.

Amancio stood up before the cluster of microphones and a wall of cameras and bright lights. There was a trace of perspiration on his brow. He held his hands together behind him to hide the slight trembling of his fingers.

From the reporters' side of the podium, however, all that was apparent was a man with a strong voice and confident smile. I marveled at the incredible leap he was making from the obscurity of his little village to sudden publicity before hundreds of millions of people. As the ordeal progressed, my affection for this brave man deepened. I was proud to stand beside him as friend and brother.

With dignity and composure, Amancio spoke through an interpreter about the morning of the tragedy. "I was having a conversation with the pastor of the Nazarene church when we heard a loud explosion. The truck went down and we all screamed and thought they had killed us. I didn't know what had happened to us until I woke up and discovered my leg was destroyed."

He concluded, "Thanks to concerned people in this country and Christian brothers and sisters, I have the opportunity to come to the United States to receive the medical attention required and to share my personal experience. As a Christian, I solely desire peace in my country so the suffering of so many families, like mine, can stop."

Rep. Bonior, Bishop Gumbleton, and I asserted that it was clearly the contras who set the mine in the road. But—by prior agreement—Amancio avoided making such a charge. He feared what the contras might do to him and his family. However, the instant Amancio finished his prepared remarks, there was a flurry of waving hands and shouted questions.

The first three questioners all hammered at the same point. "How do you *know* the mine was placed there by the contras, not the Sandinistas?"

One reporter was particularly harsh and sarcastic as he

cross-examined Amancio. I had warned Amancio that this would be the most difficult part of the press conference, but even I had not expected such an assault. Amancio's hands began to tremble behind his back. But he had been under fire before; he maintained his poise and answered every question as honestly as he could.

The story was well distributed that night and the next day. But in most cases it was carefully "balanced" by the State Department's claims that the Sandinista forces were responsible for the mine. "There is no conclusive evidence that the contras engage in systematic human rights violations," the official line went.

Some reports added a third opinion, that of contra spokesman Ernesto Palazio: "Isolated cases of abuse of civilians have occurred," he conceded, "but it is not the policy of the resistance movement to tolerate violations of human rights."

In the minds of most readers, that made the score two to one. And we were the losing side.

Back at our rooms I hugged Amancio and praised him for his presentation. He was somber and pale. "Don, I am a dead man. You will stay in the United States, but I have to return to Nicaragua. After what has just happened here today, I am sure the contras will kill me."

A week later, Amancio and his family were back at Jubilee and completely recovered from the strain of their trip to Washington. Best of all, the time came for Amancio and Elda to be fitted with their new legs. Carmen still had one more operation to undergo.

When the day came, Amancio said at the breakfast table, "This will be one of the greatest days of my life—like the day I got married or the day I became a Christian. I will be able to walk again!" The beatific smiles on the faces of Amancio and Elda as they took their first steps was more than enough payment for all of our efforts.

Some weeks after the others, Carmen's turn came. She stood between parallel bars, looking down as the final adjustments were made on her new legs. Then the attendant backed away and said, "Carmen, look at yourself in the full-length mirror." She raised her head and saw herself standing upright again. She smiled the most beautiful smile I imagine I'll ever see!

Life for the Sanchez family continued to be something like a nonstop press conference. Almost every day for the remainder of their month with us, they were interviewed by one or more reporters.

In the friendly setting at Jubilee, Amancio became quite a spokesman for the invisible victims of the war. Elda became a genuine showoff, always ready to sing and play her new tambourine or demonstrate her new walking skills in front of CNN, ABC, or any other television crew on hand. Carmen and Cristina did their best to hide.

The Sanchez family was welcomed back to Nicaragua with great fanfare. Amancio walked across a stage to the applause of hundreds of fellow pastors gathered for the 15th Annual General Assembly of CEPAD. Gustavo Parajón welcomed him back and explained to the pastors that this was evidence that many people in the United States were unhappy with President Reagan's violent policies against the Nicaraguans.

Amancio and Elda made another significant visit—to the Aldo Chavaria Rehabilitation Hospital in Managua, this time walking up and down the halls. Then they visited the new prosthesis workshop, opened just a week earlier. Already there were amputees of all ages gathering there for physical therapy, even though it would be some months before most would actually receive artificial limbs.

Colin and Karen Glenn, supported by the United Church of Christ in the United States and motivated by a deep love for the people of Nicaragua, were our primary representatives for Walk in Peace there. The International Committee for the Red Cross provided training and much of the money for the establishment of the shop. The goal was to rehabilitate five hundred people a year. Ambitious as this was, it would not even keep up with the rate at which new amputees were joining the waiting lists.

Groups all over the United States sponsored walk-a-thons and other fund-raising events to channel funds through Jubilee to Nicaragua. Each year the Walk in Peace campaign has helped the prosthetics center rehabilitate hundreds of amputees without regard to their politics. More than $1.5 million was sent to help victims of war and other disasters in Nicaragua.

Early in 1988 our Walk in Peace work led to the publication of a dramatic article in *People* magazine called "Agonies of the Innocents." The reporters started with accounts of our work, then went to Nicaragua. They followed the doctors through the Velez Pais Children's Hospital in Managua, collecting poignant photographs of children who had been shot, burned, or blasted by land mines.

The article brought the biggest response in the history of *People*—so much so that the magazine's editors considered running a follow-up article just about the response itself. It also caused a flood of calls to Jubilee Partners, mostly from people who wanted desperately to help the children somehow.

That summer I went to the Velez Pais hospital to see the situation firsthand. Because of their appreciation for our help, I was given a thorough tour by two of the administrators. That is, I was shown as much as I could take before I reached some kind of limit myself, overwhelmed by the sight of so many suffering children.

It was obvious that not all war victims had been hit by military ordnance. Indeed, most of the deaths among children were from secondary results of the war, especially diarrhea, caused by destruction of water systems and rural clinics. Widespread malnutrition—also a direct result of war—exacerbated all the other medical problems.

Velez Pais is the largest children's hospital in Nicaragua. Even it, however, could not accommodate the torrent of sick and injured children. They overflowed out of the rooms and into the halls. Makeshift beds and mattresses on the floors so crowded the halls that we had to be careful to avoid stepping on children. The crowding was intensified by the fact that almost every child was attended by a parent or relative. They were usually haggard from long days and nights of sitting beside their children.

The burn ward was full of pitifully scarred children, whimpering or screaming much of the time, their gruesome wounds open to the air. "We only recently were able to buy air conditioners for the burn ward—a personal donation from Vice-President Ramirez," said one administrator. "Before we got them, the burned children suffered terribly from the heat. If we opened the windows to cool the room a little, flies came in and spread infection."

I stepped to the side of one boy of about ten. Unlike most of the other children, he was alone. Yet he seemed content despite being heavily bandaged and having a leg in traction. When I spoke to him, he smiled back at me but said nothing.

A doctor motioned me to one side. "He was in a truck with his family a week ago when a band of contras attacked," he explained. "Direct hit with a mortar. All the others were killed, but he doesn't know that yet. He is still in shock."

In another part of the hospital, we met Dr. Denis Cuéllar, son-in-law of Dr. Parajón. In a tiny room, he was giving physical therapy to a small boy with a twisted foot. Dr. Cuéllar's cheerfulness and strength of character made the poverty of the quarters seem almost irrelevant. He was improvising a brace from a meager supply of materials. Outside, the waiting room was packed with parents who had brought their children with all sorts of physical disabilities.

The hospital's one elevator had not functioned for years. Medicine was in short supply. Great pain was everywhere. I watched a doctor reset the broken bone in the forearm of a screaming child. "Even in our operating room," I was told, "we use anesthesia only when absolutely necessary—because we have none to spare."

By the time I left the hospital, I was convinced this war would come to an immediate stop if only we could get President Reagan into the Velez Pais Hospital for half an hour.

At Jubilee we decided to broaden the focus of our Walk in Peace campaign to include all the children, regardless of whether or not they were amputees. Jubilee borrowed $50,000 for a dental clinic and other special projects at the children's hospital.

Meanwhile the U.S. Congress took the extraordinary step of appropriating "aid to children" in Nicaragua. Jimmy Carter publicly congratulated Jubilee Partners for this, saying that several members of Congress had told him that the Walk in Peace campaign and the *People* article had been the main inspiration for the action by Congress.

Our first reaction was great joy mixed with pride that we had helped at least in some small way to bring it about. Then we began to read the fine print.

The "children's aid," which was included in a $27 million contra aid bill, came with strings. The CIA was to dispense the money and it was to go only to medical institutions with no connections to the Nicaraguan government. That eliminated all but a tiny fraction of Nicaragua's indigenous hospitals and projects. The directors of the Baptist Hospital in Managua desperately needed help like all the rest. But they agonized over the matter and voted to reject their share of the aid as a matter of principle.

It was no surprise that all of the projects designed specifically to aid the contras were qualified to get the money. But inside Nicaragua most medical officials refused to accept these funds, saying they could not accept aid to heal their children from the same bill funding the contras to kill them.

What briefly looked like a compassionate departure from business as usual by the hostile U.S. government turned into a cruel joke. The very children whose suffering had initially prompted the act were left with little or no benefit. In fact, some of us who had been working all along on their behalf began to encounter the misconception in the United States that our efforts were not really needed any longer, now that Washington had pitched in with far more money than we would ever raise.

Then just when we thought nothing worse could happen, it did.

13

Hurricane

During the night of October 21, 1988, Hurricane Joan slammed into the country's east coast with tremendous force—winds up to 125 miles per hour. She screamed across the country that night and the next day. Joan wrecked everything in her path like a furious giant. Nicaragua had not had a direct hit from a hurricane since 1911; this one made up for lost time.

In twenty-four hours a billion dollars' worth of destruction was done to the little country. Hundreds of people were dead or missing. Over 300,000 were left homeless. More than two thousand kilometers of roads were severely damaged or destroyed completely, along with seventy to eighty bridges. More than a million acres of forest were leveled, crops were destroyed over a large part of the country, and the fishing industry on the east coast—a major source of income for the region—was annihilated.

In the November 12, 1988, *New York Times*, Nicaraguan commentator Sofía Montenegro expressed her country's reaction to the tragedy. Referring to the character in Greek mythology whose whole life was spent rolling a boulder up a hill, watching it fall back, and rolling it again, she called Nicaragua "the nation of Sisyphus."

Damned country! Once more in ruins! How many times will we have to rebuild what has been destroyed?

This new catastrophe, devastating but above all unfair for a country already worn down by war and enemy siege, gives one a sense that the effort to raise Nicaragua up is futile and hopeless. Against the background of aggression, the hurricane seems not a caprice of nature, but rather a joke, a hideous conspiracy by who knows what Indian gods against our absurd mortal efforts. It produces a strange and atavistic rebellion against our apparent destiny to plant again and again, without ever harvesting anything.

The White House immediately declared that—in contrast to the more than $125 million in U.S. government aid given earlier in the month for hurricane aid to Jamaica—there would not be a cent for the Nicaraguans. "The Sandinista government could not be trusted to use the assistance for disaster relief," said Press Secretary Marlin Fitzwater. He insisted that Daniel Ortega simply wanted "to use the storm as another platform for propaganda against the contras."

In Tucson an organizer in the sanctuary movement, Tim Nonn, called us while the hurricane was still raging and proposed a major relief effort by Jubilee Partners. Our friends at Habitat for Humanity lent us $40,000 immediately and in the following months expanded their program in Nicaragua to help directly with the replacement of many destroyed homes around Bluefields on the east coast. *Sojourners* magazine and Koinonia Partners agreed to put out special appeals for emergency aid. At Jubilee we soon had nearly 10,000 letters in the mail, asking our supporters to join us to help the Nicaraguans that President Reagan had shunned.

The response to our appeal was inspiring. Four days after the hurricane struck Nicaragua, we had more than seventy volunteers working vigorously at Jubilee and in

Tucson. Our telephones rang constantly with offers of aid. A thousand contributions poured in through the Comer post office. Dozens of people worked night and day to haul relief supplies to the Tucson airport and prepare them for shipment.

We rented a DC-8 and found a flight crew willing to take it to Nicaragua and back at no charge. The plane arrived at the Managua airport exactly one week after the hurricane passed through, the first aid to come from people in the United States.

"It was absolutely beautiful," reported one who watched it arrive. "It was like a huge silver bird as it passed overhead, turned, and landed just at dusk." Gustavo Parajón and other CEPAD leaders were there to help unload the plane, twenty-one truckloads of materials to be inventoried and distributed to the disaster areas.

Perhaps it was fear that prevented many fine church organizations from responding more to the suffering of the Nicaraguans. I don't know. What I do know, from Parajón himself, is that six months after the storm the combined relief contributions from the mainline Protestant churches of the United States were only a fraction of the amount our motley collection of concerned folks in Arizona and Georgia had helped channel into the disaster area.

At the height of the publicity about the storm's impact on Nicaragua, a pastor friend of Jubilee called his denominational headquarters and asked how much they were sending.

"Five thousand dollars."

"Why so little?" our friend asked.

"Well, to be honest," came the answer, "this is not a good time to emphasize an aid program to Nicaragua. We'd like to do more, but. . . ."

Money and relief materials were still pouring into our collection points, so we began plans immediately for a second flight. A smaller plane was desperately needed for shuttle flights between the Managua airport and the small east coast airport at Bluefields. All roads across the country were totally destroyed. The rivers were still too swollen for any significant amount of aid to be ferried by boat. In Indiana we located a Convair 240 just right for the job.

But the plane was not certified to fly into Nicaragua and needed a "variance" on its permit. This could be granted only by the director of the Federal Aviation Administration.

U.S. presidential elections were just a few days away. Administration officials were nervous that they might make a misstep. FAA officials insisted they could not help us without permission from the State Department and White House. "This is Nicaragua you're dealing with, you know," one reminded me.

I called Jimmy Carter. After we had talked a few minutes, he agreed to call the FAA director personally. Soon I received a congenial call from the official, assuring me it had been a pleasure to help clear the remaining obstacles from our way. "You may fly to Nicaragua immediately, if you like."

Over the next couple of weeks the Convair shuttled more than a hundred tons of badly needed materials into Bluefields and evacuated more than 650 people from there to Managua. But in what was beginning to feel like a relentless rhythm of bad news following good, we started to get reports that something seemed strange about the two pilots of the plane. As the days passed, the hunches began to give way to concrete evidence. One pilot was seen meeting with the U.S. military attaché in Managua. Then we learned that he had been a pilot for a mysterious "private" airline in Laos during the war in Vietnam.

As the story of the crew's CIA connections became clear, we insisted that they stop their shuttle flights and return at once to the United States. They refused at first, and it took several days to convince them to come home. Even after they were back, they continued to argue, offering to raise all the expenses for the relief flights if we would only allow them to use the Walk in Peace program as their sponsor.

A few days later, we received an amazing offer by telephone, from "a group of people in Palm Beach, Florida, who admire the work of Jubilee Partners." They told us that they were prepared to buy a plane "worth almost a million dollars" and donate it to Jubilee Partners for our permanent use in disaster relief projects around the world. There was only one stipulation. They wanted to take it first to Nicaragua and resume the flights we had been sponsoring there!

This was beginning to feel like some kind of elaborate joke, but it was serious and it was sinister. Parajón seemed a bit surprised that we found all of this so incredible. "We took it for granted from the beginning that the CIA would take advantage of such relief efforts to further their own causes," he told us. "We are used to that sort of activity as a regular part of our lives."

I thought back to an incident during my first trip to Nicaragua. The delegation I was coleading had talked to dozens of people on all sides of the conflict, but we had not found a chance to interview anyone who could give us a firsthand account of what was happening to the Miskito Indians on the east coast. Reagan had repeatedly charged the Sandinistas with "genocide" against the Miskitos.

As we were waiting in the departure lounge at the Managua airport, we discovered Rev. John Wilson waiting there for a flight to Costa Rica. Wilson, a Miskito and a Moravian leader on the east coast, where many people have been Moravians for generations, sat in one of the rows of chairs near one end of the lounge. More than a dozen of us gathered around him.

"What about the 'genocide' President Reagan says the Sandinistas are committing against the Miskito people?" one of us asked.

Wilson responded that there were indeed some atrocities committed against the people of the east coast—he estimated that about eighty had died since the war began three years earlier. However, either President Reagan was poorly informed or was deliberately exaggerating to suit his own political purposes. "In some ways we feel as misused by your president as by the Sandinistas," he said. He politely protested the way his people were being used as objects of propaganda by Washington, and he set the record straight with a convincing firsthand account.

While Wilson spoke, two North Americans, sitting side by side, caught my eye a few yards away. One was dressed in a business suit and the other in casual jogging clothes. Although one pretended to be reading a newspaper, both were obviously eavesdropping. They were so blatant and clumsy, so much like spies in a Peter Sellers movie, that I wanted to laugh.

I nudged another man in our delegation, Bob Van Denend, and asked, "Want to bet on whether those guys are from the CIA?"

"I was just thinking the same thing about the one backed up to John Wilson with a tape recorder," Bob replied. Sure enough, in the seat positioned back-to-back with Wilson's seat, a Latin-American man sat staring into the distance as though unaware of the tense interview taking place immediately behind him. His arms were crossed. In his right hand he was trying to hide a microcassette recorder while aiming it back across his left shoulder to catch Wilson's comments.

The whole scene was so absurd Bob and I were about to break into laughter—and so outrageous we were considering whether to blow the cover of all these "Keystone cops" by pointing them out to John Wilson. Just at that moment it was announced that Wilson's flight was boarding; before we could say more he was gone.

The three men we had spotted rushed to the other end of the lounge. There they held a quick conference in full view of us, eagerly reversing their recorder and checking to see whether they had a good record of the interview.

If all spies were as inept as these, I thought, Nicaragua should not have much to fear from them. The fact is, of course, that most of the surveillance was far more sophisticated than we saw demonstrated that day.

Late in 1987, I was on my way to Nicaragua with a friend to make a video about the amputees we were aiding through Walk in Peace. I was carrying $8,000 in cash to pay for the project, the money concealed in a belt under my clothing.

Our plane had loaded at the Miami airport, and we were waiting for the takeoff. The delay stretched on for several minutes. Then a special announcement was made over the P.A. system: "Anyone carrying the equivalent of $10,000 or more must register with the U.S. Customs officials before we depart."

"Strange," I thought. "I've never heard them make an announcement like that before." I thought back a few months to an earlier trip when Carolyn and I had, in fact, carried $25,000 in cash to Nicaragua in secret. The money had been a donation to be used for medical support for Nicaraguan children, and we had passed it on to Dr. Parajón in the privacy of his office. If there were regulations at that time requiring us to register such an amount with the U.S. Customs agents, we had honestly failed to notice them.

While congratulating myself silently that we had not gotten into trouble on that earlier occasion, I noticed two husky U.S. Customs officials board the plane and start down the aisle. As the passengers waited, the officials came slowly through the plane, looking everyone over as they came closer but saying nothing. To my surprise they came to a stop at my elbow and asked me brusquely, "Did you hear the announcement we made a few minutes ago about the $10,000 limit on cash?"

Startled, I said, "Why, yes, I did."

"Are you carrying more than that amount with you now?"

"No, I am not," I replied, beginning to feel angry. For a long moment I looked straight into the eyes of the agent standing above me—and he and I knew each other's thoughts as clearly as if we had spoken them aloud. I realized with chilling clarity that these men somehow knew more about my activities than they could afford to admit. And they saw that I knew.

There was a silence, during which I had a brief glimpse of the vulnerability that my Central American brothers and sisters must feel so often when confronted with the cold power of North American might. The moment passed, the officials left the plane without even speaking to anyone else, and we took off for Nicaragua.

As the plane moved out over the Gulf of Mexico, I continued to feel the shadow of what had just taken place, a sense that my desire to follow the teachings of Jesus was setting me on a collision course with powers I had not really taken seriously before. In fact, until recently I had imagined myself to be somehow exempt from such threats. My upbringing as a middle-class U.S. citizen had conditioned me to be somewhat nonchalant about such matters; they simply weren't part of my privileged world.

I was about to learn otherwise.

14

Trials, Jubilations, and the IRS

It was a hot summer morning, July 23, 1987. Carolyn and I were just sitting down with Tony and Robyn to have breakfast on our screened porch when two strangers appeared. They introduced themselves as James Carlan and Judith Adams from the Internal Revenue Service.

We invited them to share our breakfast or at least have coffee, but they declined. So we asked them to sit in the porch swing beside us while we finished our meal. They agreed and waited patiently while we ate and talked with the kids.

The visit was hardly unexpected. In the previous months, our relationship with the IRS had been a frequent topic of family and community discussions. Now Carolyn and I talked to Tony and Robyn about the important difference between the agents—"like Jim and Judith here"—and the evil being done with much of our tax money. We tried to be casual—as though such things happened every morning around our house.

In truth, the roots of this breakfast confrontation went all the way back to my childhood. My father was a successful Texas businessman. I grew up with all the material advantages of being a millionaire's son. I was headed toward taking over the family business when several experiences changed my course.

As a young man, I visited Palestinian refugee camps in the Middle East and Egypt. What I saw there made me realize how different from my own was life for most people in the world. I was so disturbed by the hopelessness and suffering of the refugees and of other desperately poor people around me that I returned to the United States and became one of the first to enlist in President Kennedy's newly created Peace Corps.

I spent almost five years in Asia, first as a volunteer in Malaysia, then as associate director of the Peace Corps in South Korea. While I was in Asia, the war was intensifying in Vietnam. I spent a week in Cambodia shortly before it was decimated by a combination of U.S. bombs and the brutality of the Khmer Rouge. In South Korea I was directly responsible for the safety of 125 Peace Corps volunteers near the "demilitarized zone" during frequent skirmishes with North Korea.

I had top secret clearance at that time and was involved in several emergency briefings with U.S. military personnel and embassy officials. Gradually it dawned on me that my country's role in international military and economic relationships was not always something of which I could be proud. I discovered that many of the advantages I enjoyed as a U.S. citizen were gained at the expense of people in weaker nations.

Especially troubling was the inclination of our national leaders to look on most conflicts around the world primarily as manifestations of communism. Our stock response was saber rattling, often with the unspoken threat of nuclear force. I saw that the Cold War point of view was being used to justify an arms race escalating beyond any rational semblance of "security." Nuclear weapons them-

selves—ours as well as those of the Soviet Union—had become the greatest threat of all to our security.

I was trained as an engineer, with additional majors in
math and history. So I understood the limitations of technology and of governments—and the danger of playing
the odds as we were doing. A report by Senator Mark Hat-
field revealed that our military computer system had mal-
functioned 147 times in twenty months, signaling Soviet
attacks against our country. That was, on average, one false
alarm every four days!

Some false alarms lasted several minutes while military leaders frantically tried to decide whether to launch
our missiles before they could be knocked out by those
thought to be headed our way. Once launched, they could
not be called back (a technical point President Reagan
once admitted—to a shocked visitor—he had not realized).
A Soviet response in kind would become almost certain.
On a planet stocked with fifty thousand nuclear warheads,
one such mistake could be fatal for everyone.

I began to see the nuclear arms race as a form of idola-
try. Though our money said "In God We Trust," our actions made clear that we put greater trust in Trident submarines, cruise missiles, and B-1 bombers. We were
spending over a million dollars *each minute* to prepare for
war and to pay for past ones. That was money that could
not be spent for education, housing, and health care. A
great number of people were already victims, even if we
never dropped another nuclear bomb.

My new understandings led me to a difficult decision. I
left my career as a businessman/engineer and set out to
use whatever abilities I had to work for peace and justice. I
was not interested in merely symbolic gestures; I wanted
to make a real difference. Thus began my involvement
with Koinonia Partners, Habitat for Humanity, the Fellowship of Reconciliation, Jubilee Partners, and other such

groups. I wanted to work for peace by helping to remove some of the injustices that so often set the stage for war.

I also knew I could not in good conscience claim to follow Jesus Christ, who preached love for one's enemies, and at the same time pay for wars that killed them. With almost two-thirds of the federal tax money we paid each April going to finance military and related activities, Carolyn and I decided we could no longer voluntarily support war with our tax dollars. As we began to meet individual victims of our militarism in Central America, our concern grew more intense and more personal.

For many years we were able to live simply enough to keep our income below a taxable level; simplicity of lifestyle was part of our reason for choosing to live in an intentional community. But then my father sold his business and informed me of his intent to leave me a sizable inheritance. Although I pleaded with him to donate the money to a charitable cause instead, he set up a trust fund over which I had almost no control.

Both my parents died in 1977. Even though Carolyn and I gave away the year's earnings from the trust fund and continued to live at the same level as before, the IRS regarded the money as taxable income. We had no argument with taxation in principle and had always readily paid local and federal taxes we believed would improve society. From 1978 to 1981 we filed tax forms and paid part of the taxes due, withholding an amount proportional to what would have gone to military spending. We gave that amount (and more) to charitable organizations instead.

In 1982 the IRS seized from our bank account the amount they claimed we owed, plus penalties and interest. We were faced with a new dilemma. We knew the IRS would always collect what we had withheld and more. We decided to refuse to give them information about our income; we stopped filing 1040 forms. Not wanting to be deceptive, each year we wrote a letter to then-President Reagan, with a copy to the IRS, explaining why our religious beliefs did not allow us to provide the information.

Max and Nancy Rice, who had also become part of Jubilee Partners by this time, faced a similar situation because of decisions made years earlier. Over the months, both families received increasingly threatening "last chance to pay" computer notices from the IRS. The Rices received their summons from agents Carlan and Adams seven weeks before we received ours.

It was a time of fatigue and transition at Jubilee. The Karises and Weirs had decided to leave the community and move on to other work. Recent resident partners Jim and Meg Foxvog had a new baby, born between the two visits by the IRS. Tony and three other Jubilee young people were about to leave for college. It was definitely not a convenient time to make such a watershed decision. But in our struggle, we drew closer together.

Carolyn and I spent many hours with Max and Nancy discussing our shared dilemma. Both families had begun tax resistance a full decade before we met; now our lives were converging rapidly. One big question was whether all four parents should continue to risk prison. The IRS decided for us by dropping Carolyn's and Nancy's names off the summonses. Thus the legal focus narrowed to Max and me, though we were all much involved.

About this time our family made a great discovery. We found that if we celebrated *every* new development—whether it seemed on the surface to be good or bad—we undermined the power of both the process and our fears. Most of the time we did this by going out for pizza. Bigger events, like receiving the notice that Max and I were to turn ourselves in to jail, called for our favorite, Chinese food.

We always made a clear distinction between the people who carried out the IRS tasks and the overall system they represented. We tried to develop a sincere friendship with each person. We also tried to be as open and honest with them as we could every step of the way, even going so far once as to point out errors the IRS had made in our favor. In return we felt genuine gratitude from most of these people. Sometimes they even apologized for having to cause us so much trouble.

On November 16, 1987, Max had his first hearing in Macon, before Judge Duross Fitzpatrick. Milner Ball served as Max's lawyer. Milner had been the Presbyterian campus minister at the University of Georgia—until he made the mistake of allowing student groups that opposed the war in Vietnam, as well as those that supported it, to use the Presbyterian Student Center. When dismissed, he decided to go into law as a way of continuing his ministry. Eventually he became a professor of law at the University of Georgia, specializing in the U.S. Constitution.

When he heard of our troubles with the IRS, Milner contacted us and enthusiastically offered his services free of charge. He told us, "I couldn't be doing what I am doing as a Christian lawyer if you weren't doing what you are." Max accepted Milner as his lawyer, but I chose to represent myself. "No problem," Milner said. He offered his services as my legal counsel and was by my side each time we went to court.

Milner argued that Max felt it violated his Christian conscience to produce the information the IRS wanted. And in any event, that information was filed years ago with the state of Wisconsin—the IRS could go and get it. Milner quoted one case after another reaffirming that "where a citizen invokes the First Amendment in defense of his religious beliefs, the court must scrutinize the matter, then show compelling need to force compliance."

The prosecuting attorney argued that people like Max

represent a threat to the tax system. "Voluntary compliance with taxation is already eroding. It is important to stop that," he declared. "It is asking too much of the IRS to make them go to Wisconsin to get the information which Mr. Rice could turn over himself if he would just cooperate. That is not an efficient way for the IRS to operate."

Milner retorted, "Does the IRS have the right to dismiss the First Amendment to make the collection process more efficient? That is the narrow question before us."

The judge was openly perplexed. He called for a recess for a few minutes while he retired to his chamber to think the matter through. When he returned, he ruled against Max. He said he disliked forcing Max do something against his beliefs but that perhaps the action of the court would give Max a clear conscience. Max had no choice now but to comply—the court would take the blame.

In any case, the judge argued, there was an important difference between religious *belief* and religious *action*. It was okay to hold fast to some beliefs but not necessarily to act on them. On that note, Max's first hearing drew to a close. My turn was coming.

On April 12, 1988, a jovial federal marshal drove up with a summons for me to appear in court. "Just happened to be coming out this direction anyway, so I told 'em I'd drop it by for you." He grinned—as though he was doing me a big favor. The hearing was set for June 1.

As the date approached, interest in our tax resistance grew. Articles began to appear in newspapers all over the region.

This caused one especially interesting situation. The Madison County Fairgrounds, across the highway from Jubilee Partners, was hosting the annual Memorial Day gathering of Vietnam War veterans. Called "LZ Friendly" (war jargon for "safe landing zone"), the event drew hundreds of veterans for three days of nostalgia. They camped, reminisced, sang old songs, and stood for long periods in front of the Moving Wall, a half-size model of the Vietnam Memorial in Washington, D.C. The organizers claimed it was the biggest annual gathering of Vietnam veterans in the country—in Comer, of all places, right at our entrance.

That year LZ Friendly coincided with the peak of publicity about our tax resistance. Throughout the three days of the event, all the convenience stores in the region were displaying the weekly edition of the *Athens Observer* with its headline story: "Jubilee Partners Face Prison Over Refusal to Pay Their Military Taxes." We were nervous, afraid our prominent "Jubilee Partners" sign a hundred yards from the Moving Wall might tempt someone to strike a violent blow for patriotism.

Carolyn and I felt particularly uneasy about the alienation between ourselves and the people gathered on the other side of the road. We decided to pay them a visit. As we walked slowly along the Moving Wall, looking at the thousands of names of U.S. military men who had died in Vietnam, we were deeply moved, as so many have been by the larger Wall in Washington.

We found ourselves standing beside a man a little older than ourselves. "I found his name," he said as he turned suddenly to us. "I had to ask the people in the tent over there to help, but I found his name."

"Oh?" I said. "Was it someone you knew?"

His face twisted and his voice rose with grief. "He was my son!"

As Carolyn and I shared in this father's anguish, all sense of estrangement from him and the others around us disappeared. However hard it might have been for our veteran friends to understand us, we knew our protest was on their behalf as well as for all other war victims.

In preparation for my hearing before Judge Fitzpatrick, I sent him a statement titled "Why I Should Not Be Compelled to Obey the IRS Summons." I opened it by writing,

To begin with, your Honor, I want to say that I find it very ironic that I might eventually be judged to be "in contempt of court." My attitude toward you and your court is somewhere near the opposite of contempt, and I have great respect for the Constitution and the legal system of our country. I thank God for all that is good and beautiful about our nation. . . .

At the same time, however, I want to be as clear as I can be from the outset that our nation and its legal system are neither the greatest good nor the highest authority that I acknowledge. As a Christian I believe that the kingdom of God must come first in my life, that I must make the teachings of Jesus Christ my highest authority—not just as abstract theological formulations but as the ultimate guide for what I actually *do* each day.

My case is before you because there is a conflict between that which I am asked by the IRS to do and that which I understand God to require of me.

My statement then described my journey from working as an engineer in my father's plant to my years in Asia. I told of the gradual opening of my eyes to the suffering of others around the world and the degree to which our nation was often a cause of that suffering. I described my growing alarm about the vast arsenals of nuclear weapons and the virtual certainty that we were moving closer to a worldwide disaster by placing our faith in such weapons.

Referring to Max's hearing, I continued,

It seems obvious that the IRS would not really care what Max Rice or I believe about Jesus Christ, taxes, or war—as long as we voluntarily hand over our financial information and taxes. But this is the essence of what is at stake here. Admittedly there are hundreds of matters of lesser consequence where each of us must compromise in order to live in society, but now and then there are more fundamental issues for some of us where that is not possible. To sever

204 With Our Own Eyes

our beliefs from our actions on those issues is—for individuals or for nations—to wound ourselves deep inside. That is what I am not willing to do to myself, to my spiritual core which gives the rest of my life meaning."

I explained that "the abstractions have taken on flesh." After recounting the stories of Carmen Gutierrez and her daughter Suyapa, of seven-year-old Elda Sanchez and her family, I stated, "I can no more give my support than if it were my own wife and two children being blown up by our land mines."

Then I concluded,

It's not a matter of contempt of court or of our nation that your court represents. I think, in fact, that this may be a more profound sort of patriotism than you are used to seeing—one that insists that real love for our country must be for a nation truly "under God" rather than the other way around. If we put our country first and our attempt to be faithful to God second, that would be contempt of a far more serious nature.

On June 1 the courtroom in Macon was packed, with the crowd spilling out into the hall. I was pleased to see at least half a dozen ministers, as well as friends from as far away as Canada, Europe, and Latin America. A local priest told me people were praying for us in his church nearby.

Judge Fitzpatrick made it clear from the beginning that, whatever verdict he might reach, he was taking this hearing seriously. When I told him that I chose to represent myself, he assured me he was going to see to it personally that I did not inadvertently forfeit any courtroom privileges. He also welcomed Milner Ball at my side to help in that regard.

After some preliminary questioning, the prosecuting attorney began to hammer on the same theme he had at Max's hearing.

"Has the IRS prevented you from praying?" he asked me.

"Of course not," I answered.

"Has the IRS kept you from singing hymns or reading the Bible?"

"Obviously not."

"Then how can you claim that the IRS has interfered with your free practice of religion?" he demanded.

"The free exercise of religion is more than singing songs and going to church," I insisted. "My understanding of religion is that it is much more than that. It includes loving my neighbors, even my 'enemies,' and I cannot voluntarily turn over my tax money to kill them while claiming at the same time to love them."

"But," the prosecutor pressed on, "there is no specific religious conduct you can point to that you couldn't continue. . . ."

The judge interrupted. He told us we were talking past each other "like two ships passing in the night."

Then he asked me, "Mr. Mosley, did you bring documents to present to the court?"

"I brought my Bible."

"The court takes judicial notice of the Bible." He chuckled. "Anything else?"

"I also brought an analysis of how our tax dollars are being spent, mostly for military purposes."

The prosecutor objected, the judge overruled him, and the document I had from the Friends Committee on National Legislation was allowed as evidence.

The prosecutor summed up his argument, repeating that complying with the tax laws would not interfere with the practice of religion.

When my final turn came, I stressed again that I didn't define religion as narrowly as the government would naturally hope we might. Then I rejected the prosecutor's argument that I should be more passive. "I don't believe that God says to one of us, 'You are only one of 250 million people, so you don't have any real part to play.' I believe the fate of this world is in God's hands but that God works through people who are willing to serve—through me as well as through others with whom I may disagree.

"I also want to stress that I love my country," I continued. "I have been in countries all over the world and have not found a perfect one yet. It is my firsthand observation that, for all its faults, our country offers us more freedom than most other people enjoy.

"At the Nuremburg trials after the Second World War, we argued that individuals had a responsibility to stand up against something wrong, even something ordered by their government and even if resistance might be costly. If we expect other people to follow that rule, how much more should we be willing to do so in a country where the freedom is greater and the cost is likely to be less?

"That is the essence of my defense today, whatever case law may bear upon it. If you rule against me, I am ready to take the consequences."

The judge concluded the hearing by commending my sincerity and admitting he was at least partly persuaded by my argument. He said he would take a few days to ponder the matter before ruling. Meanwhile, he instructed, I would be wise to get my affairs in order in preparation for a lengthy prison stay.

In a conversation after the hearing, Milner Ball mentioned to IRS agent Jim Carlan the U.S. land mines that were causing such torment to Nicaraguan citizens.

"Oh, is *that* what it's all about?" Carlan said. He removed a shoe, exposing a foot with a portion missing. "Blown off by an American anti-personnel mine I stepped on in Vietnam!" he explained.

The light began to dawn for him. Carlan told Milner

that the local IRS folks would drop the case against us if they had the power to do so, but they were receiving instructions from officials in Washington. It was clear people there were determined that we give in or go to prison.

After delaying as long as possible ("a few days" grew to seven months), Judge Fitzpatrick finally called Max and me back to court in Macon for a joint hearing on January 4, 1989. Our cases were now seen as essentially the same. We were content with that, since it meant we would more likely have each other as roommates during our prison time.

The judge found himself, as he put it, "between a rock and a hard place." He stressed how hard this whole matter was for him. "Neither of you is a criminal, the sort of person I'm more used to facing in this court," he told us. "In fact, you are the stuff that the early church was made of—people more like Thomas More and Joan of Arc. To tell you the truth, I just don't know what to do with you. I hate to send you to prison, but I am bound to carry out what we like to think of as justice in this court.

"I want to be sure you realize that we have reached what folks around here call 'log lickin' time'—the end of this process. The government is asking that I lock you away indefinitely, or at least until you comply with their demands. I don't know whether I will do that, but I do want to stress that if you are incarcerated, the keys are in your pocket. You can come out any time if you decide to cooperate with the IRS.

"You will hear my decision in a few days. Court dismissed."

15

Jail

As we waited for the judge's ruling, I was again amazed at the absence of fear and the great peace and joy we felt when we did what we thought we should.

Carolyn shared that feeling. "I didn't really worry about it much. That was true during the whole period of the trial as well. I don't know—maybe it was just a special gift of grace, in which Don and I were able to give it up to God and trust that God would control the situation.

"When the time came for Don actually to go off to jail, I was sad. I knew I would miss him a lot. But I wasn't devastated or afraid. I felt that grace more than anything else sustained us."

We ate a lot of Chinese food as we waited for the message from the judge. It seemed certain Max and I would soon go to prison, maybe for many months. Yet our earlier fears had dwindled, while our joy and our love for one another grew stronger than ever. Each day was a gift.

On January 24 the official word finally came: "Report on Monday morning, January 30, 1989, at 9:00 a.m., to the Milledgeville City Jail. Sentence to last 60 days."

All of us laughed, relieved to be done with the long period of uncertainty. We were thankful the judge had resisted the IRS demand that we be locked away indefinitely, or until we agreed to cooperate with them. So we were on our way to enjoy the hospitality of writer Flannery O'Connor's hometown—to experience a part of it she probably missed. Time for another celebration.

We later learned that in the forty-four years since World War II, only eighteen other people had been jailed for tax resistance and only one had a sentence longer than ours. (Our good friend Randy Kehler has since spent ten weeks in prison for redirecting his tax money to Jubilee and other humanitarian organizations.)

My last journal entry before leaving for jail was:

> January 26, 1989. These are good, full days. I feel your love with me, Father. Yesterday, for instance—as I finished my prayers, prepared to run, tore off the next page on our daily Scripture calendar and found, "God is love; they who dwell in love dwell in God and God dwells in them"—then I stepped out into the crisp, beautiful morning and looked up at a perfect sunrise sky, just as a dove flew overhead, past the beautiful moon. . . . If you were to add more beauty it would just spill over. My cup is full and overflowing.

As Max and I entered the front door of the Milledgeville City Jail, we heard the guards call down the hall. "Here come the preachers!" By this time there had been a great deal of newspaper coverage of our actions. Most people took for granted that we were preachers; after all, we talked about God an awful lot.

Our good-byes with our families in the front lobby of the jail were not easy. Soon the door closed behind Max and me. We were led down the hall and through a series of iron doors. Our personal belongings were taken from us and we were issued dark blue jump suits, the uniform of federal prisoners.

Our hosts were somewhat at a loss to know how to relate to us. "Step into that room and change, Mr. Mos—excuse me, I mean *Reverend* Mosley and Reverend Rice."

The guards were sincerely respectful. Our insistence that they didn't need to call us "Reverend" went unheeded. Max and I winked at each other and shrugged. At least we were spared the degradation of a strip search, standard procedure for the admission of new prisoners. I was officially 82571 020, and Max 82571 021.

Finally the last gate slammed behind us—how many times we were to hear that noise in the weeks ahead! We were left with the twenty other prisoners of the facility. Whatever nervousness we had brought with us soon dissipated. A few other federal prisoners were being held there—mostly white men on drug charges—but the majority were local African-Americans. We were quickly accepted as full members of the fraternity and had plenty of time to get acquainted.

In a couple of days we were familiar with the simple routine—lights on, cell doors unlocked, breakfast served, back to bed for most of the morning (except Max and me, this was our time to write letters and read the Bible), lunch, television on full blast, card games and conversation until supper, more of the same until lockdown, go to sleep.

We were reasonably happy with the arrangement, except for the constant blaring of the TV and the heavy smoking that went on all the time the other men were awake. The air was thick with smoke and the floor was covered with ashes and cigarette butts.

It seemed ironic that the worst violence we witnessed was on television—on shows like "Miami Vice," which the other men watched eagerly. They told us this was the best show for learning about new state-of-the-art weapons, silencers, and the latest crime techniques. And these same programs were being watched in living rooms all over the country!

We soon observed that there was a loose hierarchy among the prisoners. Frank, a large African-American man who had been in this jail for several months, was the undisputed holder of the top position. Fortunately, he was as good-natured as he was strong. We got along well from the first.

In fact, it was Frank who first commented on my practice of reading the Bible every day. When I told him about our experiences at Koinonia, where black and white people happily worshiped, worked, and played together, Frank was fascinated. I had some Clarence Jordan cassette tapes sent in for us. Soon he was listening to all of them on his Walkman. Every few minutes he would interrupt whatever else was happening with a loud laugh or a shout, "Man! Y'all got to listen to this, man! Whoo-hoo!" Soon there was a waiting line for the tapes.

I wrote to Carolyn,

> Every seminary student ought to be required to spend at least a few days in such a place. Great reality therapy. These men are down-to-earth, dealing with big problems, impatient with easy answers. But they are eager to talk about the Bible—at least some are. They cover the full range from college-educated to illiterate, from all over the country, some strutting and streetwise, most sad and feeling very guilty and remorseful.

I soon began to miss jogging. After a few days I decided to resume my daily exercise routine. The cells were connected by a hallway, bars along either side and a TV monitor at one end for surveillance. The hall was nineteen steps long, and forty-six round trips equaled about one mile. I started walking briskly three to five miles a day.

Max soon joined me, and after a few days Frank decided that he ought to do the same. He had only shower slippers to "jog" in, and they made a loud slapping noise as he walked.

Never one to do things quietly, Frank called constantly to the other inmates as we passed their cells, "Hey, Bo, get out here, man. You need this more'n I do. You there, Stump, get off that bed and come on out here."

Slowly Frank's recruiting efforts paid off. By the end of a week there were eight of us "jogging" up and down the hall in our underwear.

Apparently the sight of all those faces coming right at the TV camera—hundreds and then thousands of times—got to be too much for the people up front. There was an abrupt announcement over the P.A. system: "Reverend Mosley and Reverend Rice, pack your things and come out!"

One of the other inmates immediately said, "Uh huh, see there? I *told* you they wouldn't hold no preachers in here very long. You're free. Y'all goin' home!"

Then we heard a guard drop a pile of chains on the steel counter outside the cell block and knew we were not going home. We were about to be given a little "diesel therapy," as the prisoners call it—moved down the road to a different facility where we would have to start all over again learning a new system and building new relationships.

This time we got the full treatment, strip search included. After we redressed, each of us was handcuffed and shackled, with an extra chain between our handcuffs and around our waists. Finally we were placed with our faces against a concrete wall and told to stand there until called. Three men stood guard over us with shotguns. We had the impression someone was trying to tell us something. As we waited, I looked up and read a six-foot-long sign: "TREAT EVERY MAN AS THOUGH HE WERE WHAT HE OUGHT TO BE, AND HE WILL BECOME ALL HE IS CAPABLE OF BEING."

A few hours later we were checked into a state prison across the border in Florida. From there I wrote to Carolyn,

> This whole experience is a time of growth in a way that is hard to explain. Partly it's a time of prayer and Bible study and deepening of my faith. But in a very real way that same process is going on—faith deepening—while I clank along in chains with armed guards giving me orders, in a way that can't be duplicated in a "respectable" pew. I'm getting a tiny taste of what it is like to be among the outcasts (most of whom I find to be very lovable guys), carrying my own cross in a very mild way, because of my commitment to Jesus. It is a rich time, and I am genuinely grateful for it. I have felt the peace of God's presence the whole time.

Again Max and I got along well with almost all the other prisoners. Even though they weren't quite sure what to make of men who came to prison "voluntarily," most seemed to understand somewhat and respect our reasons. They kidded us about being a bad influence on them and nicknamed us "Max the Knife" and "Mad Dog Don."

We didn't try to preach to the others, but as in the first jail, we soon got into conversations about our beliefs.

After one such conversation about violence and the gospel, with several men listening silently, one suddenly said, "I just wish more people saw it the way *we* see it"—meaning himself, Max, and me.

Another said, "They'd better hurry and get me out of here. Max and Don are corrupting me."

My birthday arrived while we were in the Florida prison. The other seven men in my cell gave me a homemade birthday card. On the outside it read "YOU'RE A MAN OF QUESTIONABLE TASTE, DON"—and inside "TO SPEND YOUR BIRTHDAY IN HERE WITH US! (Happy Birthday anyway)."

Carolyn and Robyn, along with Nancy Rice and daughter Amy, made a visit around the time of my birthday. I wrote to Carolyn the next day,

> I think every one of these men is at heart a decent person who affirms good, but all people are reluctant to be open about their ideals unless someone helps to create a climate of acceptance for them. . . . Thanks for coming around to our windows and waving good-bye. As you could see, all our roommates were eager to see you—but for once there was a kind of wholesomeness about it, a sense that everybody got to share in a family visit, instead of the usual comments from sex-starved men.
>
> Max and I were very proud. "There they are, men, our wives and daughters."
>
> One man said later, "You and Max are lucky. Your marriages are going to be *stronger* because of your time in jail."
>
> Of course he was contrasting that with his situation and most of the others' here. If they have wives or girlfriends, they know they are helpless to protect that relationship, so that just adds to their punishment and remorse.

Max and I were receiving up to three dozen letters a day from well-wishers, including some from Europe, Africa, and Central America. We received more than the other 110 prisoners combined, which created a little tension—especially as the guard insisted on making a big show of it every day. He stood by our gate and called out each piece of mail as he handed it through the bars, raising his voice each time he said our names: "RICE, MOSLEY, MOSLEY, RICE, Smith, RICE, MOSLEY, Weldon, MOSLEY. . . ." Despite our repeated requests that he cut the drama, he persisted the entire time we were there.

Meanwhile, on the outside, support was coming to the community as well. Carolyn was particularly grateful for the cards and concerns from members of the Comer Baptist Church. "They went out of their way to tell me that they were thinking of us," she recalls. "I know they didn't completely understand or agree with what was going on, but they were very loving in their response to me."

Certainly not everyone understood the finer points. One neighbor said to Robbie and Chou, "You watch. If a man really stands for something, the government'll get after him every time. Take people like Ollie North and Don Mosley, for instance."

Judge Fitzpatrick eventually reduced our sentences from sixty days to forty. Just as we were congratulating ourselves, guards showed up at the bars, shouting, "Rice and Mosley, get your stuff and come with us!" Minutes later we were on our way again, this time to the minimum-security camp which is part of the Atlanta Penitentiary.

The "camp" was almost pleasant in comparison to the other jails. Several hundred prisoners accused of white-collar crimes or judged not dangerous were held there. But Max and I were soon ordered into the high-security prison next door for physical examinations. We climbed the hill to the prison with a guard and a third prisoner. The sky was overcast. Above us were the massive walls and watchtowers of the penitentiary. An officer threw a remote switch to unlock the first gate, and we stepped into a narrow roadway between high concrete walls. Heavy steel gates blocked each end and rusty railroad tracks ran through the middle.

As the first gate slammed behind us, one of the waiting guards pointed to me. "You'll do. Come over here and take off all your clothes." Slowly it dawned on me that I had been chosen from the group for a random strip search. A minute or two later I stood naked, prison uniform heaped on a chair. The guard was satisfied that I was not smuggling drugs or other contraband into the prison compound.

Then he asked gruffly, "What are you here for?"

I replied rather tentatively, "My friend and I are here because we refuse to pay our war taxes."

"Oh yeah, you doin' battle with the IRS!"

I could see he liked that. He passed the word around as I put my clothes back on.

One old man who looked more like an inmate than a guard said, "Hey, man, I know why y'all are here. Somebody wants 'Atlanta Penitentiary' on your record. You're just being set up for the next time you buck the system."

It was our moving from prison to prison that was most disconcerting for Carolyn, since there was never any warning given or disclosure ahead of time about where we were being taken. Tony, in a university a thousand miles away in Texas, was spared much of the daily ordeal, but for Robyn my jail stay was both difficult and enlightening. She says of that time,

It gave me a personal view of families that are broken up by prison. How do they support themselves, both emotionally and financially? I often say that we couldn't have done it if we didn't live in community.

We went three times when Dad was in jail. It really opened my eyes to the prison system. It was such a shocking experience to walk in the first jail and not be able to touch him, to hear him. You sit behind this soundproof glass and you talk over a phone; only one person can talk and hear at a time. The glass was all smudged from where people had kissed it. It was such a shock to know they didn't trust me enough to let me touch my father.

Then the second jail—we had driven six hours to go down to Florida. It was Dad's birthday, so I was really hoping we could see him. But they had said we probably couldn't. They let Mom sit across the table from him, but I had to stay outside. They brought him into this kind of sound chamber and opened up a speaker. We sang "Happy Birthday" to him.

The last place he was only in for a week, the minimum-security federal prison in Atlanta. We got to sit across the table from him. I got to hug him for the first time in a long time.

The publicity around my incarceration made for some interesting times for Robyn at school. Many of her classmates didn't know what to say to her about it. "I got a couple of 'I'm sorry's,' " she says. "It was almost as if he was dead or something." She remembers one incident in particular.

One guy was going into the Marines when he left school; he was ultra-military. He said, "I can't believe your father doesn't pay his taxes." Then he asked me to be sure.
I said, "Yeah, it's true."
And he said, "You're actually proud of that?!"
"Well, yeah!"
The teacher of that class was religiously very conservative. She was the adviser to one of the Christian student groups—evangelical, Republican, and really proud of it. During the Persian Gulf War, she wore a heart-and-flag pin to show her support for it.
She overheard our conversation. As I was walking out of the classroom, she stopped me and said, "Don't worry about it, Robyn. He just doesn't understand." That really touched me.

Max and I were released on March 10, just in time to celebrate Easter back at Jubilee—all the more beautiful after spending Lent in jail. I wrote in my journal:

And so the long-awaited jail sentence is now behind us. Forty days in the modern wilderness. Separated from Carolyn, Robyn, Jubilee, quiet time with a cup of coffee beside the woodstove. Sometimes separated even from any sense of peace and centeredness, with the constant television noise and shouting and clanging of steel gates. But never really separated from your love, dear God. I *knew* that even during the times when the distractions kept me from *feeling* it.

And now I am back at Jubilee, welcomed beautifully by all the community yesterday, with banners, hugs, songs, egg rolls, love. Today there is Carolyn's wonderful love, bright sunrise, piles of notes from loving friends—and a breakfast of whole-wheat pecan pancakes in a few minutes. Dear God, I don't understand why, of all people, *I* should be so blessed!

A few months later, the IRS gave up their attempt to force our cooperation by threat of prison and filed a "voluntary dismissal" of our contempt charges. But the story didn't end there.

In April 1990 Max and I were invited, along with tax resisters Randy Kehler and Betsy Corner, to be guests on the "Donahue Show." Somehow, being on TV with Phil Donahue gave us new credibility in the eyes of a lot of our neighbors. Robyn, who often felt awkward about living a lifestyle different from the other kids in school, was suddenly tinged with a bit of celebrity status.

A few neighbors were awed. One man, in whose church I had preached repeatedly and taught a Sunday school class for three years, told me, "I think I'm finally starting to understand what you've been trying to tell us!" How strange that the message comes through more clearly if one flies a thousand miles away and sends it back over television from a studio in Rockefeller Center!

In 1991 an IRS agent spent three hours, at his initiative, going over my tax records. He told me that the IRS had decided simply to "forget" two of the years for which I had refused to pay federal taxes. For the remaining year, he proceeded to find ways to excuse all but a small fraction of the taxes.

"Matter of principle," he said, "that we should contin-ue to charge you something."

When he finished, I was amazed to find that I was only being charged a few thousand dollars, probably less than 5 percent of the amount that could have been charged for taxes, penalties, interest, and court costs. Even that small amount has since been cut in half, without our having paid a cent. As the agent worked, I repeated time and again that, "as a matter of principle," I did not intend to pay any amount.

He replied, "You know, Mr. Mosley, the IRS is not like-ly to bother you any further about any of this—*if* you will just avoid promoting tax resistance by others."

These days, when I consider our refusal to pay taxes for war, I try to keep in mind the bright smile of Elda San-chez. I remember those times when I have carried her or other young victims of the weapons our taxes have bought. Then the issues become clear again.

The Cold War is officially over, but the United States continues to make weapons and to use them around the globe year after year. Our military budget is almost as large as the *combined* military budgets of all the other na-tions of the world! Most troubling is that our society is be-coming steadily more addicted to violence. As our faith in the power of love and creative peacemaking diminishes, our faith in the power of violence to solve problems keeps growing. Meanwhile the instruments of violence grow more and more expensive—affordable only if we all give our money to pay for them.

The decision to pay for war should never be casual or automatic. Just as it is a serious thing to break the law, it can also be a grave thing to comply with the law. As citi-zens, especially if we claim to follow Jesus as our Lord, we cannot afford to ignore the reality of what we are doing, whatever course we follow. I suggest that every taxpayer hold a child in his or her arms while deciding.

16

Down-Home Hospitality

As our activities caused us to be involved in an expanding range of issues and countries, our love and appreciation grew for our little hometown of Comer. Comer has just under a thousand residents. Like most other characteristics of the town, the boundary is very uncomplicated —go to the point where the railroad tracks cross Main Street and draw a circle one mile in radius. That's Comer. Anything outside the circle is the rest of the world.

Earlier this century, Comer was a bustling little town with twice as many citizens as now. On weekends it was full of wagons and Model T Fords, owned by farming families who came to town to buy supplies and to socialize. Across the street from the train station sat the Comer Hotel, full of traveling men looking to make a sale. Cotton was the mainstay of the economy, and Comer was the hub of the region's commercial activity. That all peaked out a couple of generations back.

When the younger folks take time to listen, there are still people in Comer who like to reminisce about those days. They tell about the big barbecue picnics the churches used to sponsor down by the spring at Rocky Ridge on what is now Jubilee property. The boys would slip off and swim in the pond, and the girls would spread long skirts and sit talking on the shady grass. Meanwhile the adults turned chicken on grills over the coals. Today Jubilee folks enjoy the same spot for picnics and worship services.

Norman Rockwell would have found a lifetime supply of friendly, interesting faces to paint in Comer. They are the weathered faces of hard-working farmers, of kind old grandmothers whose families have moved away to bigger towns, of postmasters and city council members and police officers who humbly serve this little community. And they are the faces of people always ready to help us welcome refugees, however formidable the language and cultural barriers.

Cliff Yarborough's patience and warmth have extended through the years. He remains a frequent visitor at Jubilee celebrations, even though he has retired as Comer's mayor. Mac Almond, principal at Comer Elementary School, and the excellent teaching staff there have always been eager to broaden the horizons of local children. They gladly welcome the few refugee children whose grasp of English enables them to attend the school. Bill Baggs, former Peace Corps volunteer and Habitat for Humanity organizer, comes faithfully every Thursday to cut firewood for us. In a variety of ways, our neighbors have extended gracious hospitality.

Jim Wilcox is one of Jubilee's favorite Comerites. A big, soft-spoken man, his open-handed generosity toward Jubilee and the refugees is demonstrated constantly. He used to be a chicken farmer but says he "finally just chickened out." Now Jim owns the Good Times Video Store in the center of town, but more important to us is his love of music. Twice a year he organizes the "Cloud's Creek Music Festival," about eight miles down the road from Jubilee. It has become a favorite part of our annual cycle of events.

When the big night comes, we load our bus and drive down Highway 22 past Georgia's two longest covered bridges, along a dirt road past Cloud's Creek Baptist Church, and finally between several of Jim's empty chicken houses. We park the bus and walk through the woods and into a delightful scene. Sloping down to the edge of a pond is a wooded hillside, covered with people scattered about on blankets or on folding picnic chairs they have brought from home. Lights hang from the pine trees, and the perimeter is lined with little stands where people sell handcrafts, hot dogs, and bluegrass music cassettes.

Down front is the stage where music groups take turns all day and well into the night, entertaining the enthusiastic audience with bluegrass, gospel singing, and other music that has its roots in local soil. There is a feeling of informality and friendliness seldom experienced in our modern society anymore.

As Will Winterfeld says, "Every year when we go to the festival, the emcee will say, 'In the group tonight are Bosnian refugees'—or whatever group we have with us—and she'll tell a little about what makes them special, and why they're here. Many local people don't come to Jubilee and don't really know what we're doing. They couldn't tell you at any given moment who's with us. So this festival has been a great tool for us to introduce each other.

"There was a Central American refugee group here with many musicians—great guitarists and tremendous voices. We took them to the festival and they really enjoyed the music. They could relate to what they would call *musica tipica*, music of the region.

"The Central Americans were invited to get up on stage and sing for everybody. Sitting in the crowd was a guy who runs a bluegrass hall in Hartwell, up the road about twenty miles. And he said, 'Could you come and sing at my music hall next week?' So they practiced through the week. They went in the bluegrass hall and they got up and did a long set, recorded by the local radio station, which right away put it on the airwaves.

"The final night, when that particular refugee group was ready to move on, all of a sudden these people from Hartwell showed up. All they wanted to do was say good-bye to the refugees. They said, 'You know, we didn't know anything about where you come from. We didn't know your stories. We didn't know that good people like you would be coming out of that situation.'

"So they made a presentation to these folks, sang some special songs as a gift. The Central Americans were really touched by that. One Salvadoran—a carver—had made a quite incredible piece out of wood, with some cloth on it, very artistic. And he presented that to them.

"So we sat around all evening. It was a great time. There was not a common language—the refugees didn't know much English, and the other people had such a different accent. But they were sitting there trying to converse with these people who had really broken into their lives. That was a great awakening."

On another memorable evening at a recent festival, we came with our bus filled to capacity with Jubilee staff and Bosnian families who had just arrived. Just a week earlier, the Bosnians had been trapped at a refugee transit center in Karlovac, Croatia, while close to a thousand rockets rained down in the vicinity. They waited, trying to shut out the wail of air raid sirens and the thunder of bombs.

When the siege finally let up, they were rushed out of Karlovac, twenty-five at a time, packed in refrigerated meat trucks. They had another long wait in a mosque in Zagreb, and finally went on to Slovenia by bus. They flew via New York and arrived exhausted at the Atlanta airport.

"I didn't even know where in the United States we were," said one of the Bosnians. "All we had heard for days was just, 'Go here' and 'Go there.' After so much trouble and rejection, some of us thought we might be arrested and taken to jail. Then I saw the Jubilee people holding the sign saying 'WELCOME' in our own language. I wondered for a moment who it was for. Slowly it dawned on me that it was for *us*—we were finally safe!"

They barely had a chance to overcome jet lag before we loaded them on the bus and took them to Jim's music festival. The scene was one I will never forget. The Bosnians quickly sensed the welcome from the local people. When the emcee explained that these families had been huddled in a war zone with mortars exploding around them just a few days earlier, the welcoming applause communicated eloquently past the language barrier.

A few minutes later, while banjos and fiddles played and a thin sliver of moon reflected on the little pond in the background, Vlasta Zhang coaxed the Bosnian children one by one to join her on a wooden platform off to one side of the main stage. Vlasta, a Baptist from Croatia who has been serving Jubilee as an interpreter, had become one of our very special volunteers.

While "Big Bird and his Split Rail Bluegrass Band" played, Vlasta led the children in improvising dances to the music. Soon the little platform was full of young dancing Bosnians, whirling and bowing, leaving the terror of war behind them for a little while. They stole the show from the music group at the mikes and brought tears to many of our eyes as we watched.

Vlasta said, "We Baptists don't usually dance, but it was so nice to help these young people relax and forget their troubles. Don't you think it was beautiful?"

We could not face the day-to-day work—and welcome such a constant stream of uprooted and suffering people—without embracing celebration as part of our community life.

We have notoriously long talent shows. They encompass everything from poetry reading to silly songs to hilarious skits making fun of everything about Jubilee's life. Even after years away at college, Tony still laughs as he describes Ed Weir's imitations of everybody in the community eating popcorn. As a community without television sets, we rely on storytelling and singing for entertainment.

Our environment also provides ample opportunities for diversion. Daily swims in our ponds help us fight the heat in summer. Down by the river are beaver ponds that occasionally freeze for winter fun. Using brooms and homemade wooden pucks, we have pulled together a Jubilee version of ice hockey. We are careful to watch out for cattails poking through the ice, and we scramble every time the ice cracks a bit. The Southeast Asians and Central Americans—who never dreamed they could "stand on water"—enjoyed it most.

Every couple of years it snows enough for us to shut down English classes. Sleds are created from cardboard, inner tubes, or sheets of metal—anything likely to slide. Makeshift as our version of sledding is, it's a thrill for refugee children from the Tropics who have never seen snow.

Volleyball is popular any time of the year, with the competition on our sandpit fiercer than some might expect to find in a Christian community. The Jubilee version has built-in grace, however, with an "Eight Rule." If your team doesn't get the ball over the net in three hits, you can do it on eight—or any multiple of eight. Games often take a long time.

A good practical joke is in order now and then, too. Tony's favorite is the time he and I cut a deer silhouette from a piece of cardboard.

As he remembers it, "In the first year or two we didn't see so many deer as we see now. We would get really excited just to find their tracks. One day Dad and I sneaked off from the others and set up a cardboard 'deer' across the meadow, so it looked like it was staring at the house where everyone was working.

"Just as we got back to the house, Rachel Weir spotted it and yelled, 'Look! There's a deer!' Soon everyone was outside, crouching and stalking slowly toward the 'deer' to see how close they could get to it. Dad and I were doing our best to control our laughter, but they figured out who had played the trick on them."

We are also hearty feasters. Will calls Jubilee a "casserole community." It's true our daily diet revolves around simple things like rice and beans, eggs from our chickens, and fresh vegetables from our large garden. But the variety of culinary cultures that pass through Jubilee makes for some fine feasting on special occasions. We eat far better than most people, and for well under $2 a day per person!

We live comfortably on somewhat less money per person than the official poverty level. But if tempted to grow smug about our success at "downward mobility," we have Blake and Sue Byler Ortman to help us put things back in perspective.

I had first heard of Blake when I was helping Jimmy Carter plan his trip to Nicaragua. He also visited San Salvador during the trip, and a friend urged me to try to arrange for him to meet Blake for a briefing while there. Blake had gone to El Salvador in 1979, established the Mennonite Central Committee program there (as well as in neighboring Honduras and Belize), and supervised several dozen volunteer workers there over the next decade. Sue was one of those volunteers. In 1986 she and Blake were married. They served until 1990 as joint supervisors of the MCC work.

Few North Americans were in a better position to know in detail what was happening in El Salvador during that tragic decade. After they returned to the United States in 1990, Blake and Sue spent most of the next year in

Washington, D.C., trying to find members of Congress who would listen to the truth about what had happened in Central America. They had little success.

"I had seen so much fear and need, so much injustice, that it just made me want to cry," said Sue. As the months passed while she and Blake searched for officials who seemed to care, she realized that a distance had developed between her and the society from which she had come. "No place felt like home anymore," she said.

One thing she and Blake longed for was the sense of community they had seen in Central America. There, especially in the rural areas, "people lived in community, not because it was the going thing, but because it was all they knew; it was the only way they could survive."

Both Sue and Blake observed community in El Salvador as closely related to the people's faith in God. "People there really trusted God and their community in ways that we in North America would almost consider absurd," Blake said.

Blake and Sue moved to Jubilee in 1991, finding links here with things they learned to value in Central America. As Blake expresses it, "Somehow the body of Christ has to be essential—as an example, not just talking about what we need to do. I look at us at Jubilee not as people who have the answers but as people who see the problems. We see clearly that things are going in the direction of individualism and materialism in the United States.

"Most of our U.S. friends," he continues, "are patting us on the back because we look so radical. But if you've been in the Third World, you know that's not true."

"There are ways in which being in the States is much harder than being in Central America—many ways. Being in Central America I felt like I was always right back with that first church in Acts. We'd read a passage, and it was happening right there around us. The story just paralleled

Acts 4 and other passages, what happened when people were arrested and imprisoned and God was with people!"

Most of the time the threats we face in North America are less dramatic than Blake and Sue encountered in El Salvador, especially if we are white. However, we have found that even in North America that can change in a hurry if we stand side by side with our black friends.

In the mid-1980s the Ku Klux Klan decided to try to recruit members in our county. Every day a few men in white robes stood handing out literature at the entrance to Madison County High School in the county seat of Danielsville, ten miles away. With the backing of the Georgia attorney general, the school principal asked the Klansmen to move off the school grounds. They moved a short distance away and continued their vigils, sometimes even climbing aboard school buses to speak to students.

Richard Haynes, pastor of the mostly African-American Springfield Baptist Church at that time, and I decided to call together a large group to attend the next meeting of the Madison County Board of Education. Two hundred people responded, mostly black parents, with a few white Jubilee faces scattered through the crowd. The response from the board members was less than we had hoped for.

We decided to call a public meeting that weekend at Springfield. I called eleven of the local white pastors and urged them to attend. Seven did, even on short notice. The church was packed, again mostly with black faces—but this time not all the white faces were from Jubilee.

To my surprise and great pleasure, every one of the white pastors went to the microphone and assured the audience they would do what they could to discourage further actions by the KKK. There was loud applause after each statement. True to their word, the pastors returned to their churches and admonished their congregations to reject the old ways of hatred and terrorism. Some even published anti-Klan statements in their church bulletins the following Sunday.

Some of the parents filed suit against the KKK. U.S. District Judge Duross Fitzpatrick, our tax-resistance judge, issued a restraining order directing the Klan to keep away from the schools. A cross was burned in response to the order, and notices began to appear around the county announcing a "KU KLUX KLAN RALLY" to be held a couple of weeks later.

"SOMETHING FOR EVERYONE," promised the posters, "BRING YOUR WHOLE FAMILY." The main attraction was to be the Imperial Wizard himself, "NATIONALLY KNOWN SPEAKER JIM BLAIR WHO IS ORGANIZING THE KLAN NATIONWIDE AND IN MANY FOREIGN COUNTRIES, INCLUDING ENGLAND." With him would be the Grand Dragon of Georgia. It promised to be quite a show with the Wizard and the Dragon both there. A pickup filled with hooded Klansmen drove back and forth through the middle of Comer to help build excitement.

One evening two women from Jubilee Partners saw a KKK notice on the window of the Bread Basket, Comer's main convenience store. The manager insisted he didn't know who had put it up.

Terry Conway answered, "Well, we'll be glad to help you take it down, then." They crumpled it up and brought it back to Jubilee.

Within an hour a car full of men cruised slowly into the middle of Jubilee. Several Jubilee people came out at once with flashlights and conspicuously wrote down the car's license number. It turned and left quickly. Three nights later the same thing happened; again the car left when people approached it.

The night of the much publicized Klan rally came. We wondered how many of our neighbors would attend. Max

Rice, who still has scars on his scalp from a beating suffered in south Georgia during the civil rights movement, couldn't help himself. He had to see how the rally was going. He and a couple of other Jubilee people drove along the highway several times past the site.

When they came home, they were laughing and full of good news. Only eight people had attended. One man was standing in the back of a pickup truck speaking to the other seven. Presumably, the Imperial Wizard and the Grand Dragon accounted for a quarter of the crowd. We were relieved the Klan had met a cool reception from our united black and white communities.

A few weeks later, someone drove past Jubilee at night, just close enough for us to hear him shout "Communists!" We smiled. We knew this was a shout from a group whose hate had been rejected by most of our neighbors.

In Comer, the churches provide the main social structure. Still reflecting the old pattern once enforced by unwritten law and now persisting mainly through habit, three churches are filled each Sunday with white worshipers and one with black worshipers—and Jubilee people. For years Jubilee folks have crossed back and forth over the invisible barriers on Sunday mornings. Slowly those barriers have begun to wear down.

The great majority of our neighbors, white and black, seem to welcome opportunities to move beyond the racist patterns of the past. We are helped in that by good leadership. Our new mayor, Dudley Hartel, continues Cliff Yarborough's tradition as a peacemaker and reconciler between all segments of Comer society.

Larry Blount, current pastor at Springfield Baptist Church (mostly African-American), says, "The best way to quiet fear—and the use of fear to separate races—is to put people together and let them know more about each other. . . . All these people are Christians; all of them have the same Lord and Savior. Their liturgy and their style of worship vary, but they all claim the same Word of God as the final authority. We have much, much more in common than we have differences."

Tom Dunn, pastor of the (white) Comer Baptist Church, agrees and adds, "On a personal level, a trust level, a friendship level, the Jubilee folks are very accepted in the community, even appreciated. They've moderated some community views. They've helped the white community and the black community speak to each other."

In the spring of 1994, we sent Will to South Africa to serve as an official monitor of the historic elections there. He was a natural choice for the job. He had worked from 1977 to 1980 in Swaziland, a little nation almost completely surrounded by the larger country of South Africa. With his big Teddy bear smile, his ready supply of songs and stories, and his love for the African people, he was a good person to help calm the waters during this tense time.

On the Sunday before his departure he stood before the congregation at Springfield Baptist Church and explained why he was going. "The South African Council of Churches has invited more than three hundred people from around the world to come as election observers. Our job is mostly to encourage fairness and to discourage violence during this transition from apartheid to real democracy.

"But I'm going for another reason as well. I want to go as a listener, as a learner. In the United States we have come a long way, but we all know there is still a lot of ugly racism here. I want to learn from the South Africans, especially from the Christian leaders there—black and white—who have led their people to this great moment.

"So I ask for your prayers not only that this will be a nonviolent election, but also that I will come home better prepared to work for harmony among our own people in this country."

The folks in the Springfield congregation shouted their approval and burst into spontaneous applause. For the next two months, we passed along Will's reports on Sunday mornings to a chorus of "Amen," "Praise the Lord," and "Thank you, Jesus." He was very much an emissary of Springfield as well as of Jubilee.

In South Africa Will and his co-workers rushed from one public event to another. They attended political rallies, church services, youth meetings, even a large birthday party, lending a conspicuous international presence to encourage peaceful behavior.

"We South Africans are like other people," said one government official. "We behave better when outside people are watching."

Finally, the great day came. Will and the other observers were recruited to help in the voting process itself. It was a formidable challenge. The great majority of the voters had never been permitted to cast a ballot before in their lives—not even Nelson Mandela, the candidate poised to win the election by a landslide.

Many of the people Will assisted were unable to read the ballot. One such elderly lady smiled and told him, "Just mark the Man for me."

Trying to follow the rules and maintain strict neutrality, Will pressed her a bit, "Which man do you mean?"

"Oh, you know," she insisted. "*The* Man."

Finally, she pointed shyly to Mandela's picture on the ballot. Will marked it accordingly. She gathered herself with dignity and moved away, proud finally to have taken part in the democratic processes of her own country.

When Will returned, his stories bound us all closer not only to the people of South Africa, but also, more important to each other right here in Comer. Apartheid took a hit on both sides of the Atlantic.

17

Not Your Usual
Small–Town Fare

From the beginning we at Jubilee have tried to cultivate genuine friendships with all our neighbors. We have found them usually eager to reciprocate. No doubt it helps that we have been involved in a wide variety of civic activities. We have built school floats, joined in construction projects at the churches, helped build a basketball court in the city park, served on local committees, participated actively in drug-awareness activities, and erected large "Welcome to Comer" signs at the edges of the town.

But we have also gotten involved in some out-of-the-ordinary activities—not your usual small-town fare. The railroad tracks that run through the exact center of Comer are only a few hundred yards from Jubilee's property. They are part of a major shipping route, with about two dozen trains a day passing along them. Many of those trains are loaded with military shipments, including ammunition and missile components. The tracks became a link for us with hundreds of people all across the South, from Memphis, Tennessee, to Charleston, South Carolina.

Jim Douglass, writer and activist, has an extraordinary commitment to the application of Jesus' teachings on nonviolence to the problems of our time. His writings began to challenge me even before Carolyn and I moved to Koinonia. We met soon after that move, and my friendship with him and his wife, Shelley, has been a source of strength and inspiration ever since.

Jim called me one day from his home near Seattle and said, "There is a train loaded with up to 180 nuclear warheads. It is apparently ready to leave the nuclear weapons assembly plant near Amarillo, Texas, on its way to Charleston, South Carolina. We have good reason to believe it may pass right through Comer. Would you be willing to help us track the train and organize peaceful protests along its way?"

Jim knew what the answer would be before he asked. Of course I needed to check with the rest of the Jubilee community, but I also knew what their answer would be. In an hour we had begun setting up a room with multiple telephones, railroad maps on the walls, and directories of telephone numbers for the news media and our network of friends throughout the South.

Our readiness to do this work grew first out of our deep conviction as Christians that the arms race is one of the most dramatic demonstrations of collective fear. The arms buildup represents national inclinations to destroy enemies rather than work seriously and creatively to make peace with them.

In addition, we were convinced that the secrecy surrounding the weapons shipments was intended primarily to keep the U.S. public in the dark about what was happening and and therefore unable to question it. There was never any doubt about whether the Soviet Union knew about the shipments. The warheads were shipped regularly from Pantex, the United States' single final assembly plant, on a long train of unique design, pulled by Burlington Northern locomotives. Every car was white. Up to fifteen special freight cars made up each train. It presented a spectacle that could be followed with ease from a Soviet satellite.

Special security cars were spaced along the length of the train, each mounted with a turret and manned by Department of Energy "couriers." According to the DOE, these guards were armed with machine guns, rifles, and hand grenades. They had orders to shoot anyone who threatened the train.

They had good reason to be careful. The most likely cargo during most of the runs we monitored were warheads for the missiles aboard the huge Trident submarines. The combined explosive power of the warheads carried each trip was estimated at between five hundred and one thousand times greater than that of the bomb that destroyed Hiroshima, Japan, in 1945.

The train was conspicuous to spy satellites. Yet few U.S. citizens were even vaguely aware that it was hauling such awesome weapons right through their towns. We resented that fact and quickly found that the majority of people along the route shared our feelings. For some, the uneasiness was little more than a preference that the weapons be transported through someone else's backyard. But many sensed the larger issue as well. They saw that there was something pernicious about such a world-threatening reality being carried on in the name of citizens themselves kept ignorant of it.

The response was often similar to that of a man in Montezuma, Georgia: "Man, somebody ought to report this damn thing to the *police!*" Sometimes local law-enforcement people themselves thanked us for telling them what was going on. They expressed frustration that they had been kept in the dark by federal officials.

We worked around the clock for almost four days as the train progressed eastward. We made hundreds of calls to newspapers, radio and television stations, religious leaders and peace organizations. The train began to encounter larger and larger crowds of protesters along its route. They prayed, sang, held banners aloft in the daytime and candles at night. After each sighting, designated persons called us with a report and exact information about time, speed, and direction of travel.

Despite our best efforts, the train made an unexpected turn in northeastern Mississippi, and we lost it. For almost twenty hours we had people looking for it across several states. Finally, with the help of a helicopter from an Atlanta television station, we were able to pick it up again in southern Georgia. The word went out again. Vigilers met it as it continued.

A group of people from Jubilee decided to rush down to Savannah to join the protesters there. John David and Barbara Borgman took their three children with them, the youngest just a year-and-a-half old. Years later the memory of that night is still vivid. John David recalls their encounter with the train.

"It was dark. And all of a sudden, I spotted the train way in the distance. We sped up to get to what we thought was the next intersection, not knowing whether it was *the* train.

"We got the banners ready. The main banner I remember was a big 'Choose Life' one. We got kind of excited. We parked the van and got out.

"As soon as the 'couriers' saw that we were there, floodlights came on. We were engulfed in light. Everything was white—eerie white. The whiteness, and the ghostliness, of this train was awesome.

"Right in the center was a turret car. They actually had machine guns. It was a self-contained arsenal. They didn't want any other protection along the way; they were able to do anything they wanted. If anything happened, they were prepared. So there was some fear—wondering what they were thinking about us. We got as close as we felt we could without feeling we were interfering with the train or doing damage.

"Our protest was, in many ways, insignificant. Somebody in that turret might have seen the sign—they obviously had everything spotted on us. But you realize how helpless we really were. We were not going to stop this train. It was just like a small voice saying something. The presence of our family as a family was, I think, at least a symbol of solidarity against something we had come to know as awesome power."

Aran Borgman, who was ten at the time, simply stuck her tongue out at the train. Barbara said the train had "another world" feel about it. She feels it was important that people stood defiantly against the secret shipping of nuclear weapons. They said by their presence, "We see you, and we know what you are doing. You can't do this in secret."

Many other people obviously felt the same way. By the time the next White Train run was about to start, we were receiving calls from all over the country about it. Television crews came from national networks, and as well as the BBC (British Broadcasting Corporation) checked with us repeatedly from London to update their reports.

The White Train made three more runs to the East Coast. We set up a computer program to help predict its progress more accurately and sent out a team each time to meet the eastbound train as it crossed the Mississippi River at Memphis. Our van followed it around the clock from intersection to intersection through the South, calling in the information to the Jubilee office. From there the word went out to organizers, and the crowds continued to grow.

As the occupants of the train became familiar with the sight of the Jubilee van, we could sense a relaxing of tension. Once in a while we actually got a friendly wave from someone through the narrow windows of the turret cars.

But someone in Washington was not pleased by the attention being paid to the train. Our Jubilee telephone bill arrived with a gap in the record for exactly those four days we had been calling people about the train. Our repeated inquiries to the telephone company brought the response that some of the records had been "temporarily misplaced." Finally a telephone official in Atlanta answered my persistent questions with, "I'm sorry, but we are not free to talk about that at this time." That portion of the bill came a month later.

There were many humorous moments as well. On one cold evening in a small Alabama town, our chase car lost sight of the train. The driver turned quickly into a driveway between two small frame houses. Jubilee volunteer Cadmon Whitty jumped out of the car and ran barefoot to the tracks that passed along the edge of the backyards. As he did so, a large African-American woman came out her back door to see what was going on. The driver quickly apologized and explained, "A train is about to come past here carrying nearly two hundred powerful nuclear bombs!"

"Well, I don't know nothing about that," the woman answered, "but I *do* know that if that boy there don't get some shoes on his feet, he's gonna catch cold for sure!"

The Department of Energy made a feeble try to disguise the train by painting the sides of the cars bright colors. But by then there were thousands of people along the tracks who could recognize the train whatever color it might have been. The train was retired from service.

The crowning irony came after the breakup of the Soviet Union a year or two later. I spotted a small story in the *New York Times* and called Jim Douglass immediately with the news. The U.S. government had just donated the train to the Russians to help them transport their weapons—presumably to collect them for dismantling. Jim and I had a good laugh about it—it was almost as if an old friend had emigrated to another country.

Despite the national attention that our efforts helped bring to the White Train, we had little feedback from local people about our part in it. For most locals, as for most people throughout the country, the arms race seemed too complex and overwhelming an issue to deal with. Therefore Jubilee's role was quietly ignored by the majority of our neighbors.

This was not the case, however, with our involvement in another controversial issue—the death penalty. That is a subject on which most of our neighbors have an opinion. And few agree with those of us at Jubilee.

The resident partners of Jubilee strongly affirm the sacredness of all human life. We believe life should be celebrated and protected wherever possible from the moment of conception. Thus it bothers us to see some of our Christian friends be so opposed (as we are) to abortion—yet show a general lack of concern about saving children from hunger and disease around the world, a readiness to kill other people in large numbers if they are of a different nation, and often an outright eagerness to execute criminals.

All the other nations we in the United States most respect abolished the death penalty long ago. There is abundant evidence that it more often serves to create a climate in which killing is acceptable than that it deters killing. In the South especially, it is overwhelmingly applied to the poor and to members of minority races.

But even if there were not all these reasons to abolish capital punishment, we are convinced it is a practice absolutely contrary to the spirit and teachings of Jesus Christ. Our opposition to the execution of criminals never in any way indicates that we excuse whatever they may have done to others. Rather, we reject the temptation of the "quick solution" or of revenge against someone who has committed a crime. Jesus taught that we should *always* work to reclaim such a person. Some people must be kept behind bars, for their own safety or for the safety of others. Yet our treatment of them must remain compassionate.

In December of 1983, John Eldon Smith became the first person executed by the state of Georgia in seventeen years. Rev. Murphy Davis, a friend of ours from the Open Door Community in Atlanta, which serves homeless people and prisoners, had been visiting Smith regularly. She told him that Jubilee had a small cemetery in which he could be buried if he chose. He sent word that he would indeed prefer that over having his body buried in the prison cemetery. The execution was highly publicized, and when word got out that Smith had been buried at Jubilee, we received several angry telephone calls and letters.

Other prisoners on death row heard about Smith's burial and asked whether we would be willing to bury them at Jubilee, too. Today the original grave of Cuban refugee Jesús Torres has been joined by a dozen more, including several men who died in poverty in Atlanta.

Josie Winterfeld expresses well the strong feeling we have each time we disregard the public disapproval and bury another person.

"What an honor it is to dig the grave of someone. I've heard before that there are other cultures in which the digging of the grave is for the very closest family and friends. It's like the last act of love that you do for this loved one. And that makes so much sense to me."

She describes the burial of Joe Mulligan, who was also executed by the state of Georgia.

"It was an incredibly powerful experience. Joe Mulligan was an African-American man. His family wasn't able to bury him in his hometown; the minister refused because the crime had taken place there. He had a large family. They didn't really know us, or what they were coming to for the burial.

"The family came dressed in their finest. We were dressed in our good clothes, too, but it wasn't quite the same. It was just written all over their faces—what kind of strange place is this, this place where we've come to bury our loved one? You could have cut the air with a knife, it was so thick. I just felt so terrible for them—how awkward this was for them. They didn't know what to say. I felt we had nothing in common.

"Then we started along the way, walking down the road, carrying Joe's body. His lawyers were here, and also people from the Open Door Community and his family. The Central Americans who were here joined us. There were people from all different kinds of places who didn't know each other.

"As we walked, someone would tap you on the shoulder and say, 'Let me take the load now.' We shared the load of carrying his body down to the gravesite. It was like something physically happened as we did that. You could feel it.

"As we stood around his grave and shared, somebody from every one of those groups talked about what had happened as we walked down the road and shared that load. We had become a community. We recognized that we were brothers and sisters.

"We didn't talk to the Central Americans very much about what was happening, who this man was, what the circumstances were. Yet at the funeral they commented, 'The power that killed this man made us flee our homes; the power that killed this man killed our relatives, too.'

"And there were the African-Americans, who probably didn't know very much about Central America, who were nodding their heads, and saying, 'Yes.' And hugs all around to the Central Americans. That was a very, very powerful experience."

Robbie adds, "When we'd have a burial here after the state of Georgia executed somebody, the Central Americans would help us dig the grave. They insisted on doing that. They did so almost religiously. For them it *was* a religious experience, because most of them had not been able to do that for their loved ones who were killed in Central America. To be able to dig a grave for somebody who had been executed in this country was a closure to an emotional process that they had never been able to have.

"Our ground here at Jubilee is rocky; it's full of stones you have to break out with a pickax. It takes a long time to dig a grave here in this rough Georgia soil. You get down so far, and there's only room for one or two people in the hole with a pickax, because you really have to swing with all your might.

"I'd be down there sweating and chopping awhile, and then I'd hand it over to one of the Central Americans. He'd be down there making the sparks fly off the rocks we were trying to break. With each stroke, he'd say, *'Este es para mi madre. . . .'* ['This is for my mother']. He'd name a litany of people who had died or been executed in El Salvador. Here were people who knew what it was to be executed by the state. And they were digging these graves for somebody else being executed by the state.

"There was real power there. Because there was a real sense, a very clear sense, of the presence of God at those burials, with all of these people rejected in one way or another—all of these people whom most of the rest of society had no use for. But that's where God was. God was there at those burials in a way I don't know I've ever experienced any other place.

"It's the old story the Bible tells. God is for the poor. God is there with the ones who the rest of the world thinks don't have any business being alive. I can't categorize it. Powerful, yes. Moving, yes. Religious experience, yes. I can't even find words to describe what all was there, but I know God was there."

Whatever differences we and our neighbors may have, we all love to gather "downtown" for the annual Christmas celebration. One year, 1989, especially stands out for me as a time when the warmth of Christmas in our little town helped to soothe the pain of the refugees.

Cristina had arrived at Jubilee in November with her two children, eleven-year-old Juan and ten-year-old Veronica. All three were gifted with radiant smiles, but it soon became clear they had been through tragic suffering not long before. Like many other families in El Salvador, Cristina's was divided by the war. Her half-brother had participated in the killing of two of her uncles.

Cristina carried the heavy responsibility of caring for the children with relatively little help from her husband. He was involved in the political struggle in ways he would not explain to her.

When questioned about why he seemed so troubled at times, he only answered, "You have enough problems with the children. These are my problems. I don't want to bother you with them."

But then he would tell her, "If something happens to me, take the children and go to Canada. I have friends who have gone there for safety, and they say it is a good place."

On May 1 of that year, the city of San Salvador erupted in strikes, demonstrations, and tense confrontations. Cristina's husband set out for work on his motorcycle as usual but never reached his office. His boss called several hours later. He suspected he had met with foul play and wanted to warn Cristina to be careful. His motorcycle was found the next day in a park about a mile from their home. There was no indication of violence, so for weeks Cristina clung to hope her husband was alive and would contact her somehow.

Her husband's boss, who clearly knew more than Cristina about her husband's political actions, kept calling and urging her to leave El Salvador with the children. In July she tried to do so, but in central Mexico they were arrested and deported. She knew they were now in even greater danger because they had tried to escape, so she went into hiding with a friend. Always she kept asking trusted neighbors around their family home to keep watch for her husband and to pass word to him if they saw him about how to reestablish contact with her.

She was able to get a letter from a church official saying she was in great danger and appealing to others to help her along the way. With the letter she went north again, traveling from church to church across Mexico. Weeks later she waded the Rio Grande with her children and was taken in by the sympathetic priest of a church in the Valley. Then she was hosted by Refugio del Rio Grande, a shelter Jubilee had helped to establish near Brownsville with a gift from friends at Koinonia.

In September Cristina called her husband's boss in San Salvador to ask whether there was any news of her husband. There was. Three days earlier he had been gunned down in front of their house when he had come back looking for his family.

After a week of grieving, Cristina decided it was time to act on her husband's advice. She tried to continue toward Canada. But she was caught immediately by the Border Patrol. Fortunately her plight came to the attention of one of Jubilee's representatives. The INS agreed to release her and the children into the Año de Jubileo program.

Shortly after Cristina and her children arrived at Jubilee, the time came for the annual Comer Christmas party. One of the joys of living in a little town is turning out for such events with our refugees, who are always warmly welcomed by the Comer people.

Everyone gathers in the parking lot next to City Hall and in front of Jim Wilcox's video store. Mary Strickland and Latrelle Ethridge from the Comer United Methodist Church preside at the huge vat of hot chocolate, while Amy Yarborough from Comer First Baptist supervises the great pile of homemade chocolate-chip cookies. Jere Ayers wanders silently through the bustling crowd, soaking up scenes that everyone will read about on the front page of next Wednesday's *Comer News*, the "oldest established enterprise in Comer still operating from its original location."

There is a traditional crescendo to the main event. After sufficient time for hot chocolate, cookies, and visiting, a public-address system sputters on and off several times. Then the announcement is made that we should all gather over by the island in the middle of Main Street. By now it's nearly dark. People are starting to get chilled. But soon they are singing along with the choir from Kingsway Bible Church—"Joy to the World," "Silent Night," and "We Three Kings of Orient Are."

It matters little that the extension cord to the amplifier keeps getting kicked loose. We alternate between the booming voice of the leader at the microphone and the crowd sounding by comparison like our voices are coming from down at the back of the pasture. The quality of the music is not as important as the fact that we are all here to keep an old tradition alive, aware that the crowd shrinks a little each Christmas as old folks die and young folks move to larger cities.

As we sing the old carols, I catch the eye of Springfield Baptist's head deacon, Frank Hall. We wink at each other. Both of us are proudly aware of the significant sprinkling of black faces among the white ones.

I look at the Kingsway choir and remember the previous year, when we had a problem getting all of our Central American refugees onto the bus and downtown to the Christmas party. We came straggling in twenty minutes after things had begun and were chagrined to learn that the Kingsway choir had just finished singing several songs in Spanish, to make our refugees feel welcome. The biggest bilingual effort in Comer's history, and we had missed it!

Finally, after the singing and a short sermon by one of the pastors about the meaning of Christmas, the big event always comes. Cliff Yarborough plugs in the lights, and the city's Christmas tree begins its annual Advent season reign over the corner of Main Street and Highway 72. More often than not, there are temporary problems with the circuit breaker or something, but in the end the tree is always beautiful.

This particular Christmas the weather had turned so cold there was some talk of canceling the event. In the end, though, tradition triumphed. A hardy crowd of about two hundred people turned out.

I led Juan and Veronica over to get some hot chocolate. I was suddenly aware of how much their lives had collapsed around them in recent months. This was their first Christmas without a father.

The high school band tried to play some carols, but the mouthpieces on their instruments were so cold the kids were having problems. The band director called it off after a couple of squeaky songs. However, Steve Sorrells, the city clerk, bravely took up his guitar and went to the microphone.

As Steve ignored the cold breeze and sang verse after verse of "Long Time Ago in Bethlehem," I realized that little Veronica had started to shiver violently. I tucked her inside my overcoat and held her tight. She was just tall enough to peek out through the lapel and was determined not to miss a thing.

As Steve sang and Cliff prepared to plug in the tree lights, I was swept by a profound sense of what a special moment this was and how incredibly blessed we were at Jubilee Partners to be at the point of convergence of all these different people. What a privilege it was to be among such beautiful but diverse children of God!

I held Veronica more tightly, trying to fill in for her missing daddy at Christmastime. As she responded by snuggling in closer, my eyes filled with tears I couldn't reach up to and wipe away. No matter. They were tears of real joy; I was not ashamed of them.

18

Against the Current— to Baghdad

It was March 1991. Our Jubilee van was on the way to the Atlanta airport to meet a brave wife and her children, the first of four we managed to reunite with their husbands in Canada.

We had been working on this family's behalf for almost a year. They were nearing the end of a long and dangerous journey—most of it "underground." It was an exciting moment for all of us. But it was one I would miss. Two hours before their arrival, I was on another plane, headed for Baghdad.

The previous August, Iraqi troops had invaded Kuwait. A month later, I was running with Jimmy and Rosalynn Carter past the peanut fields west of their home in Plains. We talked about many things as we ran, but the discussion kept returning to the volatile situation around the Persian Gulf.

Jimmy understood well the potential of the conflict to lead to a major war. In his Sunday school lesson the next morning, he emphasized how important it would be in the months ahead for the United States to avoid words and actions that might further polarize the situation and make war more likely. Along with many other people in the United States, we at Jubilee watched each step of the escalation toward the Gulf War with a stubborn refusal to believe it would really happen.

Openly breaking with the Bush administration's policy, Carter was doing his best to sway public opinion away from war. President Bush had firmly refused to support an international peace conference as an enticement for Iraq to leave Kuwait. He refused to recognize any linkage between the two issues. Carter insisted this was a mistake. As the architect of the Camp David Accords, the only lasting Middle East peace agreement, he argued that reasonable concessions on all sides would be "insignificant" compared to the devastation of war.

Carter contended that Soviet leader Mikhail Gorbachev and other key foreign leaders were being pushed to approve military action against Iraq before they were satisfied that alternatives had been sufficiently explored. He encouraged these leaders to withhold their support for military action until nonmilitary options had been given a chance.

In December 1990 a group of eighteen U.S. church leaders went to the Middle East on a mission of peace. Called together by Jim Wallis, editor of *Sojourners* magazine, Episcopal Presiding Bishop Edmond Browning, and National Council of Churches General Secretary-elect Joan Brown Campbell, the delegation represented the highest level of U.S. church leadership ever assembled in such a peace effort.

When the religious leaders returned, they issued a joint statement. They declared, "Our Christmas pilgrimage to the Middle East has utterly convinced us that war is not the answer. We believe the resort to massive violence to resolve the Gulf crisis would be politically and morally indefensible."

At the end of an impassioned argument for "serious and substantive negotiations," they concluded, "At this moment, the resolution of the Gulf crisis will take a miracle. But in this season we are reminded that the Middle East is the cradle of miracles. That miracle must be acted and prayed into being."

I had served as contact person between the church leaders and the Carter Center. I kept telling myself that, with all these good people working so hard, surely the war would be averted—especially with the great majority of the U.S. public and Congress strongly opposing it. I was terribly wrong.

I did not yet realize what great power the White House and the Pentagon had to manipulate public opinion. We were about to see a dramatic demonstration of that power.

The bombing started on January 16. Overnight, public doubts about the wisdom of intervention gave way to strong support. We felt as though we at Jubilee, living without television, were the only people in the country not watching the stream of images being beamed back from the battlefield. Wherever we went, we heard people describing what they had seen the evening before, usually in tones of awe. "Man, did you see the way they can lock onto a target with those laser beams and sock a missile right exactly on it? You can see the missile going down the beam! I watched that over and over last night."

I wanted to shout, as one protester's sign in Los Angeles put it, "TURN OFF YOUR TV AND THINK FOR YOURSELF."

The Pentagon had control over which images and information were available to the U.S. public. It established a limited pool of reporters escorted by the military rather than permitted to travel and report freely. Often General Norman Schwarzkopf, commander of the Allied forces, would preside in person at the press conferences. A few days after the bombing started, I was listening to the radio when one of these "kept" reporters was brash enough to ask General Schwarzkopf or one of his aides, "Can you give us an estimate of how many Iraqi civilian casualties there have been?"

The instant response was, "We're not going to get into body bag counting in this conflict. Next question." When I heard that exchange, I felt a stab of pain and anger. Something fundamental to our system of democracy was being destroyed right before us. Once again—as when I heard of trainloads of nuclear warheads being transported through the country—I felt a strong urge to resist. But it was not yet clear what could be done.

Jubilee Partners hosted a two-day meeting of people searching for a constructive way to respond to the war fever sweeping the country. We all agreed we were feeling weak and ineffective as peacemakers. Jim Douglass reminded us that, at just such times, we should be most ready to turn to God in prayer. He decided to go to Washington to fast outside the Capitol building. Several of us in the room decided to join him.

A few days later, on Ash Wednesday, February 13, Nancy Rice and I represented Jubilee in a circle of twenty-two people on the east lawn of the Capitol. We all felt frail and small before the magnitude of all that was going on. Our hope came from confidence that God was ultimately greater than all the forces at work. As we prayed together I kept asking, "Lord, please show me some compassionate way to respond to this tragedy."

I had parked our Jubilee car down the street from the Capitol. Every hour or so I had to slip away from the prayer group to put more change in the parking meter. Once, as I did so, I realized it was exactly five o'clock. I slipped into the car to listen to the news headlines. I turned on the radio.

"My wife! Oh, my wife! She was such a good woman who hurt no one. . . ." The anguish in the man's voice cut through me. I stayed to find out what had happened.

The reporters began to give the terrible details of the destruction of the Ameriya shelter in Baghdad. "Struck during the early morning hours by one or more missiles . . . probably hundreds killed . . . claims by the Iraqis that it was filled with women and children . . . too hot to begin rescue attempts."

Then there was a repeat of the interview with the weeping man whose family was still inside the destroyed shelter. For the first time since the bombing sorties began, I also wept, grieving with this man who had lost the wife and children he loved.

Then my sadness mixed with anger as I listened to the immediate response from the White House. Press Secretary Marlin Fitzwater declared, "We don't know why there were civilians in that shelter. But we do know Saddam Hussein does not share our belief in the sanctity of human life." Not a trace of shame, no hint of confession that we had made a great mistake—only self-righteous boasting about our own high principles.

I knew of nothing to make me admire Saddam Hussein. But I knew it was wrong to censor the news, dehumanize the enemy, then justify whatever we did to them by such statements. As Jim Wallis insisted, "The evil of Saddam Hussein does not make us good. Nor does everything we do in the name of fighting him become morally acceptable."

A week later I agreed to lead a delegation to Baghdad as the representative of the Fellowship of Reconciliation. I felt I needed to meet face-to-face with the victims of our bombs. I wanted to reaffirm their humanity and ours. And, still angry that the Pentagon was being allowed to manipulate news of the war, I wanted to challenge its censorship and bring back firsthand reports about what was happening to the Iraqi people. Our delegation of five included writers and a professional photographer for that purpose. I also agreed to take several tons of medicine to the Iraqis and the Jordanians, as other FOR delegations had done during the previous months.

At Jubilee we got a wild idea. We wondered what would happen if we invited all the people on our mailing list to send a letter of apology to the people of Iraq. We weren't sure. The war was still raging. We knew some people would probably ask to be taken off our mailing list. But we hoped to get some positive responses in the few days remaining before my departure.

Two days later we sent out 9,500 letters by first-class mail, apologizing that some would likely not even reach the addressees before our deadline for a response. Each included a form letter in English and Arabic that began, "Dear Friend in Iraq—For just a few moments I would like to forget the political differences of our two countries and communicate with you simply as one person to another." It went on to assure the recipient that there were millions of people in the United States saddened by the suffering of the Iraqis being killed and injured by our weapons.

"It is tragic that the people of your nation and the whole Arab world have experienced Christianity so often in history as a source of violence rather than as a source of love and understanding," the letter continued. "In that way we have gone absolutely against the teachings of Jesus. He was a man of great compassion who taught his followers to love all people. It may be that you, whether Christian or Muslim or of whatever religion, can help us learn to be more true to our own faith."

The letter closed by expressing our hope that we could at least reduce the chances of our children fighting against each other in the future. "I ask you to forgive, and I prom-

ise to work in my own country to promote greater understanding and compassion toward your people."

The response far surpassed even our most optimistic
expectations. Not just hundreds but thousands of letters
poured in, so many it took a dozen people every day to
open all of them and prepare them for delivery to Iraq.
Hundreds were sent to us by Federal Express or UPS, including one package of three hundred from our sanctuary
movement friends in Tucson. They told us that if they had
been given another week, they "would have had half of
Tucson sending letters!" More than four hundred came
through our new fax machine, tumbling onto a big pile on
the office floor.

Positive responses to our mailing had outnumbered
the negative almost five hundred to one. When the day
came for me to leave, I was carrying 8,200 letters to the
Iraqi people. Nothing we had seen at Jubilee had demonstrated so clearly the yearning of most for peace and reconciliation.

The one hundred-hour ground war had taken place
while we opened the letters and prepared for the trip. Iraq
now lay smoldering. Our little delegation flew to Amman,
Jordan, where we managed after some days to get special
permission to enter Iraq. This in itself was a miracle, because all other foreign reporters were being refused entrance. The doors remained closed to them until we came
out almost a week later.

We traveled as guests of the Jordanian Red Crescent.
Our van followed a modern highway along the ancient
caravan route across the desert, passing oases that have
hosted travelers since the time of Abraham. Hour after
hour we passed the wreckage of war. We saw bomb craters, shells of destroyed power stations, ruined relay tow-
ers, and the blackened remains of buses and trucks. Our
two Jordanian drivers, Ali al-Hadi and Mohammad al-

Bodawi, reached back and tapped me on the knee from time to time to be sure I saw it all. I nodded, took pictures, and jotted notes.

I soon noticed that Ali, especially, was a warmhearted man who obviously suffered with the people we saw along the highway. They would hold up empty gas cans or beg for rides. Ali would apologize eloquently to them by hand and shoulder motions as he drove past. A hundred miles west of Baghdad we began to see hungry children running desperately out on to the highway, waving their arms and begging for food. Ali seemed almost in tears, carefully steering the van to miss them, rocking upturned hands in helpless sympathy, and sighing deeply again and again. "You see this!" he exclaimed. "This part of the war your President Bush never hears about."

When we finally reached the Euphrates River, we discovered that the bridge ahead had been bombed. Its shattered remains were suspended high above the water like a hammock, a section in the middle hanging from bent reinforcing rods that could give way at any moment. As we reached the highest point above the river, our driver glanced back at us, shifted into low gear, and went over the edge onto the suspended section of the bridge, scraping bottom loudly as we tilted forward. Down, across, and back up. And we were on solid concrete again. In unison, we all took a deep breath.

A little while later we entered Baghdad. In contrast to the little encampments of Bedouins with their goats and camels we had seen in the desert, Baghdad is a large, modern city. Wide boulevards are lined with homes and apartment complexes like those found in any major U.S. city. With few exceptions, those buildings seemed totally unaffected by the bombing that had pounded the city for most of the previous two months.

Not so with the taller public buildings. They had been

the chief targets of the cruise missiles and laser-guided bombs. They were now towering piles of twisted steel, sitting in the middle of neighborhoods littered with the debris blasted from them. Most bridges across the wide Tigris River were either destroyed or seriously damaged.

For the next several days, we were taken around Baghdad by our Red Crescent hosts, usually with one or more Iraqis joining us. It soon became clear that the Iraqi people were afraid to criticize Saddam Hussein's government openly, although a few did so to us privately. We were not given freedom to move around the city as we would have liked, although individuals from our group did manage to break away and make brief tours alone. Despite my repeated requests, we were never given a map of the city.

I had been in scores of countries around the world, including several at war, but I had never before felt such a strong atmosphere of fear and intimidation as I did among the Iraqis on this trip. But we were representatives of the powerful nation that only a few days earlier had been raining thousands of tons of bombs down upon this city. Not only had our forces defeated the Iraqis, but our leaders persisted in hurling insults at them daily, even while we were there.

If the situation were reversed, how receptive might we in the United States have been to a group of Iraqis touring our battered capital, notebooks in hand and cameras clicking? Under the circumstances, the people were gracious and trusting.

We visited Iraq's largest children's hospital. The director, Dr. Q. M. Ismail, told us that his little patients were among the first fatalities of the war. The evening of the initial bombing raids, there was a general panic among the mothers. They rushed about pulling IV needles from their babies' arms, taking them from incubators, and rushing to the basement to escape the bombs. While bombs thundered here and there in the city, about fifty babies died, even though the hospital was never directly hit.

"And now our patients continue to be the hardest hit, even though the actual fighting has been concluded," Dr. Ismail said sadly. "This is the central hospital for children in the whole country. But we have almost no milk for them; the milk factory was bombed as a 'military target.' Our generator does not produce enough electricity. The surgical ward is able to function at about half capacity. And worst of all, we do not have nearly enough medicine."

Before leaving the children's hospital, we saw those who were enduring the worst suffering of all, the children in the burn ward. Most had been burned or scalded by the makeshift lights and stoves their parents had rigged to compensate for lost electricity and fuel.

I saw Ali break away from the group and go outside. A few minutes later I went to find him. He was leaning against the van with a look of helpless anger on his face, tears in his eyes. "I cannot look on such suffering in little children," he said. "They did nothing to deserve this!"

I stood with him for a few minutes, feeling close to this Jordanian Muslim brother and sharing his grief. "Ali," I finally said, "I can only promise you that I will tell as many people as possible about it back in the United States."

We visited the Athamiya neighborhood, a densely populated section of Baghdad along the edge of the Tigris River. Soon we were in the middle of a crowd of local people, who were being led over the rubble where two bombs had been dropped on the evening of February 24. The people said they had heard a plane but never saw it. "I was knocked off my feet by a powerful blast, stood up, and was knocked down again by a second blast," said one man as four or five others nodded in agreement. "We all ran away in confusion."

All that night and the next day they had worked to rescue their neighbors and friends. Forty were dead and many more injured. Nine houses were completely destroyed. "I will never forget the burned face of my friend who died right here where we are standing," said one man. Minutes later this same man invited me graciously into his home, introduced me to his family, and urged me to join them for a meal. Outside, the others were already waiting in the van to go to the next site. I reluctantly declined the invitation and joined them, bewildered by such unexpected generosity.

The hardest part of the trip was just ahead. We headed to the Yarmuk Hospital in western Baghdad, where we were greeted by Dr. Paul Boghossian, director of the surgical unit. Educated in Baghdad, England, and Walter Reed Hospital in the United States, he was an articulate and impassioned speaker. He knew more than most U.S. citizens about key people in our government and how they reach decisions.

Boghossian had directed the removal of the charred bodies from the Ameriya shelter—fifty-three the first day, more than ninety the second day, then a ghastly stream of others for many days thereafter. He told us that all were the bodies of women and children, and a few elderly men.

"When we had the first bodies laid out for identification," he told us, "I sent a truck to the El Rashid Hotel to bring the TV crews. The BBC cameraman declined to film one child's body.

"Why?" I asked him. "Is it humane to do the deed but inhumane to show it afterward?"

Suddenly Boghossian said, "Come, I will take you to the shelter myself."

After a brief ride in the van, we parked in front of a one-story concrete building surrounded by piles of twisted, charred rubble, the remains of beds and furniture. To one side was parked a fire truck, pumping dirty water from inside the shelter out on to the ground.

"They are emptying the water from the lower levels," Boghossian explained, "where we expect to find the remains of many more people. We have no idea how many. The water was pumped into the shelter while they were still fighting the fire and trying to cool the building enough to rescue the few survivors."

We entered through two sets of heavy steel doors and felt our way through the ruins toward the dim light in the center of the room. As we made our way, Dr. Boghossian continued, "This shelter was designed to withstand a nuclear attack from Israel. There are others like it around Baghdad. As you can see, the roof and walls are very thick, and the doors were very strong."

The room was eerily lighted by the sun's rays filtering down through the hole blasted through six feet of reinforced concrete. It had been penetrated by the first of two heavy laser-guided bombs, which depended more on their great weight than on the explosive charge they carried to pierce the concrete. The first had blown the hole through the roof at about 4:30 in the morning, instantly killing most of the occupants of the large room in which we were now standing.

A few of the survivors of the first blast made their way in the pandemonium through one set of steel doors, only to find the outer doors locked. About four minutes after the first explosion, a second bomb plunged precisely through the hole made by the first, drilling on down to the lower levels and killing everyone except a few then trapped between the two sets of doors. Many of those died from the heat before rescuers managed to open the outer doors hours later.

Boghossian explained that the shelter had been reserved initially for people like himself—doctors, administrators, professors, and government officials. However, he said, after the first few days of the war, they had decided they did not like hiding in the shelter while other people, such as his patients at the hospital, had no such place to go. As the VIPs stopped using the shelter, the families of the Ameriya neighborhood requested and received permission to move in.

Although the total capacity of the shelter was said to be around two thousand, we heard estimates all the way from five hundred to fifteen hundred people that were actually killed in the attack. I was painfully conscious as I examined this horrible place that I was standing in the ashes of hundreds of innocent people, the wives and sons and daughters of the men still living in the neighborhood all around us. I took a deep breath and braced myself to go out to meet them.

As we emerged from the charred interior of the shelter, an imam began his plaintive call to prayer from high up in a minaret across the street. His call fit my mood exactly; I would have liked more than anything else right then to be able to go to a private place to pray.

Instead we found ourselves surrounded by a crowd of excited people. Word had spread that Americans were in the shelter, almost certainly the first visitors from the West they had seen since the bombing had stopped. We were told that this street was now referred to by some as the "Street Without Women," the wives and girls having been incinerated by our laser bombs.

Our Jordanian friends and Dr. Boghossian stayed close beside us, translating the comments from the crowd. "How can human beings do such things?" one of the men kept shouting. "My wife and children were destroyed by your great weapons. Why? What did they ever do to you?" As he spoke, an old man beside him stood silently, tears running down to his chin.

A second man confronted me, speaking excellent English. "My family was also in the shelter," he said. "What has happened to the higher values of America, to the values of Lincoln and Franklin Roosevelt and John F. Kennedy? These," he said waving toward the shelter, "represent the values of the CIA. And not only were the actions brutal, but George Bush and General Schwarzkopf continue to insult us daily with brutal language as well."

Of all the victims we met, the man whose life reflected the suffering of the Middle East most clearly was Mohammad Ahmed Khader. A member of our party found Mohammad without the benefit of our guides, and we managed to spend several hours with him in private.

A Palestinian, Mohammad was forced to become a refugee early in life. He went to Libya, where he got a master's degree and married Adiba. Later they moved to Iraq, where they bought a home in the Ameriya neighborhood. Mohammad became a professor at the University of Baghdad. When the bombing became more than they could bear, he sent his wife and four daughters to the Ameriya shelter. They tried once unsuccessfully to go to Jordan to live with relatives in Amman. They returned to Baghdad, where they made preparations to try again on February 14, but for Adiba and her daughters that was one day too late.

After the bombs struck, Mohammad joined the grieving, helpless men in front of the burning shelter. Indeed, it may well have been his voice that I had heard on the radio in Washington. Then he returned to his empty house and tried to burn himself to death. A neighbor intervened and saved him. Now, even though his wife and daughters had been dead for weeks, Mohammad could not help going to his front gate some afternoons, hoping that somehow nine-year-old Ghana, the youngest, might still come skipping around the corner from school.

As I took a picture of Mohammad seated beside the

portraits of his wife and four daughters, he said softly, "They were all so beautiful and so intelligent. But now. . . ." He choked and fell silent.

After the long interview with Mohammad, I went outside into the night and walked the dark streets of Baghdad, trying to sort out my feelings. I felt as though I were full of broken glass. After a while I became aware of the full moon shining down through the date palms and the eucalyptus trees. I noticed that the sweet smell of jasmine was everywhere.

Just then a jet plane thundered overhead. Flying without lights at low altitude, it was the nightly reminder to the millions of residents of Baghdad that Iraq was defeated and the U.S. Air Force controlled the skies. For a few minutes I struggled with rage on behalf of thousands of children so terrified by these nightly fly-overs. Parents told me of children screaming and trying to hide under beds each time it happened. Now I shared the impotent fury of the parents and wanted to curse the plane.

But as I gradually calmed down, I realized I had to learn from the example of many of the people I had met the previous few days. These were people who, despite grief and frustration and anger, almost always concluded our interviews with a handshake, a smile, or even an invitation to dinner. Despite all the calculated humiliation they had suffered, there was still the urge to forgive and to build friendships.

Earlier that afternoon I had delivered my heavy suitcases of letters to the head of the National Women's Federation. I showed her some of the many pictures drawn by children from all over the United States and the awkward requests that we be forgiven for our part in what the Iraqi people have suffered. She received them graciously and promised to distribute them through schools and other channels to the people of Iraq.

"But," she said sadly, "it seems such feelings have come too late to prevent the war."

I agreed with her, but as we talked further we also agreed that we should begin working right away to prevent the next war.

Three days later I was back in Amman. I picked up a copy of the English-language newspaper, *The Jordan Times*. I found an interview with a U.S. Air Force pilot who had returned from his nightly flight over Baghdad, quite possibly the very flight that had startled and enraged me.

"What is it like to fly over Baghdad at night like that?" asked the *Times* reporter.

"Boring," was the answer. "Just routine. Not exciting like the bombing raids were."

The Gulf War initiated a period of painful soul-searching and disorientation for people who oppose war as a way of settling international conflicts. President Bush, whose popularity soared after the war, boasted about putting an end to the "Vietnam syndrome," including all the questions about whether it is proper for the United States to assume the role of righteous policeman of the world. The country was swept by euphoria about this war in which we suffered so few casualties. There was little remorse or even knowledge about the massive suffering of the Iraqi people.

In a society nurtured for years on violent video games and movies, this conflict took on a surreal quality. Unlike earlier wars, it entered our collective memory as an assortment of bloodless blips, brilliant laser beams, and precision weapons scoring direct hits while the fascinated public followed the show live on CNN. The slaughter of retreating troops after Iraq had formally surrendered was passed off as a "turkey shoot" by our triumphant Air Force pilots.

Christians committed to following Jesus' way of peace

felt battered by Gulf War developments, just as did their secular counterparts in the peace movement. Although the conflicts in Vietnam and Nicaragua had lasted an agonizingly long time, there was evidence that people troubled by our policies in those conflicts were able to have some mitigating effect on them. There was little evidence of such effect in the Gulf War. From the offices of religious leaders to the protesters in the street, from Congress to the Carter Presidential Center, those who had argued that we should take time to search for a less violent response had been swept aside as irrelevant "fuzzy thinkers."

19

Other Fronts

A few months after the Gulf War, the Soviet Union lost control of Eastern Europe, then broke apart. What seemed to many a sudden collapse was, in reality, largely the result of nonviolent movements with roots going back many years. Often with the church leading the way, successful nonviolent revolutions swept Poland, East Germany, Hungary, Czechoslovakia, Bulgaria, Latvia, Lithuania, and Estonia. Still exulting over the Gulf War victory (and ignoring the fact that our violent actions had made Saddam Hussein all the more a hero in the eyes of millions of embittered people in the Arab world), President Bush proclaimed this another success of U.S. might and right.

For those of us in the United States committed to nonviolent peacemaking, it was both an exciting and a painful time—a time when we found ourselves increasingly out of step with most of the people of our own society. It was a time for reexamination of our basic beliefs and recommitment to peacemaking. Some of us were still deeply involved in this soul searching when the conflict in the Balkans added still more difficult issues to the list.

Yugoslavia had been formed after World War I, a confederation of Serbs, Croats, Muslims, and other ethnic groups of the region. During the Second World War, Hitler made a great strategic error when he sent part of his troops to capture Yugoslavia on their march to Moscow in 1941. They never managed to take the whole country. The attempt cost the Nazis so much time they faced disaster in the cold of the Russian winter.

Marshal Tito emerged from World War II the undisputed leader of Yugoslavia. He led the country until his death in 1980. Without Tito's iron-fisted leadership, the country slowly came unglued.

In June 1991, while Desert Storm troops were still returning home from the Middle East, Slovenia and Croatia declared their independence from Yugoslavia. Within a month Slovenia managed to drive back the Yugoslavian army, but the battle between the Croats and the Serbs was destined to last much longer. Bosnia-Herzegovina is trapped between them, affected not only by the larger regional struggle but by internal warfare between the three major ethnic groups.

After the bloody fighting had been going on in the Balkans for a year, I got a call from an old friend, Bill Clarke. Bill and I had worked together for years in Habitat for Humanity and other organizations. Now, as chairman of Refugees International, he had just had a meeting with Mrs. Sadako Ogata, the United Nations High Commissioner for Refugees. Mrs. Ogata pleaded with Bill to help bring together Christian, Muslim, and Jewish leaders to pray publicly for peace in the region. Bill called me, and soon Jubilee was organizing another delegation.

In December 1992, ten of us—two Muslims, one Jew, and seven from a variety of Christian backgrounds—converged on Zagreb, Croatia. The city was beautiful under a light blanket of snow, with attractive architecture and winding streets along which Christmas decorations twinkled through frosted windowpanes. As I watched cheerful shoppers greet one another and eat pastries in cozy cafes, I wondered if I had somehow come to the wrong place. It was hard to believe we were within easy range of Serb mortars and rockets.

But over the next few days the reality of the conflict became clear. We spent many hours talking with relief agency officials, United Nations representatives, and others who could help us understand this complicated war. Speaker after speaker stressed that it was not fundamentally a "religious war." Yet the great majority of the casualties and refugees were Bosnian Muslims under attack by Orthodox Serbs or (less frequently) Catholic Croats. The most grievous victims of all seemed to be the hundreds of thousands of families of mixed marriages between the three ethnic groups.

We learned a lot of facts from the officials, but the strongest impressions came from meetings with the refugees. In Croatia, a country with a peacetime population of less than five million, there were close to a million refugees and internally displaced people. We spent many hours interviewing them and heard in great detail about Europe's worst atrocities since World War II.

We went to a convent and talked with an indomitable Croatian nun who had been a nurse for fifteen years. For the previous eighteen months, Sister Silvija had been giving most of her attention to victims of rape by Serb soldiers. The great majority of the women were refugees from Bosnia-Herzegovina.

"For almost two years my phone has rung constantly with calls for help," she told us. "Often there is nothing I can do for the women except hold them in my arms and pray for them. But that is what they need most."

Silvija said that she was sure, based on stories the women had told her, of at least four "rape camps" in Bosnia. The victims are women and girls of all ages. Some were released only after they were several months pregnant, or so ill that they were near death.

Silvija takes the women in, nurses most of them back to better health, and tries to find rooms around Zagreb where they can live. She confessed to us that she is sometimes "a little dishonest" when looking for rooms for her patients. "I go up to the house in my nun's habit and say, 'I am hungry and have no place to stay.' When they invite me in, I tell them about the other women. They are usually ashamed then to say no to the others after they have said yes to me."

Silvija told us a miraculous story about a thirty-five-year-old Muslim mother of five, a rape victim also suffering from cancer. She had become almost insane with suffering—screaming constantly, pulling her hair and pounding her head against a wall.

When Silvija came to the poor woman, she screamed, "Pray to your God to save me!"

Silvija took her hand and prayed with her for half an hour. "In that half hour she found peace and she was healed!" Silvija reported. "She said, 'Your God is alive. He gave me peace.' A few days later she was released from the hospital, healthy, with no medical explanation for what had happened."

After more than two hours of wrenchingly painful stories—interrupted frequently by other nuns on Silvija's staff coming to confer with her—she concluded, "I get my strength from God. We have an hour each day of prayer for the women. I couldn't do this work without God."

One evening we gathered at a large church for the ecumenical service that had been the initial idea behind our trip. Father Mirko Matausic, leader of the Franciscans in Croatia, led the worship. Our delegation sat on the platform with local religious leaders of many backgrounds. There was a wonderful spirit as we sang and prayed together. As one Orthodox priest put it, our effort was small on the overall scale of things, but "a little bit of light dispels a lot of darkness."

Near the end of our trip, we drove forty kilometers from Zagreb to Karlovac, the main United Nations transit camp for prisoners released by the Serbs. Ice covered everything—trees, ponds, and the highway along which our driver raced at high speed. We flew past two accidents, one involving a United Nations truck that had flipped over, scattering relief supplies all over the highway.

Our destination was a large, three-story barracks in the center of Karlovac. Across the street from it stood the ruins of an Orthodox church. "Let's be honest," said our guide, "many Croats have dynamited Serbian houses and churches." Ken Sehested, director of the Baptist Peace Fellowship of North America, remembered and quoted the statement of a seventeenth-century European general:

> The first act is an atrocity, the subsequent acts are mere justice . . . leading to a self-perpetuating cycle of violence. No one remembers the first act; and thus every new act is rationalized in the mind of the perpetrator as eye-for-an-eye justice.

A thousand men had arrived at this building a few hours before, brought directly from the horrible Serb prison at Omarska—a name we were to hear many times over, spoken always in tones reserved for places like Dachau and Auschwitz. Although none of us knew it at the time, three of these men were the first Bosnian refugees to arrive at Jubilee six months later.

Hundreds of people were gathered in front of the building, many of them wives searching frantically for husbands. From time to time there was a scream of joy as couples found each other. We also witnessed those who heard their worst fears confirmed as reported by the survivors—their loved one had died in the camp.

We pressed through the crowd to a small room where we were briefed by the U.N. director of the transit center, Alexandra Morelli, an extraordinary young Italian nun. High on the wall of the room where she spoke was a hand-lettered sign. "THIS CAMP NEEDS THE WORLD BUT THE WORLD NEEDS THIS CAMP AS WELL."

Sister Alexandra finished her talk with the question that seemed to be on the minds of most of the people we met. "I don't know what's happening. . . . Why can't we stop this?"

Some of us went upstairs and made our way through one crowded room after another, talking to the newly released prisoners. Everyone in the building seemed to be smoking at once. Once we jokingly pretended to be choking on the smoke, and the men laughed and said in English, "No smoking, no smoking!" But they obviously had been looking forward to this moment for a long time.

We met in a hallway with a twenty-six-year-old man. His face was a gaunt record of suffering past and present. Yusof had an injured foot, but he stood as he talked to us, leaning against a dirty window. His niece, a beautiful, sad-faced child of about eight or nine, held his hand as he spoke.

"I was in a prison camp for ninety-two days," he said. "Then the Serbs loaded many of us onto eleven buses and a truck. 'No harm will come to you,' they told us. 'You are going to Travnik to be released.'

"We were taken to the base of Vlasic Mountain, where they told us to get out and drink from the creek. The women and children were taken away in some of the buses, but about 260 men were left behind. Then they cursed us and forced us to squeeze into two buses. They drove a few hundred meters down the road and stopped beside a cliff."

From time to time Yusof was overcome by emotion as

he spoke. He bit his lips and stared past us. His niece stroked his hand and pressed close beside him. Then he resumed the grim story.

"After five minutes passed, I heard rifles and machine guns. I couldn't see what was happening. Then the front door of my bus opened and they began taking men out, three at a time. 'You, you, and you,' they would say. There would be shots. Then again, 'You, you, and you,' and more shots. I still hear that in my sleep—'You, you, and you.' "

Yusof was one of the last to be taken off the bus. "In a state of shock, I stepped outside—facing seven Chetniks [Serb soldiers]. I looked at them face-to-face for a moment. The three doing the shooting were cursing. They ordered us to turn our backs to them. I hardly had time to turn before I felt the bullet."

Here he paused and pulled his shirt open to show the scar where the bullet had passed through him, just above his heart.

"When the bullet hit me, I fell over the side of the road and down a cliff. . . ." He had to stop for a minute or two before he could continue speaking. "There was a pine tree that broke my fall. It kept me from falling about thirty meters, as many others had. I landed among corpses and some men who are still moving. About twelve more were executed after me. Then a Chetnik climbed down to a place where he could shoot anyone still alive. I tried to move under a bush and he shot me in the leg. Finally the shooting stopped, and I heard the buses leave."

After some time passed, Yusof managed to get down to the creek. Two other men had survived the massacre. One stayed with Yusof. Both had leg wounds but were able to crawl slowly along the creek at the bottom of the valley. They did this for five days before Yusof became so weak he sent the other man ahead.

For two more days he struggled on alone. His wounds

were badly infected and he lapsed in and out of consciousness. Finally he was found by a group of soldiers. "I thought they were going to kill me. But then I saw the 'chessboard' [Croatian coat of arms] on their uniforms." A few hours later, he was safely in a hospital.

As we listened to one story after another of gruesome torture, grotesque sexual assaults, and murders of children as they begged for life, I realized we were hearing of things that I wanted to believe were impossible. At least I wanted to believe abominations on such a scale had disappeared forever with the defeat of the Nazis half a century before.

I returned to Jubilee Partners unable to express clearly the emotions that filled me and tempted me to cynicism. My feelings of helplessness after the Gulf War had been intensified by this trip. I had never felt so inadequate in the face of such great evil and suffering.

I was distressed that Christians are so often the attackers in one conflict after another. On a collective scale, instead of modeling the compassion of Jesus of Nazareth, we are all too often behind the controls of the weapons attacking the people of non-Christian nations.

Our delegation found inspiring exceptions to that, of course, including the small Baptist community in Croatia. At Jubilee we started raising funds to help buy relief supplies. These were then distributed through a network of Croatian Baptists and Bosnian Muslims to villages so isolated by the war that the U.N. was unable to reach them.

We teamed up with the International Rescue Committee, founded sixty years earlier by Albert Einstein to help Jews escape the Nazis. The IRC has been helping thousands of refugees from Bosnia-Herzegovina to find new homes in host countries in Europe and North America. We began to host them in the summer of 1993. More than two hundred have come to Jubilee since then. We have also helped hundreds of others reunite with families divided by the war.

Working, playing, and celebrating with these Muslim brothers and sisters has enriched our own Christian faith. We do our best to demonstrate a side of Christianity that all too few of them have ever experienced.

One evening Jubilee was hosting members of a group touring through Georgia called Murder Victims' Families for Reconciliation. All had lost a loved one to murder. And all had worked through grief and bitterness to the realization that their own healing lay partly in learning to forgive the killer. They were sharing that message around the state just before the 1994 congressional elections, a time when the language of vengeance was rampant.

George White spoke to the Jubilee community one evening about the murder of his wife in southern Alabama. Even though George had been wounded by the gunman, the local court convicted him of the murder. He spent several years in prison before he was able to prove his innocence. During that time his teenage children stood by him and helped him to overcome the hatred he felt toward the killer and all who had been part of the gross miscarriage of justice that almost destroyed his life.

While George spoke to us, I was watching a sixteen-year-old Bosnian with limited English struggle to follow what he was saying. When he finished, I leaned over and asked her, "Could you understand?"

"Yes," she replied. "I understand—but I don't understand. A man kill your wife, and you forgive that man? I don't understand how is it possible!"

She stood up, her eyes filled with tears. "I hope," she began haltingly, "I hope I can forgive the Serbs like that in ten years."

I called George over and told him what she had said. He put hands gently on her shoulders and said, "Honey, you have to try. It's the only way to heal from this mess."

20

Invaded by Love

In November 1993, Jubilee Partners sponsored another delegation to Central America. Josie Winterfeld and I served as coleaders of the group. We spent a few days in Guatemala, then moved on to Nicaragua, the main focus of the trip.

I had been going to Nicaragua once or twice a year for a decade. In the summer of the previous year, Carolyn and I had spent more than a month working with Jim and Sarah Hornsby. They had moved to Matagalpa, a town in the mountains of north central Nicaragua, where they had founded a branch of Young Life, an international evangelical youth organization. Carolyn and I helped with the construction of a new Young Life camp.

Jim and Sarah's home was in Matagalpa itself, less than a block from that of Amancio Sanchez and his family. Elda often participated in the youth activities, and Amancio worked among local churches to increase understanding and support for the Young Life program. He also began to serve in an informal role as a pastor to the staff, sometimes leading them in prayer retreats. His humility, goodwill, and joyful work as a bridge-builder between groups was contagious. His home and the Hornsbys' home were busy places, with scores of young Nicaraguans attracted by the love and hope that stood out in such contrast to the general sense of discouragement settling on the country.

My visits to Nicaragua had lasted from a few days to a few weeks at a time, giving me a kind of kaleidoscopic view of events there. Like scenes from an old epic movie, there had flashed on the screen the great dreams and tremendous efforts, then collapse and dreadful suffering, and natural calamities occurring at a rate beyond all statistical probability. Now the country was marked by political chaos and economic disintegration.

As we visited one town after another, seeking out old friends whose determined struggle against the odds had inspired us time and again, we could see that hope was dwindling in Nicaragua. The spark of determination we had always observed in the eyes of Nicaraguans was dimming, replaced by the dull look of great disappointment.

Even though the Sandinistas lost the election in 1990 to the U.S.-supported candidate, Violeta Chamorro, powerful conservatives in the U.S. government continued to do all they could to strangle the Nicaraguan economy. Senator Jesse Helms fought relentlessly against one aid package after another, arguing that the Sandinistas were still being allowed too much influence in the government. He contended that the wealthy Nicaraguans who had moved to Miami after Somoza was overthrown should have their original holdings restored to them.

It was apparently irrelevant that much of that land had been mortgaged to the banks before the flight of the "Somocistas." And most of it had long since been divided among thousands of formerly landless peasants, including many who now lived in houses built in a dozen Habitat for Humanity projects.

By the time of our trip late in 1993, more than 60 percent of all Nicaraguan workers were unemployed. The per capita income of most people had fallen to the equivalent of less than one U.S. dollar a day! Masses of poor people crowded around our cars at intersections, trying to sell pitiful little handfuls of chewing gum or trinkets. Boys clambered up on to the hoods of the cars while the drivers protested. They quickly washed the windshields, then begged to be paid a coin or two. The gulf was growing much wider between the poverty of Central America and the wealth of the United States, ironically at the same time that our own news media were full of reports of growing anxiety about economic matters here.

We discussed the situation with Gilberto Aguirre, the executive director of CEPAD. "You are so rich, you don't even know how rich you really are!" he insisted.

Gustavo Parajón made the observation that as a medical doctor, he had noticed a distinct difference between most of the illnesses being treated in the United States and those he saw among the poor of Nicaragua. U.S. health problems are more often associated with overeating, lack of exercise, anxiety. In Nicaragua the problems are usually related to poverty—to polluted water, malnutrition, lack of prenatal care for mothers and simple immunization programs for children.

When we visited friends in projects with which we had worked for years, we saw a heightened level of desperation in their pleas for help. They knew well that their work depended on whether they could persuade us to find funds for them back in the United States. The economic crisis was creating an awkward, embarrassed competition with other worthy projects also deserving our support.

I found that most painfully clear as I talked to my old friend, Amancio Sanchez. "I still preach to my little congregation about hope," he said, "but there are many times I feel like a clown with a fake smile painted on my face. The people of my church are mostly women and children, and they are very poor and hungry. I try to encourage them. But I don't have any jobs for them or any way to help them out of their poverty."

As I stood before Amancio, noting his sad smile, I could think of nothing adequate to say. I had already decided to gather funds to be used as an emergency fund for his congregation, but the best we could do would be hardly more than a gesture. As with the many other Nicaraguans we had been meeting all week, the economic wounds among Amancio's little congregation were too deep to be treated with Band-Aids. I hugged my old friend, promised to pray with him for help, and turned away with a feeling of great heaviness.

By the final evening of the tour, our delegation members were struggling not to be overwhelmed by the apparent hopelessness of it all. There was little enthusiasm when I announced that we would spend the last evening in one of Managua's poorest barrios, Batahola Norte. Like most visitors from rich nations, we were feeling a strong temptation just to close our eyes and rush to the airport for the escape back home.

More than ten thousand people live in Batahola Norte. They are crowded into little houses jammed one against another, with narrow dirt streets and footpaths winding among them. We had passed along the periphery of the barrio many times in earlier visits to the nearby Aldo Chavarria Hospital and the prosthetics industry which we had been supporting through the Walk in Peace campaign. On one of my early trips to Nicaragua, I had even attended a service in the little open-air church there. My main memory from that visit was of the way the pastor had led that service with a guitar in his hands and a joyful sparkle in his eyes. But I had forgotten how poor were the surroundings.

The church has three open sides, and birds fly through during services. The congregation sits on simple pews and benches, facing a platform backed by a colorful mural. The picture is a primitive painting of the baby Jesus in a manger, surrounded by humble Central Americans, Archbishop Oscar Romero among them. From a distance, Augusto Sandino looks on from beneath his broad sombrero.

The church compound had grown since my earlier visit, with several new adjoining buildings all covered with bright murals. Everywhere we looked were colorful paintings and flowers.

As we entered, we passed a group of young girls practicing on their plastic flutes, producing a cacophony of squeaks and shrill notes. On one end of a pew sat a teenage boy playing a French horn, studying the musical score with such intensity that he seemed not even to notice the group of foreign visitors filing past him. Out beside the church, surrounded by a garden of ornamental and medicinal plants, two young musicians were receiving instruction on cellos. Within minutes, our fatigue and discouragement were replaced by fascination with this place. Our spirits were lifted by the colors and the happiness that we could see on all sides.

The Batahola Norte Center grew out of the vision of a Spanish Dominican priest, Angel Torrellas, and a North American nun, Marge ("Margarita") Navarro. They had come to this barrio ten years earlier, while the war was still raging and an invasion by the United States seemed imminent. They decided to counter the tragedy of war by launching a center where faith would be expressed through the beauty of music and other arts.

Angel, a trained musician, brought together some of the youth and began teaching them to play simple instruments and to sing as a choir. Margarita started other classes, which gradually expanded as new teachers were recruited. Students could learn painting, typing, computer technology, sewing, cooking, electronics, health services, and many other skills.

Several dozen young people gathered for the evening's rehearsal. Angel arrived, guitar in hand and characteristic twinkle in his eyes. Without a moment's delay, he took his seat in front of the youth and began to lead them in one lively song after another.

We were enchanted. The joyful intensity of the singing drew us in immediately. Angel had the full attention of the young people. The love between him and them was obvious. We felt like very privileged guests. As we reveled in this little island of beauty and hope, we forgot for the moment that we were surrounded by a sea of hardship. It seemed impossible that these kids with beaming faces would disperse later in the evening to crowded little houses so inadequate for human occupancy that most would be condemned and bulldozed if in U.S. cities.

As the singing continued, we were so moved we left our seats and went to the edge of the platform. The young Nicaraguans smiled in response and poured their souls into their singing. They charmed us completely. When they sang "*Cuando Venga La Paz, Mi Amor*" ("When Peace Comes, My Love"), we were deeply touched, even though most of us could not follow all the words in Spanish. These beautiful children, who had known only war and poverty, drew tears to our eyes as they sang with such feeling of the day when the streets would be filled with flowers and even the rivers would sing.

After the rehearsal, Margarita introduced us to the singers. She explained that our delegation was sponsored by Jubilee Partners, the same community that had worked through the Walk in Peace campaign to help Nicaraguan amputees receive artificial limbs. The young people exploded into the most sustained applause of the evening.

My eyes would not stay dry. I thanked God for leading us to this demonstration of love among the barrio children. Several of us agreed at once that these kids had something we needed back in the United States. Meanwhile I just wanted to go down the row, hugging every one of them.

Back at Jubilee, we soon decided to invite the Batahola Norte choir to come to the United States for a concert tour. The Nicaraguans agreed wholeheartedly, but they told us that they had already been refused visas three times. During the Reagan years, friends in New England had twice failed to get permission for them to come for a singing tour. Under Bush's administration, they had been blocked even from flying to Canada for such a tour, because their plane would have touched down briefly in Los Angeles! They had rescheduled that tour and flown with an airline that went nonstop from Mexico City to Vancouver.

I called the State Department and was assured that times had changed under Clinton. The necessary visas would be issued. But each of the Nicaraguan youth had to go in person to the U.S. Embassy in Managua and swear to return home at the end of the trip.

After months of intensive preparation, the big day of their arrival finally came. The plane landed at the Atlanta airport, and there they were: three leaders and thirty-eight beaming young Nicaraguans, three-quarters of whom had never been outside their own country before that day. They ranged in age from twelve to twenty-six, most of them teenagers. Angel was smiling as broadly as anyone at the airport, repeating over and over, "A miracle! This is a miracle!"

The next eighteen days were a blur of exuberant concerts, "folkloric" dancing in colorful costumes, dozens of standing ovations, enthusiastic hospitality in one city after another. And always there was the steady refrain from Angel, "Miracle. It's a miracle!"

We traveled in the Jubilee bus and a van, with Carolyn driving the van most of the time while Max Rice and I took turns driving the bus. Our adult staff was rounded out by Dorothy Barnhouse, who had come with the choir from Nicaragua to serve as the voice coach, and Helene Hill, a vigorous woman in her seventies, who had been a volunteer both at Bathahola Norte and at Jubilee.

Between concerts we packed in as much sight-seeing as possible, from the red hills of Georgia to the red leaves of Vermont and New Hampshire. Mountains, caverns, museums, monuments—in less than three weeks they saw more of the Eastern United States than most U.S. citizens ever do. Several times a day we offered thanks to God for the blessings of love and hospitality along the way.

In Washington, D.C., the choir gave a concert on the west steps of the Capitol, though not without some difficulty first in getting a permit. The authorities apparently found it hard to believe that an event connected with Nicaragua could be anything but a "demonstration." For several days prior to the concert, they refused to give a permit for the use of musical instruments—apparently afraid they could be used as weapons! When they actually saw the smiling kids in their beautiful costumes, they relented, and the concert proceeded.

Margarita and I alternated as emcees during the tour. My turn came at the Capitol. As I spoke, I thought back to the many times we had come to this place to lobby for peace in Nicaragua. I felt deep pride and satisfaction as I announced each song, then watched these three dozen young Nicaraguans sing their hearts out—beginning as usual with "You Are the God of the Poor," from the *"Misa Campesina"* (Peasants' mass).

As they proceeded to *"Señor, Ten Piedad"* ("Lord, Have Mercy"), I looked up past them to the room where Amancio Sanchez had endured a barrage of questions from hostile reporters. I thought of President Reagan's warning of an invasion from Nicaragua and of Tomás Borge's re-

sponse. *Here it is*, I smiled to myself, *the "invasion of love"
Borge promised!*

Finally, on the lower steps of this huge building in
which the fates of other nations are routinely decided,
these young Central Americans closed their concert with
an act of gentle defiance. They sang a song of love for their
own country, *"Nicaragua, Nicaraguita"* ("Nicaragua, My Little Nicaragua"). The happiness on their faces as the audience applauded was worth all the effort the trip had taken.
Angel told me softly, *"Estoy contento*, Don" ("I am satisfied").

The choir sang at ten universities, a dozen churches,
and in several other schools and civic centers. As a cultural
exchange and public relations effort on Nicaragua's behalf,
the choir tour was successful beyond our greatest hopes.
But somewhere along the way, I became aware of something more subtle taking place.

The first indications came from the people in each city
who hosted the choir. After the concert each evening, we
divided the choir and sent small groups of from two to
four Nicaraguans to spend the night with local hosts. More
often than not, the hosts gave each of the young people a
private bedroom. Almost invariably, they told us, they
found them the next morning together in a single bedroom. The youth explained, "We have never slept alone in
a room like that. In fact, our whole house is not as large as
some of these bedrooms."

As over and over I watched hosts drive off with the
youth in cars only the wealthiest of Nicaraguans could afford—sometimes calling ahead on their cellular phones to
say they were on their way—my misgivings about the ef-
fects of all this on the young visitors grew. Their own family incomes averaged only about one-*hundredth* that of the
median family income in the United States.

For years (with similar misgivings), we at Jubilee had

introduced refugees to the wealth of North America. But this was different. For better or worse, the refugees were on their way to become part of U.S. society, sharing in the wealth as they chose to and were able. By contrast, every one of these youth was sworn to climb aboard a plane at the end of the tour and fly back to households with monthly incomes less than many of the hosts were accustomed to spending on a family meal in a restaurant. I was anxious about whether they would be seduced by all the abundance and become bitter back in Nicaragua.

As it turned out, I need not have worried.

In one church an opportunity was provided for the Nicaraguan choir members to have a discussion with a dozen young people of their age from the local community. After some initial awkwardness, an earnest dialogue began to take place. One local teenager asked a question straight from her heart, "Are you ever bored?"

There it was again. Ever since the comment of the U.S. pilot in the Middle East, I had been noticing echoes of this theme, especially from young North Americans. "Boring" is about the most damning epithet that can be thrown at a movie, a class at school, or another person.

The Nicaraguans seemed a little puzzled by the question. In the end they decided boredom was not among their main problems.

But getting an education was. "What is it like to be a student in the United States?" asked one choir member. After some glances at his friends, one local fellow answered somewhat hesitantly, "Well, I guess we don't really think much about it. We pretty much just go to school because we're expected to."

The Nicaraguans found that hard to understand. Jairo Ampié responded on behalf of the others, "In Nicaragua we are lucky to be able to finish high school. Only the luckiest of all ever get to attend college. Please tell your friends," he added softly, "that in most places kids are not so lucky as you are here."

As I listened to this sincere exchange between the two groups of young people, my heart went out to all of them. Until then I had been preoccupied with problems caused by the extreme material poverty of Nicaragua. Now I was getting a deeper insight, largely through the eyes of the Nicaraguans, into a different kind of poverty and suffering among the youth of my own country. Jesus' words "Blessed are you poor" took on new meaning.

Still fresh on my mind was a survey done shortly before the choir tour in a town not far from Jubilee. Nearly three hundred middle and high school students in a predominantly middle-class neighborhood were questioned by a professional survey team. Parents and local officials were shocked by the level of unhappiness found among them by the team. About one-third of the high school girls and almost half of the middle school girls said that in the past year they had considered committing suicide. About one-fifth of the boys said the same.

The Centers for Disease Control in Atlanta added that in the United States as a whole, the number of suicides among people ages from ten to nineteen has more than doubled in the past decade. Suicide has become a leading cause of death among young white people. It is estimated that for every actual suicide, there are twenty unsuccessful attempts. Despite our tremendous wealth as a nation, anxiety and stress are on the increase. As one of the CDC researchers put it, our "support systems" are breaking down.

As the concert tour came to an end, Angel and Margarita were concerned about possible "reentry shock" for their young friends. But they were worried as well about the mood of the dozens of choir members they had left behind in Nicaragua.

On the flight back to Nicaragua, the Batahola Norte

youth were amazed to find that their president, Violeta Chamorro, was on the same plane. For reasons known only to her, she never acknowledged the presence of her lively young compatriots. She seemed unable to realize that they had just completed one of Nicaragua's most successful public relations efforts in years. No matter—there was also a handsome, young rock star from Puerto Rico on the same plane. The youth preferred one of his autographs rather than three from the president!

When the plane rolled to a stop at the Managua airport, the welcome deck was crowded with cheering, waving people. President Chamorro smiled brightly and waved back, likely surprised that so many had come to welcome her home. Well she might be, since most of the crowd was there from Batahola Norte. They had rented and borrowed half the vehicles in the barrio to come meet the choir!

There was a triumphant procession back to the Batahola Norte Center, where more people were gathered to cheer the returning heroes. Then the youth were treated to a feast of home-cooked rice and beans. They were entertained by songs and dances by those left behind who had been practicing for three weeks. A perfect homecoming.

Months later Sister Margarita was still excited about the way things turned out. "There is such a beautiful spirit among the kids," she reported, "that new ones are joining the program in droves. They are organizing community service projects and teaching music to kids in other barrios. We are so thankful for the way the Lord is blessing us!"

The first epistle of John began to occupy my thoughts more and more during these days as I watched all of this unfold. For me, John communicates the message of Jesus Christ in a way as eloquent and as exciting as any writer in the Bible.

"It was there from the beginning," he opens his letter. "We have heard it; we have seen it with our own eyes; we looked upon it, and felt it with our own hands; and it is of this we tell. Our theme is the word of life" (1 John 1:1-2a, NEB).

"God *is* love," John announces repeatedly—and those who "dwell in love" are "dwelling in God," and God is dwelling in them (4:16). He emphasizes that "love must not be a matter of words or talk; it must be genuine, and show itself in action" (3:18).

But neither John nor Jesus himself ever suggested that such a life would be free from problems. Jesus said there would be plenty of problems for his followers. He also promised he would be with us through even the worst of them. In the late spring of 1995 we saw that illustrated dramatically.

In mid-May Amancio Sanchez was riding in the back of a truck once more, along a rough mountain road just a few miles from where the road mine had blown off his leg almost a decade before. Again there were preparations being made for a wedding; Amancio's oldest daughter was soon to marry the young man driving the truck.

Suddenly the truck hit a large hole and skidded off the road. Amancio was thrown from the back of the truck and was crushed as it rolled over him. He was taken quickly to a hospital in Managua, placed in intensive care and given the best treatment available. For a few days it looked as though he might pull through again.

Jim and Sarah Hornsby called us at Jubilee. We agreed to raise funds to help provide any medical care that would improve his chances of survival.

Jim went to Managua to see Amancio. He was in a coma, barely clinging to life with the aid of a respirator. Jim stood by Amancio's bed, weeping and praying for his friend. After he left the hospital, he met Dr. Parajón, who told him that Amancio was so badly injured doctors gave him little hope of survival.

The next afternoon, on Saturday, Jim was back in Matagalpa leading a youth group in Bible study. They were reading in Matthew about the Sadducees arguing that there is no life after death. "You are wrong," Jesus answered them, "because you know neither the Scriptures nor the power of God." Our God, he said, "is God not of the dead, but of the living" (Matthew 22:29, 32, NRSV).

"At that moment," Jim told me, "something strange happened. You know I'm not a very mystical person. But at that moment, the young people around me just sort of faded and I began to weep. I'm sure the kids wondered what was going on. Then I had a strong picture in my mind of Jesus and Amancio meeting—laughing and hugging and so happy to see each other. They seemed to be standing on a veranda. Amancio was strong and healthy and had two good legs again.

"I immediately sensed that this meant Amancio had just died or was about to. I called out, 'No, Lord, please. We need Amancio with us in the youth work. His family needs him. We have to have him on our pastoral team. . . .' "

Jim choked up and had to wait a moment before he could go on. "It's all still so strong it's hard to tell about it," he explained.

"Then I had this overwhelming sense of the intimate closeness of Jesus," he continued, "just right there with me, as he answered, 'It's all right, Jim. You aren't losing Amancio at all. He *and* I will be right there with you as you work.' I felt the most wonderful sense of love and peace!

"When I became aware again of the young people around me, I couldn't express what I had just experienced. Later that evening we got word that Amancio had died."

During the night Amancio's body was brought to Matagalpa. On Sunday morning a wake service began that lasted more than twenty-four hours, as hundreds of people streamed into town to participate. During the service Jim shared his vision with the crowd.

More than a thousand people gathered at the church on Monday. They carried Amancio's body two miles to the cemetery in one of the largest processions the city had ever seen. There they held a great celebration of the life of this humble man who had grown to be such an inspiration to all of them. They told how he had been a pastor in the little village of Pantasma until the contra land mine had almost killed him. While they spoke, Carmen and Elda and the rest of the family listened, all of them reliving their own painful memories of that terrible day.

The speakers told of how the Sanchez family had come to Jubilee, then went on to Washington, where Amancio had spoken boldly on behalf of the many war victims back in Nicaragua. They recalled the way he had returned to lead and inspire other Christians at home, serving as president of his denomination, teacher in a seminary, pastor to many, and a constant reconciler among different groups of Christians. Finally one speaker told of Amancio's great dream, that of educating young Nicaraguans to enable them to become Christian leaders, men and women who could help rebuild Nicaragua.

Amancio himself had been unaware that others of us were starting to work toward that same goal. He did not know that Margarita had called me one Saturday morning in February. "I really hate to bother you about this," she apologized, "but I am calling because I don't know what else to do. Twenty-seven of our young people have just finished high school—our school year ends in December, you know—and they would like so much to be able to continue their education.

"I have called other friends in Canada and the United States, but so far I have only been able to raise funds for six of them. And Monday morning is the deadline for them to register for college!"

Hesitating, I asked her how much it would cost to pay for a year of college for one of the students. As the father of two college students myself, I was used to tuition rates in the United States. I braced myself for the bad news.

"About five hundred dollars a year," she answered.

"Margarita," I said with a surge of relief, "would you please be sure that *every one* of those students gets registered for class Monday morning? What was it that Jairo said that day, that 'only the luckiest of all get to go to college'? Well, tell him and the others to get their notebooks ready. They are going to be among the luckiest of all."

Monday morning I began sending out fund-raising letters to people who had heard the youth choir sing. Soon contributions rolled in. Some people gave a full five hundred dollars to cover the year's expenses for one student. Most gave smaller gifts or pooled their money with others to cosponsor a student.

An exciting idea developed among some of the U.S. students who had heard the choir sing on their campuses. They were uncomfortably aware that as many as two or three *dozen* Nicaraguan students could get a college education for the equivalent of what just one student spends in many of our colleges and universities. They began to contribute from their own pocket money to give the Nicaraguan students the same opportunity. For about ten dollars a week, they could sponsor a fellow student in Nicaragua.

Our dream now is to expand the scholarship program in Batahola Norte and beyond, to help young people from Matagalpa and other rural communities. Amancio would be thrilled. The Walk in Peace campaign that he helped to launch—and that has provided aid for amputees and hurricane victims, medical programs for children, and many other projects—can now help in this new way to build a promising future for these young Nicaraguans.

21

We Have Seen It
with Our Own Eyes

Today thousands of visitors come through Jubilee to
see what is happening here. Some come for from three- to
five-month terms as volunteer workers. They receive their
food, a simple room, and ten dollars a week. With such a
pay scale, they are obviously motivated by high ideals and
a desire to serve in a Christian community.

Most of our work is centered on the refugee program.
So far, nearly two thousand refugees have come through
Jubilee from a dozen countries around the world. Most of
the arrivals now are from Bosnia, Muslim families who
have been driven out of their homes by the relentless campaign of "ethnic cleansing." We are working hard to offer
them hospitality and love in this Christian community—to
demonstrate a love that is not merely "a matter of words or
talk."

Larry Blount, speaking to his congregation of mostly
African-Americans, recently described the work this way:
"You folks know all about the way some of our own great-
great-grandfathers and grandmothers had to run for their
lives and their freedom through the Underground Railroad, don't you?"

There were murmurs of agreement from around the room.

"Okay, I want you to know that the same thing is happening right here in Comer today, over at Jubilee. It's different folks who are looking for a new life, but the idea is the same—putting our love into *action*, just like the Bible tells us to! And it's up to all of us to help out when we can."

The support from our local neighbors, both black and white, and the gradual disappearance of barriers between all of us, is an exciting part of our lives in Comer. As we help paint a church or provide bus transportation for one or another of Comer's churches; as they gather clothes for our homeless guests or help us build a new basketball court for the refugee kids; as we do all this and more—we know something good is going on here. It is something that goes against the general trend across the South and around the country today. And we are full of gratitude.

Several years ago we adopted a "Statement of Faith" that tries briefly to express what is at the heart of our community. "We affirm that Jesus is Lord. Our life together is a response to the life, death, and resurrection of Jesus Christ. We joyfully order our lives in the belief that he calls us to love God and to love our neighbors as ourselves."

We know a lot more now than we used to about what it means to live by faith, "in scorn of the consequences." We are still learning.

We have learned a lot about the scope and the power of evil in this world, more than we privileged children of North America had ever suspected. Along the way we have lost some of our earlier illusions about quick and easy solutions to the world's great problems. All of this could have caused us either to be paralyzed by fear, or to seek escape in the popular religious and cultural ways of denial.

Instead, we have discovered a deeper faith in the great

power of God's love to overcome the worst that evil has to offer. We are all the more committed to doing what we can to be faithful and effective channels of that love.

We have discovered, as theologian Walter Wink puts it in *Engaging the Powers*, that

> [w]e are not called to do everything, to heal everything, to change everything, but only to do what God asks of us. And in the asking is supplied the power to perform it. We are freed from the paralysis that results from being overwhelmed by the immensity of the need and our relative powerlessness, and we are freed from messianic megalomania, in which we try to heal everyone that hurts.
>
> If we are sharply attentive to what God wants of us, we can then very modestly, in the strength of God, anticipate the impossible: we can expect miracles. . . . We should expect miracles, because the God who has called us to act at this precise point also is at work within us (p. 307) .

In one of his sermons at Springfield Baptist, Larry Blount warned about working without that faith, without a sense of God's enlivening presence in what we are doing. "Our work becomes drudgery, and in a little while we ourselves become *drudges*," he warned, "and that leads to what is popularly known today as 'burnout.'

"But what a difference," he continued, "when you work as a person who is *on duty for the Lord*! Then, as Paul says, we can give thanks for every occasion to serve the Lord."

Over in Plains, Jimmy Carter often challenges the people in his Sunday school classes to consider what will happen if we devote ourselves to compassionate service to others. "Not a dreary life when I break out of my own little self-centered world—but a life of adventure, unpredictability, and excitement!"

We haven't been as effective as we once hoped at stopping wars in Central America or the Middle East or in Bosnia. Despite our best efforts, nuclear weapons still threaten all life on earth. In our country, the death penalty is gaining popularity. The ancient tradition of providing sanctuary for war victims is being replaced by a mood of resentment against refugees, whose worldwide numbers have doubled since we started our own work with them. A movement toward "resegregation" is reversing many of the gains made during the time of Martin Luther King Jr., Clarence Jordan, and the nonviolent army of lesser-known people of courage and vision.

But at just such times, when things are most discouraging and we have reached the limits of our own power, God hears our prayers and works miracles among us. In ways that don't always compute in the halls of power or show up on the evening news, things begin to change in response to acts of love. New strength, new hope, and new vision emerge where before there had been only despair and exhaustion.

That's not merely wishful thinking. That's reality. We know what we are talking about. We have seen it with our own eyes!

Appendix

Chronology of Events

1979: February 19: Koinonia delegation buys 258 acres in northeastern Georgia, to launch Jubilee Partners.

July: Decision to establish a Welcome Center for refugees at Jubilee.

July 19: Sandinista victory in Nicaragua*.

September 26: First refugees arrive at Jubilee, 14 Cubans from Miami detention.

1980: *January 20: Ronald Reagan inaugurated as president.*

March 24: Archbishop Oscar Romero assassinated in El Salvador.

September 26: 39 Cuban refugees arrive at Jubilee.

1981: Vietnamese, Laotian, and Cambodian refugees go through the Jubilee program.

1982: *Gen. Efraín Ríos Montt seizes power in Guatemala, violence intensifies.*

---

*Items in italics are national or world events which set the context for Jubilee-related developments reported in normal type.

January: Congregation of Southside Presbyterian Church, Tucson, votes to declare their church a sanctuary for Central American refugees.

November: Jubilee launches the Año de Jubileo program.

December: U.S. Congress passes Boland Amendment— "No U.S. funds to be used to overthrow the Nicaraguan Government."

1983   January 19: First Central American refugee group arrives at Jubilee.

March: First death row inmate buried at Jubilee.

November: Witness for Peace begins in Nicaragua.

October 11-14: First nuclear weapons train chase by Jubilee.

1984   *January 21: Reagan's second inauguration as president.*

February 4-22: Delegation to Nicaragua and Honduras, cosponsored by Fellowship of Reconciliation and Witness for Peace.

February: Jubilee friend Stacey Merkt and others arrested for "aiding and abetting" undocumented refugees.

April 7: Meeting with Jimmy and Rosalynn Carter; he decides to serve on Board of Directors of Habitat for Humanity.

1985   *January: Phoenix grand jury indicts 16 sanctuary workers, including John Fife and Jim Corbett.*

May 1: President Reagan announces trade embargo against Nicaragua.

June 12: Congress votes $27 million in "nonlethal" aid to Contras.

1986   January 9-11: Habitat for Humanity conference hosted by Jubilee.

February 3-13: Carter trip to Central America—cease-

fire between Sandinistas and Contras almost achieved by Jimmy Carter.

February 19-21: last run of nuclear weapons train.

August 13: Congress approves $100 million for Contras.

October 5: Hausenfus plane shot down in Nicaragua.

October 20: Road mine explodes near Pantasma, Nicaragua—three members of the Sanchez family lose legs.

October 20-November 1: Jubilee delegation to Honduras, El Salvador, and Nicaragua.

October 30: Hausenfus trial begins.

November 25: "Contragate" revealed—money from Iranian arms sales had been diverted illegally to the Contras.

1987   February-March: Sanchez family at Jubilee—Press conference in Washington. Walk in Peace Campaign launched.

Summer: Iran-Contra hearings.

June 4: IRS agents deliver court summons to Rices.

July 23: IRS agents deliver court summons to Mosleys.

November 16: IRS vs. Rice court hearing.

November 25: Ollie North relieved of duties because of "serious questions of propriety."

December: By this time the U.S. was providing half a billion dollars a year to the government of El Salvador, 80% of the Salvadoran budget.

1988   *February: PEOPLE Magazine article about Jubilee's work and suffering of the Nicaraguan children—huge response, including from U.S. Congress.*

May: Jubilee sends $50,000 to Nicaraguan Velez Pais Children's Hospital.

June 1: IRS vs. Mosley court hearing.

October 22: Hurricane sweeps Nicaragua.

October 24: Jubilee launches hurricane aid effort for Nicaraguans.

October 29: Walk In Peace airliner reaches Managua with 30 tons of aid—three more shipments follow in the next two months.

1989 January-March: Max Rice and Don Mosley in prison for 40 days.
February: George Bush inaugurated as president.

1990 *August: Iraq invades Kuwait.*
September-December: sustained attempt to bring 200-300 women and children from Central America to Canada to reunite families—only four families eventually reunited.
November: Last Año de Jubileo group (Number 60) arrives at Jubilee.
December: Delegation of 18 church leaders goes to Mideast in attempt to head off Gulf War.

1991 *January 16: Bombing attack on Iraq begins.*
February 13: Bombing of Ameriya shelter—hundreds of women and children killed.
February 20: 9,500 letters sent out from Jubilee, inviting people to apologize to the Iraqi people—more than 8,000 replies.
March 23-April 3: peace delegation to Baghdad.

1992 July-August: Mosleys in Nicaragua.
October: Fundraising efforts by Jubilee raises $200,000 for Nicaragua.
October 26: U.S. decides to admit Bosnian refugees.
December: Delegation to Croatia.

1993 June 17: First Bosnian refugees arrive at Jubilee.
November 9-20: Jubilee Delegation to Guatemala and Nicaragua.

1994 April 4-May 13: Will Winterfeld monitors South African elections.

September 10-29: Nicaraguan Youth Choir Tour—
28 concerts.

October 1-15: Journey of Hope—tour of Murder
Victims' Families for Reconciliation.

1995   February: Batahola Norte scholarship program
started in Managua.

May: Amancio Sanchez killed in accident—massive
funeral.

1996   March: Jubilee delegation to Nicaragua—Amancio
Sanchez Scholarship Fund established in Matagalpa—total of more than 70 Nicaraguan students in colleges with support of Jubilee schol-
arships.

The Author

Don Mosley was born in Texas and educated at Baylor University and at Texas University, where he earned an M.A. in anthropology. For several years he worked as an engineer in his father's manufacturing business. His experiences in the Peace Corps in Asia as well as in other travels around the world sparked a concern for the victims of poverty and war.

In 1970 he and his wife, Carolyn, moved to Koinonia Partners, a Christian service community in southwest Georgia. During his time as director of Koinonia, Don helped found Habitat for Humanity, serving on its executive committee for its first seven years.

Don was national chairman of the Fellowship of Reconciliation from 1984 to 1986. In 1984 he helped lead an FOR delegation to Nicaragua. This changed his life and resulted in more than a dozen such trips to Central America since then. He also led groups or went on peace missions to other war zones in many parts of the world.

In 1979, Don and Carolyn and their two children, Tony and Robyn, joined two other Koinonia families to found Jubilee Partners in northeast Georgia. They established a refugee center there which has since hosted thousands of visitors and about two thousand refugees from all over the world. The main goal of Jubilee community members is to follow Jesus Christ as faithfully as they can through compassionate service to others.